W9-AEN-442

HOMEMAKERS

Rae André

PATRICK & BEATRICE HAGGERTY LIBRARY
MOUNT MARY COLLEGE
MILWAUKEE, WISCONSIN 53222

HOMEMAKERS

The Forgotten Workers

The University of Chicago Press
Chicago and London

86-1493

Rae André is assistant professor of industrial administration at the General Motors Institute.

The University of Chicago Press, Chicago 60637
The University of Chicago Press, Ltd., London

© 1981 by The University of Chicago
All rights reserved. Published 1981
Printed in the United States of America
85 84 83 82 81   5 4 3 2 1

Library of Congress Cataloging in Publication Data

André, Rae.
    Homemakers, the forgotten workers.
    Bibliography: p.
    Includes index.
    1. Housewives—United States.   2.   Displaced home-
makers—United States.   I.   Title.
HQ759.A5   305.4'3   80-21258
ISBN 0-226-01993-4

305.43
An2
1981

To Peter

Contents

Preface

In my work as an organizational psychologist there is emphasis on improving the quality of working life for employees in business organizations. This is an important goal—really a social mandate—but my contemplation of it has raised some questions. What about workers outside this system? What happens to workers who have no organizations at all? Or who have no "business"—no way of earning money? Of course a large group of such workers is homemakers. An entire book could be written about the importance of homemaking—about homemakers' contributions to their children, to their communities, and to society. This is not that book. I focus, instead, on problems and solutions. A number of authors have touched on homemakers' problems, but to date none has concentrated on what can actually be done to improve the homemaker's status. I hope that this book will be useful in describing and analyzing a wide range of proposed actions, from action the average homemaker can take to improve her personal life to action that can improve homemakers' status worldwide.

The book's orientation toward change derives from my own values as a researcher. I am interested in studying people's working lives because work is one of an individual's strongest bonds with society and a primary source of psychological well-being. And, for the same reasons, I am interested in improving people's working lives. There is nothing as practical as a good theory—but we ought to make sure that theory does lead to practice.

To create a broad conceptualization of change for homemakers, I have chosen to go beyond the academic discipline I know best. Although dealing only with the psychology of housework would have been easier for me, I believe it would have seriously distorted the reader's view of viable solutions that, while based in the psychology of change, have goals that are economic and political and sociological. For me this exercise has been challenging and worthwhile. In the end, as women's studies has always told us, real people tend to lead interdisciplinary lives.

Acknowledgments

During the three years this book has been in work, I have incurred many debts, none of which can be fully repaid by mere thanks. Early in the project, Joseph Pleck and Graham L. Staines at the Institute for Social Research provided valuable advice and access to their meticulous collection of related literature. Richard H. Price, professor in the University of Michigan Department of Psychology, encouraged me to develop a first outline as a course project and made important suggestions about organization. Throughout, several University of Michigan professors and colleagues have been generous with their time and expertise. All read portions of drafts and provided valuable feedback. Some provided significant amounts of hand-holding as well. Many thanks to Eugenia S. Carpenter, Mary I. Edwards, Deborah S. Freedman, Keith J. Holyoak, Robert L. Kahn, James V. McConnell, Donald N. Michael, Barbara S. Morris, Sally Smith, and Peter D. Ward.

I am especially indebted to Tish Sommers and Laurie Shields for their inspiring example; to Cynthia Marano and the staff of the Baltimore Displaced Homemaker Center for introducing me to their fine program; to Cindy Obron, Mary Berger, Nancy Jablonski, Lori Weinberg, to the homemakers they interviewed, and to Hattie Hogeterp for numerous insights; to the members of the editorial board of the Feminist Press for their encouragement and careful criticism; to Kathy Jones and Scotti Lucasse for performing so admirably on that diabolical machine; and to the University of Michigan Center for the Continuing Education of Women and the Ford Foundation for a timely supporting grant.

Introduction

Margaret Sandler is thirty years old. She has a master's degree and has worked full time outside the home for several years. She helped put her husband through graduate school. Margaret is four months pregnant now, and she has decided to stay home full time. And Margaret Sandler is a little bit afraid.

She says she is afraid of "being isolated and lonely and useless." She says that she likes to work, to have her own money, to feel needed, and that the idea of one person staying home to care for one baby in one house strikes her as a misuse of resources. Margaret is not afraid of childbirth or motherhood. She is not afraid of working hard, or of meeting daily crises, or of taking on a lifetime responsibility. What she is worried about is stepping into a particular role, a role that has been created for her and for millions of other women. She is afraid that by stepping into this role she will lose some of her dignity, her autonomy, her self.

Margaret Sandler is afraid of becoming a homemaker.

One wishes there were someone to blame for Margaret's predicament. Somehow, homemaking in American society has become a low-status, low-security, low-power job. But there is no one villain to point to. The creation of the role of homemaker in both its positive and its negative aspects is bound up with sex roles and economics and reproduction and historical accident, and there are no simple solutions.

The women's movement has recognized homemakers as important contributors to the health and welfare of children and families and society, and many feminist reforms have had direct impact on women in the home. Yet feminism often gets the blame for homemakers' low status. One need only pick up a current newspaper or magazine to find statements by women who say in effect that they cannot support the women's movement because feminists are against homemakers and against homemaking.

Such assertions are based on a simplistic view of the relationship between feminism and homemaking. After all, one would not necessarily assert that the federal government is "against homemakers" be-

1

cause it taxes homemakers more heavily than other dependents, and one would not say that the federal legislature is fully "antihomemaker" because, for example, it has not allowed homemakers to qualify for Social Security disability payments. Instead, one recognizes that many government policies that now have the effect of being antihomemaker actually originated in a different era, an era when the assumption was that women were willing dependents and that a man was duty-bound to support his wife and children. Of course, times have changed. These assumptions are less valid, and the policies based on them now need to be modified. But the time lag between the realization of the need for change and the implementation of new policy is not usually seen as reasonable justification for statements about the antihomemaker bias of the persons and agencies involved.

Similarly, feminism's treatment of the homemaker must be understood in context, which in this case is the women's movement of the last decade and a half. The doctrine of choice has been one of the prime movers of the movement: feminists have asserted that women should be able to choose freely between careers as homemakers and careers as wage earners, or that they should be free to choose some combination of these. In the late sixties the women's movement got its primary impetus by challenging the feminine mystique, the belief that the highest value and the only commitment for women is the fulfillment of their own femininity. Betty Friedan went to the heart of the matter when she pointed out that the idolization of femininity was nothing new, that "the new image this mystique gives to American women is the old image: 'Occupation: Housewife.'"[1] Feminists rejected the implications of the role of housewife-mother not because they objected to the role itself but because, in the two decades after the Second World War, it was for all practical purposes the *only* role permitted to women. Women could easily choose careers as homemakers, but because of educational and other cultural barriers it was difficult for them to choose any other kind of career. Thus, feminists came to believe that their first task should be to develop real possibilities for women in paid careers, and they embarked on the continuing campaign to equalize paid work opportunities for women.

The feminist emphasis on the importance of paid employment has not precluded feminist support for women who choose to stay at home—not, at least, in theoretical terms. But, in all fairness, it must be said that neither have feminists often been strong advocates for homemakers. Feminists have not made an error of commission in their policies for homemakers—they have not been antihomemaker—but they have perhaps made an error of omission. Although they have helped homemakers, particularly with respect to marriage and divorce, credit, Social Security, displaced homemakers, and most recently battered wives, until lately feminists had done very little to help homemakers *in the name of* homemakers. Improving homemaking as a career choice for women has not been a primary feminist goal.

In the early days of the movement the home came to be viewed as the place of women's confinement, a pleasant enough place but a prison nonetheless. Women who sought other outlets for their talents became acutely conscious of efforts to help them "adjust" to their role as homemaker, and in their desire to break away from these influences many of them embraced what seemed to be the only alternative: paid work. The choice was not made without compunction, for, in emphasizing employment as a solution, women were painfully aware that they were to some extent embracing a system that might be alien to their own values about power.

In the movement today the question remains whether women who choose to join the existing system will be coopted by that system, or whether they will be able to maintain the integrity of their own values and their own characteristic modes of operation. In retrospect, it would be instructive to consider whether feminists could have devoted equal energies and resources to improving the choices of women both within and outside the home and still have gained the power and momentum necessary to achieve the changes of the last decade. However, I must leave these highly interesting theoretical issues to other writers. The purpose of this book is not to grapple with this aspect of the women's movement, though that might prove instructive, but rather to examine the current and future trends in women's efforts to expand their options in terms of homemaking.

Among feminists today the realization is strong that an important contribution of the movement is the continuing reexamination of popular values and the reaffirmation of so-called feminine or, more accurately, humanist values. To achieve this, and to continue the momentum of the movement, feminists are becoming more equally attentive to both sides of the choice model they have always espoused. Interest in homemaking and homemakers, and in associated values and problems, has been renewed. Today the women's movement is actively advocating the cause of the homemaker as never before. Eleanor Cutri Smeal, a full-time homemaker, was elected president of the National Organization for Women in 1977. Major resolutions supporting efforts to improve the status of the homemaker have been supported at NOW's national conventions ever since that year.[2] And among feminists NOW is not alone in its concern. The Martha Movement was established to provide women with a forum for discussing the homemaker's dilemma. The international organization Wages for Housework has worked to raise consciousness and to get money and security for work done in the home. In the past few years dozens of bills for homemakers have been introduced in state and federal legislatures, and homemakers themselves have reasserted their belief that their job deserves to be treated with respect. Most recently the NOW Legal Defense and Education Fund sponsored the National Assembly on the Future of the Family, which brought together professionals and leaders from many fields to discuss such issues as changes in and prospects for homemaking, marriage as an economic partnership, and balancing the demands of workplace and family. In her *New York Times* article published the week of the conference, Friedan wrote: "With the same mix of shock and relief with which the women's movement began in the 1960's, feminists at the end of the 1970's are moving to a new frontier: the family . . . . The second feminist agenda, the agenda for the 80's, must call for the restructuring of the institutions of home and work."[3]

These recent efforts constitute the beginning of a new homemaker movement. They represent a new and welcome thrust of feminism, a renewed emphasis on real choice for both women and men.

It is important to point out that the issue of the homemaker also goes beyond feminism. Millions of women who do not call themselves feminists are homemakers, and many of these women are well aware of the low status and minimal security of their position. As far as many of these women are concerned, the new homemaker movement is neither feminist nor antifeminist: it is humanist, and a social movement in its own right. As such the movement already has a widespread constituency with the potential to create powerful coalitions for change.

The new homemaker movement will have social implications far beyond the home. Most home workers are women, while most employed workers are men, and we usually say that the ensuing inequities are the result of sexism. However, the domestic double standard, that ideology that permits society to pay lip service and nothing more to home work, is not a result of sexism alone. As it becomes clearer that all people working in the home, irrespective of sex, generally have a low status, while those who work outside the home "at least have a job," we can see that there is a second system of inequities in operation and that this system is based on our cultural values about what kinds of activities are worthwhile. For example, when we find that unpaid labor, however strenuous or time-consuming, is usually considered less socially valuable than paid labor, it is evident that earning money has been adopted as the main criterion for measuring the worth of an activity. People who do unpaid work like child-rearing could reasonably argue that this is a narrow and socially irresponsible criterion, and that to treat them as less worthwhile than wage earners is to perpetrate a system of inequities that, like sexism, is based on an outmoded way of thinking. Yet there are many such inequities entrenched in our American work ethic, including imputations of increased value to outside labor as opposed to home labor, full-time versus part-time work, and work that includes production versus work that is primarily service. The new homemaker movement will be a challenge not only to sexism, but to the very foundation of our American work values.

It is unfortunate that inequities based on sex have remained primarily women's issues. The inequities based on the work ethic, however, are more obviously the concern of both men and women, a circumstance that may work to the benefit of homemakers and, indeed, to the benefit of all working women. The middle manager who has devoted twenty years to his company only to be laid off can see the parallels between himself and the fifty-year-old woman, mother of grown children, who faces a bleak future in a tight job market. The man who works in a service-oriented or "soft science" job in a highly technological society is, like the homemaker, likely to suffer from a technological inferiority complex, to say nothing of unemployment. The man who understands the limitations of his traditional work role can begin to understand the woman who is experiencing the limitations of homemaking. It is from their common interests as workers that a coalition of men and women may be forged to change the status of housework.

Thus the constituency for change in work values ranges from homemakers to assembly-line workers, from white-collar employees to management. For instance, unions that are campaigning for a shorter workweek are beginning to realize that workers may need some assistance in learning to deal with large amounts of leisure time; people may need to adopt new ideas about the status and contribution of work done without wages—work like housework—in order to manage large amounts of leisure time and still maintain self-esteem and a sense of purpose. Management is open as never before to new ways of integrating their workers' homelives with their employment lives.

All these people have an interest in what happens to the homemaker. The same work values that affect her affect them: her legitimation as a worker may lead to important new ways of looking at their own working lives.

The new homemaker movement has many difficult tasks ahead of it. One of these is instigating ideological change: breaking old stereotypes and creating new ways of thinking about homemakers. Another is achieving wide-ranging research—meaning, in some cases, lobbying for the mere inclusion of homemakers as a population in existing studies and, in other cases, creating original designs and samples. Yet another task is designing action research models—explorations from which both change and scientific knowledge can be expected to emerge. And, finally, there is the realm of action alone, the complicated task of encouraging individual awareness, commitment, and involvement, and the responsiveness of organizations and society.

We need to begin to think systematically about organizing these tasks, and I offer this book as one contribution. Basically, I have two purposes. The first is to assemble in one place a representative portion of the research and policy thinking on homemaking that now exists in many different sources. The integration and analysis of this information here should provide a reference resource for researchers and should stimulate ideas among policymakers.

A second purpose of the book is to demonstrate the usefulness of a broad theoretical model for understanding and pursuing change in the homemaker's status. Such a model can help us to overcome various forms of parochialism—our socialization to sex roles, the tunnel vision of single academic or professional disciplines, the singular view of the world as seen by homemakers themselves.

A broad theoretical model will also guide us to consider the possibility and methodology for changing not only individuals but whole systems. For example, if, in our research, we keep in mind an individual's relationship with social systems, we are therefore encouraged to consider such notions as homemakers and organization, or homemakers in the world society. We see the possibilities for homemakers' organizing and, too, the effect of organizations on homemakers.

My theoretical orientation here is simple. My perspective is based on the fundamental assertion that an approach that simultaneously considers both individual change and system change is more likely to be successful than an approach that emphasizes only one aspect of change. To give an example from recent feminist history, consciousness-raising would have accomplished little without legislative reform. Conversely, without consciousness-raising, legislative reform would most likely have been overturned. Thus I advocate neither micro nor macro theory alone but a systems approach to theory. I encourage both micro and macro theorists and policymakers to be aware of their contributions in as broad a context as they can manage. Those who work with individuals are admonished to be aware of homemakers as a community force. Those who are homemaker advocates on a policy level in this country are encouraged to consider the international implications of their work. And at all levels we must be aware that our primary concern is for the welfare of individual human beings.

In keeping with this model, the materials in the book are arranged on a micro-macro continuum, from concerns and change strategies involving primarily individual homemakers and their families to those involving groups and organizations of homemakers, and, finally, our society and the world society. Naturally, within this sequence there is some overlapping, reflecting the eternal dilemma of focus in systems approaches.

The model is in contrast to disciplinary approaches: it does not focus on, for instance, the psychology of homemaking or the economics of homemaking, but instead weaves these concepts, where pertinent, through each of the various levels of the social system. Some readers will miss a historical account of the homemaker research in their respective fields. I hope they will be encouraged to write such much-needed volumes themselves. The disadvantage of this systems approach is that it will sometimes neglect, out of ignorance or lack of space, the depth and breadth and maybe even the cutting edge of the disciplines, instead culling from them the ideas and policies that seem most pertinent to the problem at hand. Naturally, however, I believe that its advantages outweigh this disadvantage. The systems approach highlights the units of change: the entity that acts is the individual or, perhaps, the group or the society, but not "psychology" or "economics." To a point, for the purpose of action research, focus on the social unit rather than the discipline makes sense.

In addition, the systems approach encourages interdisciplinary thinking on a social problem, which—while not necessarily better than single-disciplinary thinking—does seem to be progress of sorts in a world that feels overspecialized. Tomorrow, of course, the fashion may again be specialization. At any rate, I hope there will be disciplinary spinoffs based on my integration efforts here: increased efforts by disciplines to see full systems perspectives, stimulating challenges to the efficacy of my own approach.

The specific plan of the book is as follows. It opens with a brief chapter cataloging basic issues. Chapter 2 describes the work of some of today's prominent theorists on homemaking and suggests more implications of a social systems approach.

Chapter 3 begins the micro-macro continuum with a discussion of ideology: how the individual tends to think about homemaking and how this ideology can be changed. Changing the way we think about housework and homemakers is a necessary companion to taking action to improve the homemaker's position. To do this we need to better understand the scope of homemakers' problems and to analyze traditional conceptualizations of these problems.

Chapters 4 through 11 undertake successively broader explorations of homemakers and social systems. Beyond the reconceptualization of housework lies the sphere of action, to which most of the rest of this book is devoted. Most of what you read here will concern primary change strategies that are today being discussed and developed, beginning with chapters on the more individual and family-oriented strategies and concluding with chapters on the possibilities of community, state, federal, and to some extent even world change. Chapter 12 is a summary of problems and future directions, emphasizing the homemaker's potential importance in emerging decentralist philosophies. It may well be that, as individuals with close community ties and knowledge, homemakers will be key figures in implementing a "small is beautiful" world view.

The Domestic Double Standard

1

I want some adult companionship, a feeling of accomplishment; having the cleanest floor on the block isn't the greatest thing that can happen to you.

Jane, age thirty-five

I don't know where to turn. I'm alone with no assets. Except for part-time jobs as a waitress I've never worked outside the home and find now that I am not qualified for a self-supporting job. I can't bear the thought of welfare.

Margaret, age fifty-seven

I came out of the divorce court with a cash settlement of $2500 and was told I was lucky to get it. I figured it out: 23 cents a day for 31 years of hard labor.

An American woman in her fifties

These women are homemakers. They are members of that widely lauded, largely neglected group of people who make the beds of the country.

America's homemakers wash a trillion dirty dishes a year. They clean millions of homes every day. They raise our children.

They have been told that their contributions are priceless, but most of them have earned neither salary nor security for their work. They have heard that they are valuable members of society, yet they receive few of the benefits our society provides even its lowest-paid members. Homemakers have been victims of a way of thinking that in the popular ideology has put them on a pedestal, but that in reality has relegated them to second-class citizenship; they have been victims of a domestic double standard.

At some time in their lives most women will refer to themselves as homemakers. Some men are beginning to assume this role as well, but more than 99 percent of all homemakers in the United States still are women. Together these people represent a significant proportion of the population whose interests have often been overlooked and, worse, exploited. The problems arising from the domestic double standard have direct impact primarily on them and on their dependents.

In recent years women have been entering the paid labor force in large numbers, and today about half of American women over sixteen years of age are employed or want a job.[1] Because of their direct effect on the job market, the labor pool, and the unemployment statistics, and because their recent move was so unexpected, women who are working for a wage have received a great deal of attention from the media, the women's movement, and the legislatures. Yet these women represent *only* half of the adult women in this country. The fact remains that in the United States approximately 35 million women—57 percent of all married women—are unpaid homemakers.[2]

Today's domestic double standard for homemakers is one of the many historical double standards for the sexes that have influenced everything from sexual behavior to work roles. If we look specifically at the double standards for women's work, we find that a century ago separate standards of behavior for the sexes were even more encompassing and, for women, even more debilitating than they are today. For instance, when Harriet Martineau wrote *Household Education* in 1880, she was a strong advocate of women's education. She intended her book to be the ultimate text on the education of the Victorian female. Yet, in arguing for women's education, she could manage only a very narrow view of women's work: "Men do not attend the less to their professional business, their counting-house or their shop, for having their minds enlarged and enriched and their faculties strengthened by sound and various knowledge; nor do women on that account neglect the workbasket, the market, the dairy, and the kitchen."[3] In other words, in 1880 education was permissible for a woman only if it did not interfere with her primary role as home worker. Even girls from wealthy families were strongly encouraged to become homemakers. Martineau saw a "natural desire and a natural faculty for housewifery" in every girl, and she warned that these tendencies should not be suppressed. She exhorted all benevolent parents to help their female children satisfy what Martineau believed was the girls' fondest wish:

> I am sure that some—perhaps most—girls have a keener relish of
> household drudgery than of almost any pleasure that could be offered
> them. They positively like making beds, making fires, laying the
> cloth and washing up crockery, baking bread, preserving fruit,
> clear-starching and ironing. . . . It will be a treat to them to lay the
> breakfast-cloth, and bring up the butter from the cellar, and toast the
> bread; and when the breakfast is over, to put everything in its place
> again, and wash the china, and rub and polish the trays. They may do

the same again at dinner; and while the servants are at meals, they may carry on the ironing in the laundry.[4]

Nearly a hundred years would go by—another century of washing dishes and dirty underwear—before women would assert that housework is political. In 1974 sociologist Ann Oakley declared, "'Housewife' is a political label after all, a shorthand symbol for the convenience to a male-oriented society of women's continued captivity in a world of domestic affairs—a one-word reference to those myths of woman's place which chart their presence in the home as a natural and universal necessity."[5] Pat Mainardi had already written her widely circulated *Politics of Housework,* in which she reminded women that participatory democracy begins at home and that women's liberation signals liberation from housework.[6] Today there is a surge of interest in homemakers and their work, and there is a growing movement to improve the psychological, economic, and legal status of homemakers. More and more women are challenging the domestic double standard.

Even if they work full time in the home, more and more women are refusing to call themselves "housewives." Many prefer the term "homemaker," which is nonsexist (obviously men can call themselves "homemakers") and more closely reflects their extensive family and household responsibilities. When asked if they are housewives, some women still say, "Yes, I'm just a housewife," but many others have new answers like "No, I'm not married to a house," and "No, I'm not a housewife—are you a househusband?" Women are finding that even the term homemaker has its limitations because of its longtime association with home work that is unpaid, undervalued, and disparagingly called "women's work." Such terms as "domestic manager" or "household technician" carry less of this traditional stigma and thus may be more useful, they feel, especially in business transactions. A woman I know who has worked in the home all her life has repeatedly gotten credit in her own name by using the occupational title "household manager."

A 1976 poll showed that only 3 percent of seventeen-year-old women in the United States want to become "housewives."[7] On the surface this sounds like a major change from, for example, the fifties. But we need to examine such results cautiously. Do these young women have a real understanding of the broad cultural forces, including sex discrimination and our American work values, that have defined the homemakers' role? Or are they merely reacting to the negative implications associated with the term itself? In other words, to what extent are these young women making an informed choice? Campaigns against "housewifery" may have the unfortunate tendency of emphasizing only the problems of domestic, unpaid work, thus turning such young women—and young men—away from a realization of the pleasures and contributions of homemaking. It remains to be seen whether men and women will grasp the message that what homemakers need and want is not the abolition of "housewifery" but the revitalization of homelife for both men and women on an equal basis.

Change will not come easily or quickly. To a large extent the battles in the new homemaker movement will be fought in the home, an arena far removed from the legal supports and sanctions that, in the public arena, have been prerequisites to women's progress. Individual women, often working alone, will have to bear the responsibility of being the agents of change. Often their efforts will be resisted within the family and unrecognized outside it. And, when public changes are made on the homemaker's behalf, planning their implementation and gauging their effect will be difficult because of homemakers' separation and isolation. In short, there will be no easy answers to a problem that is so basic to the fabric of American society, yet so removed from that society's controlling institutions.

Presenting Problems

The homemaker's problems begin with the deceptively simple fact that she receives no salary for her work. Yet she does receive support, she does spend money, and sometimes she even has financial resources of her own. How does this economic marvel take place? Instead of grappling with the economic and psychological complexities of the husband-wife relationship, many economists have chosen to ignore the problem. They usually deal with the household as a unit instead of with the individuals who compose it, a focus that obscures the contributions of the individual homemaker and the problems that each homemaker faces as a citizen.

And there are problems. Consider the homemaker's job security and benefits. Most people who work, even those who make a minimal amount of money, are covered by Social Security in the case of disabling illness, and by unemployment insurance in the case of job termination. Not the homemaker. As Kirsten Amundsen writes in *The Silenced Majority*:

> Woman as a housewife is, in this sense, the most underprivileged of all laborers. That she may and often does share in the income and prestige coming to her husband does not change the fact that this award is meted out voluntarily. The housework performed by her is

not recognized as sufficiently socially useful to require the governmental protection extended to other types of labor. For her efforts she gets whatever marriage can offer—with no guarantee of either salary, benefits, or tenure in office.[8]

Unlike a salaried worker, a physically or psychologically disabled homemaker receives no federal support. She becomes dependent on her husband or family. Dependents of disabled salaried workers can also receive federal benefits; not so if the disabled worker happens to be a homemaker. Private disability insurance is difficult to get. What happens to children of disabled homemakers—homemakers whose work was probably essential to maintaining the husband's salaried work? What happens to disabled homemakers whose husbands fail to support them? We need to find out more about these human costs of homemaking. Unfortunately, it is difficult to obtain information, because it is the Social Security system that compiles such data, and the disabled homemaker is not included in this system.

Compensation for overtime is virtually unknown in homemaking. The homemaker's complaints of overwork may be greeted with responses ranging from the blatantly ignorant "Overtime! All you do is sit around the house all day!" to the plaintively passive "Well, honey, that's great, but just who is going to pay you?" The idea of a homemaker taking a vacation is usually more fantasy than reality. Often for her the family vacation is simply more of the same—cooking, picking up, watching the children. In reality, going to work in an office would be more of a change.

The thought of unemployment insurance for homemakers is such an unusual notion that many people greet it with derision. And yet the homemaker needs protection from the whims of her employer and the vagaries of the market as much as and perhaps even more than the salaried worker. Today there are more than a million divorces a year, and a quarter of all divorces are filed after fifteen years of marriage. If her husband chooses to divorce her—and changing divorce laws have made this fairly simple in many states—the homemaker is as good as fired: she is out of a job, and her home-oriented skills are not readily transferable to the salaried labor market.

Even when the marital relationship stays intact, we cannot be sure that the homemaker is protected. What compromises must a woman make to keep her sole means of support? Does she dress the way her husband wants her to? Cook and eat what he likes? Decorate in his favorite colors? Cater to his sexual preferences? Does she usually do the things *he* thinks are most important—or the ones he is most likely to complain about if she doesn't do them? Does she, in the best tradition of "pleasing her man," in reality bow to him—and thus lose her individuality, independence, and self-respect?

The degradation of the homemaker's dependency was well summarized in 1917 by Emma Goldman:

> Marriage is primarily an economic arrangement, an insurance pact. It differs from the ordinary life-insurance agreement only in that it is more binding, more exacting. Its returns are insignificantly small compared with the investments. In taking out an insurance policy one pays for it in dollars and cents, always at liberty to discontinue payments. If however, women's premium is a husband, she pays for it with her name, her privacy, her self-respect, her very life, "until death doth part."[9]

Whether the fault should be attributed to the institution of marriage itself is debatable. Even without a marriage contract, women tend to be homemaker-dependents more often than men. It is they, more often than their divorced husbands, who live on alimony and perhaps a poorly paying part-time job while at the same time raising their children, thus foregoing the possibility of establishing a career for themselves when they are young. It is they, rather than their brothers, who tend to stay home to care for elderly parents, living on the retirees' Social Security while acquiring no security in their own right.

But, whatever her living arrangement, when the woman who is a homemaker is out of a job she is out of luck. The existence of her job depends on a personal relationship; the dissolution of that relationship leaves her unemployed and relatively unemployable.

The problems of the older unemployed homemaker are particularly acute. Her job skills, which may once have been acceptable in the traditional job market, are now outdated or, at best, unpracticed. She faces discrimination based on both age and sex. Considering the lack of security and benefits available to these women, it is no wonder many of them face a life crisis: they must relinquish their accustomed standard of living, and usually society values neither them nor their skills. Among mature women who worked full-time for a full year in 1974, the average income was $7,773—only slightly more than half what men forty-five years or older were earning.[10]

A spokesperson for the Social Security Administration tells us that "the reasoning behind the social security law is that women in their 40's and 50's are able to go out and get jobs."[11] Unfortunately, the once seemingly reasonable (but always inequitable) law does not meet the needs of today's women. A Labor Department study released in August 1976 reported that women who have attempted to enter the job market at a "mature" age have a hard time finding work. The reasons cited include outmoded skills, little or no recent experience, inadequate counseling, and lack of job contacts.[12]

Though many mature women need to collect crucial Social Security quarters toward retirement, there is a sharp drop in employment for women in their fifties. In 1972 the labor force participation rate for women aged forty-five to fifty-four was 53.9 percent. It was only 42.1 percent for women aged fifty-five to sixty-four.[13] As Tish Sommers, national coordinator of the National Organization for Women Task Force on Older Women, has explained, "Just before retirement time, we hit rampant job discrimination because employers, mostly men, prefer the women around them to be young, part of their own aging hangups. So we give up and take early retirement, thereby condemning ourselves to lifelong poverty. Yet from a strictly legal point of view, all of this is perfectly equal."[14]

The homemaker is particularly disadvantaged when the time comes for her to retire. (Whether she actually does retire is debatable: if all our homemakers are retiring, who is doing the housework for our senior citizens?) At any rate, the age of awakening is often sixty-five, the year in which she may—or may not—become eligible for Social Security benefits.

For many women, and particularly for the woman who has spent most of her adult life "keeping house," retirement years are likely to be poverty years. Elderly women on their own make up the poorest segment of the American population.[15] The median income for those over sixty-five is $312.50 per month for men and $158.33 for women. Fourteen percent of all aged women have no income whatever, compared with 1 percent of the men. And of those persons on Social Security, a shocking 42 percent of the women receive less than $120 per month, or $1,440 a year, compared with 19 percent of the men.

Close to 4.3 million elderly persons live in poverty. More than two-thirds of these people are women.[16]

The Social Security system is primarily designed to benefit paid workers, and most women have not been active members of the paid labor force. Ninety-one percent of all men are insured as workers in their own right for Social Security retirement benefits. Although the number is growing, only 45 percent of women were so insured in 1970. Probably most of the 55 percent of uninsured women were homemakers.

Many of these women may be covered by a spouse's Social Security. At age fifty-five, if certain conditions are met, they are entitled to a benefit equal to exactly half of their husbands' benefit. Unfortunately, the crucial conditions are, first, that the husband must also have reached retirement age and, second, that the couple must have been married for at least ten years. Thus the woman who is married to a man younger than herself must wait until he reaches retirement age to collect any benefits. In addition, unless she has worked outside the home in her own right she will not be able to get hospital insurance without paying a monthly premium.

Unless she has been married to the same man for at least ten years, the divorced woman will not be covered at all by her husband's Social Security. Whether she was married for one year or nine years, her credits toward retirement are exactly the same: zero. In the face of today's high rate of divorce, this homemaker is in a particularly precarious position.

One rationale underlying Social Security is that the American people will not stand for handouts, that they want an earned retirement, not welfare for the elderly. The logical question, then, is whether the homemaker has earned her retirement. Among other things, homemakers raise children and create a pleasant environment for the family wage earner, helping the wage earner to devote his or her best energies to the job. While this division of family roles is perhaps not ideal, it is nevertheless the model for many families today, and, furthermore, it is the accepted, even the cherished model. Homemakers have been told, and rightfully so, that their role in the family is important, but the nation's retirement plan has not reflected this belief.

An especially poignant example of the pitfalls of the homemaker's dependency is the case of 119 widows who lost their coverage in 1974 because their husbands had not been properly divorced from former wives. One of these women, a seventy-three-year-old widow, had been married for forty years. Had their contribution to society, rather than their dependency on their husbands, been the criterion for these women's Social Security payments, probably all of them would have been covered. Such women are not looking for handouts; they are only looking for the decent retirement that they deserve.[17]

Among those women who have worked most of their lives in the home, some have also spent a number of years in outside employment, usually before and after raising their children. If they happen to have earned wages for enough years to be eligible for Social Security retirement on their own records, they will still find themselves at a disadvantage because the calculation formula for their benefits will penalize them for the years spent outside the labor force.[18]

Thus benefits may be lower than they would have been if the woman had worked outside the home throughout her life.[19] When determining a person's average lifetime earnings, the five years of lowest earnings are exempted, but all other years of nonwaged work are averaged in. The average amount determines the amount of benefits paid. Thus, if a woman spends more than five years as a full-time homemaker—a likely pattern if she stays home to raise children—she is penalized for those years. The victims of sexism and age discrimination on the job, homemakers already have lower salaries than men and thus lower benefits when they retire. Their problems are compounded by the fact that, because of their short job tenure, they are less often covered by company pensions. If women and men had the same waged-work lives, twice as many women would receive the highest Social Security benefit and only 11 percent, as opposed to 24 percent, would receive minimum benefits.[20]

These days more and more women are becoming eligible for Social Security insurance in their own right.[21] Labor Department statistics in 1970 indicated that only 56 percent of women between the ages of sixty and sixty-four were covered for Social Security retirement, while 66 percent of all women between the ages of forty and forty-four were already eligible for coverage.[22] (Of course this means that 34 percent of all women in that age bracket—and that means millions of women—were still not covered.) Exactly how many of these women will be penalized for their years of homemaking is unknown. If the present formula for benefit calculation continues in use, the answer is that any one of them that spends more than five years outside the work market will suffer the consequences in reduced retirement payments. This is but one more instance of the domestic double standard: homemakers, revered for their priceless contributions, are rewarded with yet one more economic disability.

Housework as Work

For all its disadvantages, one might guess that housework must have some redeeming characteristics. Otherwise, why would so many women work at it? Indeed, housework does offer significant advantages for some women, particularly for those who are economically and educationally disadvantaged to begin with: housework provides more autonomy and variety on the job than almost any other work they can get.

Approximately 42 percent of all women in the paid work force are clustered in ten occupations: they are typists, cashiers, secretaries, food-service workers, noncollege teachers, salesclerks, bookkeepers, personal-service workers, private household workers, and professional nurses.[23] Not all these jobs are routine by any means, but most of them are. And few of them have any semblance of a promotion track. Further, the narrow scope of these kinds of jobs—many of which require skills related to housework and child care—is a measure of the exclusion that women face in other areas of employment.

The idea of staying home to raise a family can become attractive indeed when a woman is faced with monotony, low wages, low status, and outright discrimination. Thus, a woman "decides" to stay home "for a few years," and at first homelife looks good. The conditions on her paying job probably included inflexible hours and much sitting or standing. On her new job as homemaker her working conditions are greatly improved. She now has relatively flexible hours and a variety of both active and less active tasks. She is chauffeur, domestic servant, and dishwasher, but she is also, if she wishes, teacher, craftswoman, and gourmet. Most important of all, her job satisfaction seems to be under her own control. Standards for performance are more her own and, though influenced by family and friends, at least reflect a part of the culture that is familiar to her. These standards might be in sharp contrast, for instance, to the typing accuracy demanded by a critical boss or to the standards set for teacher behavior by an imperious school principal. In short, at home she can assert her own values and make relatively independent decisions. She has more job autonomy.

Yet, if working in the home is relatively rewarding, why is it that a Gallup poll taken in 1962 during the height of women's indoctrination to homemaking indicated that 90 percent of American women would not want their daughters to live their lives the way they did but would prefer to see them get more education and marry later? Why is it that a group of women married to top business and professional men revealed in 1970 that if they could do it all over again they would pursue careers?[24] The problem may be that the homemaker's short-term gains—her initial escape from an unsatisfactory job and her acquisition of new job satisfactions—are counterbalanced by longer-range effects of housework that can be unpleasant and even disabling. These long-term hazards of homemaking include the kinds of financial dependency I have already discussed. They also include boredom, isolation, and low status.

It is important to remember that the homemaker's dissatisfactions have a long history. They did not originate, as is sometimes believed, in the post–World War II era. Women should not delude themselves into thinking that their wholesale indoctrination into the role of homemaker was only a nation's emotional reaction to the Second World War, a rekindled desire for the peaceful haven of a homelife. Rather, convinc-

PATRICK & BEATRICE HAGGERTY LIBRARY
MOUNT MARY COLLEGE
MILWAUKEE, WISCONSIN 53222

ing women to go back into the home was a necessary condition for postwar return to the economic status quo. The returning army of men wanted the women's jobs, and government and the unions wanted the men to get them. With various rationales, this preference for male workers has existed for decades, even centuries.

Neither were homemakers' dissatisfactions caused, though they may have been complicated, by the technological advances of the past thirty years. The homemaker's boredom is not merely a result of having fancy gadgets that do much of her work. The truth is that her dissatisfactions have existed for as long as women have been indiscriminately molded into the role of housewife, or, as social scientists Sandra and Daryl Bem put it, for as long as women have been "homogenized."[25]

More than fifty years ago Lorine Pruette was motivated by "curiosity" to write about what women were doing and about what they might be doing. Actually her work included feminist thinking on topics ranging from birth control to part-time work, and Pruette discussed frankly the dissatisfactions and disadvantages of the job of homemaker. A sobering thought is that today some homemakers are still in the same situation Pruette described:

> Many of the tasks of the home have been lifted from their shoulders, with the result that some women are without any job at all, some on no better than a quarter- or a half-time job, while some are working double time.
>
> Now these women who are on the part-time jobs are growing fat and intellectually flabby; they are cajoling themselves into believing that the care of a small household is a full-sized job, their minds are going soft like their bodies. Not all women! Not all, but a very great many . . . .
>
> But they are not satisfied, these women on the part-time home jobs. Some, it is true, do appear as placidly contented cows deep in green lush grass, but many bear upon their faces the mark of irritation, of restlessness, of longing for something more.[26]

Today, although buying and maintaining elaborate gadgets can fill much of a homemaker's time, housework that does not include child care is often only part-time work. The essentials of housework—the cleaning, the cooking, the clothes-washing, the appliance maintenance—are often boring and unrewarding and can be accomplished in a few hours a day. And while the nonessentials like crafts and gourmet cooking are interesting and can consume the rest of available work hours, they remain nonessentials. They are little valued by society, and the reward for doing them is usually meager. The American home is often the only showcase for the homemaker's talents, and

86-1493

yet the rewards to be gained there are few: relatively few people are available as an audience, and for all her work in the home the homemaker earns very little or no money, the primary currency of accomplishment in our society.

So, unless and until our society changes its ideas about the importance of work, the homemaker knows that she *must* work and that she must do "real" work in order to feel valued. Though she sometimes convinces herself to the contrary, basically she has known this for a long time. As Elizabeth Barrett Browning wrote in 1856:

Work man, work woman, since there's work to do
In this beleaguered earth, for head and heart,
And thought can never do the work of love!
But work for ends, I mean for uses; not
For such sleek fringes (do you call them ends?
Still less God's glory) as we sew ourselves
Upon the velvet of those baldaguins
Held 'twixt us and the sun.[27]

When the real work in the home—the necessary housework—does not fill her day, the homemaker sometimes attempts to professionalize her job, to expand it by studying it in detail and to improve it by doing it perfectly or creatively. Often others see through this attempt and ridicule her for it: Dagwood Bumstead and his friend Herb are flabbergasted when Tootsie creates a planter out of Herb's bowling ball. Others praise her for being such a "good" homemaker, and—as the sales of Marabel Morgan's book *The Total Woman* demonstrate—homemakers are desperate for this kind of support. But as a whole the culture is not forgiving. Work must serve a culturally legitimate purpose or go unrewarded. The homemaker who realizes this but sees no way out of her job often begins a downward spiral of boredom, despair, and depression.

Ironically, our very affluence contributes to a homemaker's dilemma by making possible the two-generation nuclear household. Whether she lives in an apartment or in her own home, today's homemaker tends to live with spouse and children; older generations and other relatives live in other households, not necessarily nearby. Her isolation is a particularly important characteristic of her working conditions because it compounds the other problems. It exacerbates the homemaker's boredom. And, because they are isolated in both space and time—each household is on a different schedule—homemakers often fail to communicate with each other about their common problems and interests. If she is lucky the homemaker lives in a neighborhood or apartment building in which she finds other homemakers like herself. If she is very lucky she will find homemakers who are conscious of their isolation and who are looking for change, who plan regular collective housework and child care, creating, in essence, an extended family. But if she is not lucky, and if it is true that a crucial aspect of working life is social interaction, then the homemaker's working conditions must be dreary indeed.

In summary, we have seen that the homemaker's on-the-job security is minimal, that her retirement is tenuous at best, and that her working conditions seldom meet even minimum standards for rewards, advancement, and social interaction. An additional strike against her is that she contributes service, not money, to her family and to society, and in our society service is less valued than cash. Finally—need we even say it?—the homemaker is usually a woman, not a man. In American society all these characteristics of the homemaker add up to one thing: low status.

Status: Homemaker

The homemaker's low status becomes apparent in various insidious ways. I have already mentioned that much of women's paid work is really housework performed outside the home, and that it has a correspondingly low evaluation. Even women in paid jobs that are not obviously related to housework often are relegated to the housework role while on the job. Take the case of Iris Rivera, a secretary in the Office of the State Appellate Defender in Illinois. Rivera was fired because she asserted that her job as a secretary did not include making coffee. Her boss made the counterassertion that he paid lawyers "a lot" to practice law, not to make coffee.[28] The unspoken message is that the secretary's job includes personal services for others in the office. This is housework—"women's work"—in another guise. The problem here is that the message is implicit—bound up with the traditional assumptions about who secretaries are (women) and what they can do (women's work)—rather than explicit—asserting the full nature of the work and the true value of the service aspects of that work. The work is the same whether it is done in the home or in the office. The sexism is the same whether it is applied to the role of homemaker or to the role of secretary.

Women's part-time work, even if for wages, is accorded lower status than part-time work done by men. Men's part-time professional work is often described as "consulting" or as "committed time," while women's is simply "part-time work." As Hilda Kahne, labor economist and assistant dean of the Radcliffe Institute, points out, "Unlike women's experience, there is no implication that if fewer than 35 hours a week are spent in a particular activity, it is less important, less serious or less of a contribution. There is need to ascertain why this terminological discrepancy exists and how much it is related to perceptions that only paid labor market activities are useful. Once we are able to acknowledge and assign value to unpaid work in the home, this double standard in valuing work may diminish."[29]

Though her status remains low, in the home itself the homemaker's responsibilities continue to be high. There is the child care, of course, and one can only begin to evaluate the importance of this activity. In addition, older persons are more likely to live with their daughters than with their sons, "possibly because the daughter is not employed, is underemployed, or is under greater social pressure than males to forego paid employment to care for a parent."[30] At any rate it is the woman who tends to assume the responsibility for aging parents, whether they are at home or in a nursing home, and yet it is likely to be the sons who can most easily afford the financial aspects of these responsibilities. What kind of logic is it that compels those not employed or those underemployed to give up the only work they do have, thus jeopardizing their own future security, to remove the burden of such responsibility from a person who is already better off?

Even her own family is likely to remind the homemaker of her low status. Columnist Erma Bombeck, writing about her feelings of guilt over leaving the home for outside work, sums up neatly what many women soon realize. She writes:

> I don't think I'll ever forget the day I had written a column, lectured at a luncheon, come home, made beds, put in a load
> of clothes and started dinner when my son said "Why don't you make some lemonade?"
> "Why don't you make it" I said?
> "It's your job," he retaliated.
> I thought about that one for a long time and decided what did it profit me to be an expert lemonade-maker—when I failed to raise a child who respected me as a person.
> I've never felt guilty since.[31]

Differences by Class and Race

The domestic double standard might be expected to act differentially upon different classes and races, indeed, upon any subcultures. Various studies have shown that it is essentially universal but that today its strength may differ by class and that its effects differ by both class and race.

A study by Cornelia Butler Flora comparing role expectations for middle-class and working-class women in 1970 and 1975 found that during this period role expectations for middle-class women moved away from valuing dependence and ineffectuality (inability to complete a task undertaken) and toward valuing independence.[32] As the middle-class woman's labor-force participation increased, jobs came to be seen as a good alternative to marriage. In contrast, among working-class women passivity was relatively valued and general conservatism increased. At the same time, according to the study, labor-force participation declined among women with less than a high-school education.

The author's explanation for this is based on the differing assessments of the wife's employment role in the two classes. The middle-class employed wife is often seen as fulfilled in her job and as an asset to her husband, whereas in the working-class household an employed wife is often seen as an indication that the husband has failed in his provider role. Thus we see that the domestic double standard is more likely to be found in the lower-class household, and perhaps to be intensified there. Flora notes (borrowing in part from Harry Braverman):

> The "double day" for working-class women, especially lower working-class women, is more alienating at work, where they hold ununionized jobs as matrons, waitresses and other lowpaid service jobs, and more difficult at home because greater segregation of household tasks by gender leaves housework solely to the women. Male roles are also more difficult in such insecure economic settings and, despite the need for extra income, the already fragile marital bond is severely threatened when the wife assumes an economic (read male) as well as a domestic (read female) role. Thus the very structure of *male* work in lower working-class homes requires a concept of the ideal female who can be economically controlled at home, when all control is taken away in the work place.[33]

The notion that the homemaker role is one that must be financially affordable (read middle or upper class) is obviously challenged by this kind of research. It suggests that the relationships among spouses, money, and power are hardly simple and, specifically, that while a paid job may tend to equalize the balance of power in the middle-class household it is likely to increase polarities in the lower-class household. Very likely this is because the middle-class woman can get a relatively well-paying job and thus more security.

Flora asserts that "the very alleviation of oppression of middle class women...may lead to a deterioration in the relative situation of less advantaged women. It may close avenues of active participation previously open to them, with the resulting symbolic reaction which glorifies traditional passive female roles."[34] (The main reason cited for this potential class conflict is that the entry of middle-class women into the labor force increases the credentials required for all jobs, leaving only the most menial, if any, jobs for the lower classes.) In other words, at bottom we continue to find the problem of the economic and emotional exploitation of homemakers. Lower-class women are especially susceptible to the domestic double standard.

In a secondary analysis of survey data collected by the Institute of Social Research at the University of Michigan as part of the longitudinal *Panel Study of Income Dynamics*, Audrey D. Smith and Joyce O. Beckett have been able to examine the effects of both race and class (income) on wives' employment status.[35] Their analysis indicates that, for working-class white wives, employment is inhibited by the presence of children, the husband's income, and his attitude about his wife's employment. The same is not true for the working-class black wives. In their preference for outside employment, white wives (in the middle class) similarly are more influenced than are black wives by the husband's present income, by having small children, and by the husband's preference for the wife to remain at home. The authors conclude that the black wives may be responding not only to husband's present income, but to the smaller lifetime earnings of black husbands and the greater instability over time of black husbands' employment compared with that of white husbands.

Thus it seems that, regardless of class, the black wife is somewhat less likely than the white wife to be victimized by the domestic double standard. Indeed, Smith and Beckett note that, where sharing housework is concerned, whites are more egalitarian in attitude, but blacks are more egalitarian in practice: black husbands of both employed and unemployed wives spend more time on household tasks than their white counterparts; the median number of hours per week for all black husbands was five, compared with three for white husbands. However, the authors are quick to point out that, even when wives are employed outside of the home, usually full time like their husbands, they still spend on the average three and a half times as many hours on housework as their husbands do if they are black and five and a half times as many hours if they are white.

Women's Two Jobs

Many women believe that taking a job outside the home will provide a solution to the domestic double standard. Indeed, one of the main thrusts of the feminist movement of the last decade has been the fight for equality in jobs. The point has been to get beyond the feminine mystique and provide women with a choice of careers both outside and inside the home.

Somewhat less attention has been devoted to the assumptions women have made about the interaction between housework and outside work. Yet this interaction is crucial: housework does not go away merely because outside work appears. Women have believed—quite reasonably by any standard of equity—that by holding down a paid job they would achieve equality with their mates. They have believed that this equality would mean, among other things, equal rights and responsibilities in making family decisions, equal treatment under the law, and, last but not least, equal housework.

Equality in the sharing of housework is a basic measure of a woman's liberation. After all the rhetoric and all the consciousness-raising and all the legislation, dealing cooperatively with housework requires getting down to the difficult task of personal change. In spite of the women's movement, and in spite of the rapid increase in the number of women in the paid work force, in the majority of households today sexual equality in housework has not been achieved.

The popular ideology would have us believe otherwise. It is antithetical to the American sense of decency that, in a household in which two adults work full time for pay, one of them comes home to work a second full job, essentially as the servant of the other person. And yet most of the recent data indicate that this is precisely what is still happening in the American household.

A study done in 1955 in the Detroit area indicated that in more than two-thirds of all households the wife alone was responsible for making the husband's breakfast, doing the evening dishes, and straightening the living room. Husbands and wives shared grocery shopping and bookkeeping more equally, but still only about a third of the wives reported that they and their husbands actually did these tasks equally. Tasks that were predominantly men's were shoveling the sidewalk in winter, mowing the lawn in summer, and making home repairs.[36] In 1971 a similar study showed that while husbands were participating somewhat more in getting their own breakfasts, they helped less with the evening dishes and showed no change in straightening up the living room. While her bookkeeping chores were somewhat diminished, the wife was taking on more of the grocery shopping and more of the home repair. The authors of the second study concluded that there had been no trend toward equalization of housework.[37]

Some other interesting research in this area compares time diaries kept on comparable days in representative samples of American families in 1965–66 and 1975–76. People were asked to write down all their activities for several different days. Later their responses were summarized to give us a picture of how the typical American wife and husband spend their time. In 1965–66 this research showed that men were doing about 11.3 hours per week of family work. Housewives (the term used by the researchers) were doing 53.2 hours of family work per week, and women employed outside of the home were doing 28.1 hours of family work per week. By 1975–76, men's average time in family work had increased only 6 percent, or *six minutes a day*. Furthermore, the men do the nonroutine tasks. The routine work and the dull tasks are still the women's work.

The research indicates that some change is occurring. If a man's total number of family work hours does not go up when his wife works, the proportion of housework that he does is still going up, since the number of housework hours she is spending has gone down. (Some quick arithmetic will demonstrate that he is still doing far less than his equal share.) And there is some indication that the type of work done by the sexes is becoming less stereotyped. Some men are doing more cleaning and more meal preparation, and less yard and car care.[38]

Interestingly enough, more husbands than wives report that they feel husbands should do more in the family than they do now. In families in which both husband and wife work outside the home, a recent study shows, only 65 percent of the wives, but 79 percent of the husbands, report that husbands should do *some* housework. The men's consciousness has actually been raised more than the women's! A 1976 Gallup survey indicates that men are split almost evenly on the issue of whether husbands should do as much housework and child care as their wives if their wives have paid jobs: about half said that they should, but half said that the husband should do "none, or at most a little" or "he should help her out part of the time."[39]

Do women themselves wish their husbands would give them *more* help with the household chores? A national survey indicates that, overall, only 19 percent of women responded yes to this question in 1965–66, and in 1973 23 percent answered yes—only a tiny gain. Among wives who said that their husbands had given them no help with the housework during the previous week (and about a third of the women said this), in 1965–66 only 24 percent said they wanted more help. Their consciousness had been raised slightly by 1973: in that year 35 percent of all women who had received no help from their husbands reported that they would like more help from them. Over this period only black women had a majority who wanted more help: 58 percent in 1973, up 35 percent from 1965–66.[40]

All these figures leave us with a sizable proportion of women who do not want any change in the amount of housework they do. While it is not within my main purpose here to explore the reasons why so many women prefer the status quo, the importance of their viewpoint and the evolution of their view should not be overlooked in future research. Why do these women assert that they do not want more help from their husbands? Is it because they believe so wholeheartedly in the traditional sex role ideology that woman's place is in the home and man's is in the outside workplace? Is it because they wish to keep their roles separate from their husbands' in order to maintain some integrity in their work—some pride in the personal accomplishment of a well-defined job? Perhaps they do not wish to deal with the resistance—and determined, even bitter, resistance it may be—that they are likely to get from their husbands. Or perhaps they are so economically dependent that they literally cannot afford to challenge their sexist household system.

The new homemaker movement is seeking to change all this. It is in the process of designing and implementing strategies for achieving the system of equality that is today being sought by the millions of American women who are already aware of their need. But in our work here let us not forget those others who do not see the need—or who see it in a different way. In a sense they are a part of the audience—not the audience who is already listening, but the audience who, I hope, will come to hear.

Perspectives on Housework

2

What is needed now in the new homemaker movement is not primarily traditional research or analysis, but more action research and change. We need more women who see their common problems as homemakers and who set out to change their status, whether their efforts are directed at their own families or at their legislatures. We need more men who are willing to eradicate sexism in their own homes and who will stand alongside their women and say to the world, "I too am a homemaker."

However, it is likely that action taken without some theoretical guidance will be relatively ineffective. Like any movement for social change, the new homemaker movement needs to develop and coordinate its efforts so as to avoid wasting valuable energy. We need to think about where we are going in order to minimize false starts and wrong turns.

Some authors have attempted to establish theoretical guidelines specifically for homemakers, and among theorists who have done the same thing for women in general there are a few whose work has special relevance for homemakers. Consider some of the change strategies advanced by theorists Ann Oakley, Mariarosa Dalla Costa and Selma James, Jessie Bernard, Elise Boulding, and Juliet Mitchell.

Ann Oakley. In one sense, sociologist Ann Oakley is one of the more radical of the theorists. In *Women's Work: The Housewife, Past and Present* (1974), she asserts that we must break down the equation "woman equals housewife." Oakley believes there are three radical political statements that point the way to the liberation of housewives (her term): (1) the housewife role must be abolished; (2) the family must be abolished; (3) gender roles must be abolished. Let us follow her reasoning for a moment. She writes that, to start with, we must abolish the housewife role: housework lacks any motivating factor, she asserts; it gains for the housewife neither self-actualization nor earned recognition. In Oakley's opinion, many less radical strategies to help the housewife have failed, including: (1) efforts to improve the conditions of housework through building better houses and buying more machines; (2) attempts to raise the housewife's status by using the term "homemaker" instead of "housewife"; (3) attempts to elaborate housework into something more difficult and therefore more rewarding; and (4) paying women for their work in the home. She feels that paying housewives for their work will maintain the status quo of equating women with the housewife role. Oakley states that the only strategy that will have any effect in the last category is improving domestic workers' status.

Oakley goes on to say, "It becomes clear that a second political statement follows from the first: the abolition of the housewife role calls for the abolition of the family . . . . Women's domesticity is a circle of learnt deprivation and induced subjugation: a circle decisively centered on family life."[1] Because the family provides a direct apprenticeship in the housewife role, Oakley believes it should be abolished. She says that a necessary corollary is to abolish marriage—not merely the idea of marriage, but the legal trappings as well.

Finally, Oakley says, we need to abolish gender roles. She suggests that this is to be accomplished primarily through raising people's consciousness about them.

Dalla Costa and James. The rhetoric and the change strategies of Dalla Costa and James are also among the more radical in the movement. Mariarosa Dalla Costa and Selma James are members of the international organization Wages for Housework. Their book *The Power of Women and the Subversion of the Community* (1972) is one of the primary documents to come from the Wages for Housework theorists. Like Oakley, the authors assert that eventually the housewife role must be abolished, but they believe that until homemakers receive wages for their work they will be powerless to abolish their role.

The only strategy that will make it possible for women to reject housework, they say, is paying housework a wage. That wage must come from the government. Pensions alone are not adequate, they believe, but rather will serve to institutionalize exploitative housework. Once housework is paid, the authors assert, it will also be clear that domestic work is productive work.

The authors challenge some time-honored assumptions about our life-styles. For instance, they assert that the community is not an area of freedom and leisure that is separate from the workplace but rather is "the other half of capitalist organization, the other area of hidden capitalist exploitation, the other, hidden, source of surplus labor."[2] Therefore they assert that women must stop presenting themselves only as wives and mothers; that is, they must stop meeting their husbands and children only at mealtime after they have come home from the outside world. The movement must be seen everywhere: "Every place of struggle outside the home, precisely because every sphere of capitalist organization presupposes the home, offers a chance for attack by women: factory meetings, neighborhood meetings, student assemblies, each of them are legitimate places for women's struggle."[3]

The authors believe that working outside the home for a wage is not the answer:

> But those of us who have gone out of our homes to work because we had to or for extras or for economic independence have warned the rest: inflation has riveted us to this bloody typing pool or to this assembly line, and in that there is no salvation.... The struggle of the working woman is not to return to the isolation of the home, appealing as this sometimes may be on Monday morning; any more than the housewife's struggle is to exchange being imprisoned in a house for being clinched to desks or machines....
>
> The challenge to the women's movement is to find modes of struggle which, while they liberate women from the home, at the same time avoid on the one hand a double slavery and on the other prevent another degree of capitalist control and regimentation. This ultimately is the dividing line between reformism and revolutionary politics within the women's movement.
>
> It seems that there have been few women of genius. There could not be since, cut off from the social process, we cannot see on what matters they could exercise their genius. Now there is a matter, the struggle itself.[4]

Dalla Costa and James believe that the result of women's struggle will be the demise of the nuclear family: women's exploitation through domestic work is tied to the nuclear family, so women must break out of the nuclear family and be seen as individuals.

> The housewife's position in the overall struggle of women is crucial, since it undermines the very pillar supporting the capitalist organization of work, namely the family.
>
> So every goal that tends to affirm the individuality of women against this figure complementary to everything and everybody, that is, the housewife, is worth posing as a goal subversive to the continuation, the productivity of this role.[5]

Jessie Bernard. Theoretical guidance for the new homemaker movement can also be found in the writing of some authors who have taken a broad perspective on women's issues. Since 1970 Jessie Bernard, professor emeritus of sociology at Pennsylvania State University, has written several books in which she touches on issues important to the homemaker. Her primary interest has been in women's roles as wives

and mothers, though to say that these are the only roles she deals with
would be to misrepresent her very rich and broad work.

When it comes to planning for change, one of the main themes that
recurs in Bernard's writing is the importance of men and women's
learning to share roles that have traditionally been sex stereotyped. In
her 1972 book *The Future of Marriage,* she does say that sharing roles is
not a panacea. Because of the nature of the original marital commitment, the nature of the sexual encounter, and other factors influencing
life-styles, marriage cannot be easily perfected, especially by one simple
strategy. Nevertheless, Bernard does come back again and again to the
idea of sharing, and in *The Future of Motherhood* (1974) she suggests
that, whereas sharing the housework seems like a relatively mild
change, in actuality it will entail a revolution in "the whole concept of
work for both men and women."[6] Bernard feels that hours for work
outside the home will have to become more flexible to allow husbands
and wives, mothers and fathers, to share their responsibilities more
equally, though she points out that changes in work schedules will
come about not because parents wish it but because industry will discover the benefits of "flextime" for both employees and employer.
Longer time periods—months or years—out of the paid work force will
become accepted practice for both men and women. It follows that
justifying women's lower pay on the basis of their longer absences from
the work force will no longer be possible.

Because women's work in the home is increasingly cut off from old
support systems—from family support, both psychological and financial, from neighborhood networks, and from community helping
systems—new provisions must be made for homemakers. Bernard believes that a new relationship must be created between homemakers and
"the exchange world," that world in which there is a very direct
relationship between money and services. Bernard laments this: she
would prefer to see the "love or duty world leaven the exchange
world,"[7] instead of vice versa. But she feels that today the reality is that
we need to make available to women in monetary form the help that is
no longer available through mutual aid systems. Benefits included in
this monetary aid system would be income maintenance while
mothering, and various kinds of insurance for the special hazards to
which women are vulnerable—rape, abortion, unexpected pregnancies,
abandonment, desertion, and physical violence in the home.

In her 1975 book *Women, Wives, and Mothers,* Bernard disputes the
view that a better world system will come about simply through in-
corporating more women into it. She points out that a widely accepted

view has been that if women were to gain positions of power they would vastly improve society through their nurturing, person-oriented, and less belligerent characters. The idea is no longer tenable, Bernard feels; no one can be better than the system. "If women are in positions of power they have to act according to the logic of the system; anyone who occupies a strategic position has to act according to the rules of the game, regardless of sex."[8] She does not argue that one should therefore abandon attempts to gain power; using power as it is now constituted is in itself a reasonable avenue for effecting change.

Beyond those strategies already discussed here, and others that she mentions briefly, Bernard sees two primary ways to promote change. For one thing, she is sympathetic to a new style of motherhood, one in which women become more active in political affairs and social movements. The new aggressive style of motherhood began to develop in the 1960s when mothers with various social backgrounds saw that they must confront policymakers whom they saw as responsible for threats to their children—threats like war, drugs, and poverty. "An increasing demand being made on the mother role was the ability to confront the enemies of children. Participation in the political process became a legitimate part of the mother's role. Mothers were coming to recognize that learning how to acquire and use power was one of their maternal responsibilities."[9]

Bernard also describes the power of technology that has tempered the outside world in the past century: "It is no longer the same world as that of early industrialism; the individualism is no longer permitted to be so rugged; dogs are not permitted to eat dogs, at least in such quantities; and, in general, the most brutalizing kinds of work have been gentled, if not wholly tamed or eliminated."[10] Further, it may not be women's commitment to their ideals that will create a new social order; rather, a developing technology that calls for those values women espouse may be the primary impetus to change: "In the postindustrial or cybernetic age, the traits associated with femaleness as we know it today will be in demand. The basis of society in the cybernetic age will be an information net, the effective functioning of which calls for an honest, cooperative society and greater acceptance of what have been called female characteristics."[11] On the other hand, Bernard does not wish to put all her confidence in technology: "As in the case of Marx's inevitable triumph of the proletariat, a little help from women cannot be out of order."[12] Obviously women can make and are making gains through their own efforts; improved technology may be necessary, but it is hardly a sufficient condition for the expression and acceptance of their ideals.

Elise Boulding. Elise Boulding has written extensively on women, and her work is often pertinent to homemakers. In *Women in the Twentieth Century World* (1977), Boulding sees as an ultimate social goal the movement toward a gentle society, a society that is, among other things, androgynous and peaceful. She lists four points of leverage to manipulate in achieving such a society. The first three are the major ones. Boulding believes that these leverage points are most likely to be effective in the affluent Western world, and she asserts that to identify Third World strategies is beyond her "competence" at this point. (I put the word in quotes because I dispute it: apparently we do not yet have the kind of information necessary to develop such strategies, but if we had it Dr. Boulding would surely be competent to use it.) The first leverage point is the redefinition of gender-based social roles; by this Boulding means that we need to move toward equal parenting and work sharing and, where desirable, to create extended families. Like Bernard, Boulding gives major priority to this leverage point. The second leverage point she mentions is the early-childhood school setting. Boulding feels that women can have tremendous influence here, and she emphasizes the possibilities of apprenticeships between the children and their communities. Through such apprenticeships, teachers and others influential in this setting can make sure no particular skills belong to only one segment of the community, and they can also see to it that children learn a variety of practical skills. Also important in this setting will be using male volunteers to help avoid gender-based stereotypes, textbook reform, and teaching children to help other children learn.

Boulding's third leverage point is the community. We need to establish more neighborhood self-help networks, she asserts, and we need continuing education for all ages in a variety of skills, especially to help people learn to perform more labor-intensive economic activity when necessary. In all of this community activity, women need to be active leaders.

Boulding's fourth leverage point may be harder to use effectively. This is the implementation of those principles that have been set forth, usually internationally, through declarations and covenants on human rights. She believes women can and should use these declarations, which have been made in organizations like the United Nations, as leverage to expand their participation in public areas.

Juliet Mitchell. The last theorist I will discuss is Juliet Mitchell, whose article "Women: The Longest Revolution," appeared in *New Left Review* in 1966. Mitchell's theory is the oldest of those we have considered; it is also the most comprehensive. She points out that women are essential and irreplaceable, fundamental to the human condition, yet at the same time marginal in their economic, social, and political roles. This combination of fundamentality and marginality has been fatal to them, she asserts, because "the one state justifies the other and precludes protest."[13] In other words, women's exclusion from other roles is justified by their having their own sphere in the family, where they are essential and irreplaceable. When a woman seeks to enter economic or social or political roles she is turned away either with the admonition that she is neglecting her family role or with the consolation that the family role too is important.

Mitchell believes that women's liberation today is a viable concept only in the highly developed societies of the West. Further, she believes that revolutionary change will be possible only through simultaneous change in the several structures in which women are integrated—the systems of production, reproduction, socialization, and sexuality. Modifying only one of these structures at a time will merely change the character of women's exploitation.

Within the first structure, the system of production, Mitchell points out that, at present, women's role is virtually stationary. Women's jobs continue to be lower-status and lower-paid and less often are career positions. Young women continue to get less pertinent education. Automation promises the technical possibility of offering women equality in jobs because physical strength will be outmoded, but Mitchell believes that "under capitalist relations of production, the *social* possibility of this abolition is permanently threatened, and can easily be turned into its opposite, the actual diminution of woman's role in production as the labour force contracts."[14] She believes that, where capitalism leads to growing unemployment, women—the group seen as having the least legitimate claim to employment—will continue to be the first fired.

The second structure that continues to need improvement is reproduction. Mitchell indicates that the effect of oral contraception is only beginning to be felt, that it needs to spread across all classes and all countries, and that it needs technical improvement. She points out that, in spite of the existence of oral contraception, the ideology of the family remains strong, and that the sudden increase in the birthrate in the United States in the fifties was an indication of this.

This brings her to her next point—that increased awareness of the critical importance of children's socialization should lead us not to reaffirm women's place in the home but to reconsider the best modes for that socialization. Obviously children need permanent, intelligent care, but unfortunately this need has been used to perpetuate the idea of the family as a total unit in a time when its other functions have been visibly declining. "Socialization as an exceptionally delicate process requires a serene and mature socializer—a type which the frustrations of a *purely* familial role are not liable to produce. Exclusive maternity is often in this sense 'counterproductive.' "[15] Both for their own good and for the good of their children, women's options must not be restricted to the family.

Finally, Mitchell asserts that the liberalization of sexual relationships is threatening marriage in its classical form, and that the production and work ethos that has been standard throughout the history of the United States is today taking on aspects of a consumption and fun ethos. Sex is at the center of the new way of thinking. The new sexuality can, she believes, contain a great potential for liberation; but, again, it cannot be successful alone. Change in all four of the structures she discusses must be integrated.

What does this four-part analysis mean in practical terms? Mitchell combines systems in this way: the family can be seen as a combination of sexual, reproductive, and socializing functions (the woman's world), all of which is embraced by production (the man's world). This entire structure is determined, she asserts, by the economy. Thus, when it comes to change, women must still concentrate on the economic element. To Mitchell this means they must enter fully into public industry; the most elementary economic demand is not the right to work or even to receive equal pay for work, but the right to equal work itself. And to achieve jobs of equal status with men, women must achieve equal education, which Mitchell feels is at present "the main single filter selecting women for inferior work roles."[16] The family must also change to become compatible with equality of the sexes. Sexuality and reproduction must be clearly separated, and marriage should be separate from parenthood. Furthermore, we need to develop a diversification of human relationships rather than limiting ourselves to a single social form. Mitchell says that "Couples living together or not living together, long-term unions with children, single parents bringing up children, children socialized by conventional rather than biological parents, extended kin groups, etc.—all these could be encompassed in a range of institutions which matched the free invention and variety of men and women."[17]

Perspectives on Change

We are only beginning to understand the dynamics of change for homemakers. Obviously each theorist has a slightly different perspective, and there is still much room for debate. Perhaps the only surprise at this point is that so few have addressed the problem with any kind of methodical and comprehensive analysis.

A fruitful next step would be to generate some discussion of the central issues. It would be instructive to have Dalla Costa and James debate other theorists on the merits and pitfalls of women's entering the paid work force. Mitchell feels such entry is a must; Bernard seeks only some relationship with the exchange world. It would be interesting for several writers to get together and attempt to establish priorities: Should women work to gain equality at home first, or should they enter the political arena as soon as possible? What are the policy implications of Mitchell's contention that all systems must change simultaneously? Is there not perhaps some ideal point of entry? Boulding and Mitchell both agree that our educational system should become more egalitarian. Is this to be done all at once, or piecemeal? And, if piecemeal, which aspects of education should take priority?

To date, each author seems to be making suggestions out of her individual perspective on the problem—an important beginning. The next crucial step is for them to synthesize their experience and recommend strategies for action. One suggestion for such a synthesis is offered in table 1, which organizes the solutions suggested by the foregoing theorists according to the social-system level at which they are most likely to be implemented.

Studying these suggestions by level, it is clear that women have definitely moved away from the perspective that change is solely the responsibility of individual homemakers and that change should adapt to traditional role patterns. A few suggestions have been made to encourage women to work on personal change—but these are nothing more than ideas to help women combat a socialization that is no longer useful; they are not suggestions for a primary strategy for change. The idea of adaptation to old role patterns has been successfully abandoned.

At the same time, the idea of working for system change has been successfully adopted. Theorists are emphasizing a scope that includes not only homemakers themselves but their families, their workplaces, and institutions outside the home as well. This broader conceptualization of the problem is a step in the right direction. Individual women, women in isolation from their families and communities, could not effect significant change. It is essential to include families and institutions in strategies for change.

But perhaps we can go beyond even this. The most frequently mentioned areas for change are basically personal (see table 1). Broader perspectives are mentioned by fewer of the theorists—perspectives like political change, community organization, participation through exercising human rights, and advancing technology. Why have topics like these not been considered at all in some cases, let alone in the same detail as topics like sex roles, education, and family?

In table 1 there are noticeable gaps at various levels of solutions. No one author has encompassed all levels of change. Furthermore, at a given level the range of ideas is rather narrow. For example, at the organizational level the suggestions include only government wages for housework, employers' implementation of flextime and leaves, a general reference to increasing power for women, and some educational issues. Not only is this a rather narrow range of ideas, but it also is limited to existing organizations and does not even consider the possibility of homemakers' own organizations.

Conversely, the effect of a given idea has not been considered across systems levels, and, while not all ideas will have major effects at all levels, the possibility should at least be considered. Role sharing, for example, is not simply the concern of the nuclear family. It will directly affect the extended family and peer groups; I argue elsewhere (chap. 5) that, unless peer groups change along with couples, the changes are likely to be short-lived. Role sharing will have important person-power effects at the organizational and societal levels as well.

As to what the major content areas are, or should be, we are probably only at the brainstorming stage, but the five theorists have given us a start. Summarizing the content areas they mention yields the following major categories: technology, the family, gender roles, economics, employment, and education. It also yields the minor categories (mentioned by only one theorist) of individual development in nonhomemaking roles, entering traditional power structures, improving community networks, using human rights declarations, and the methodological issue of achieving simultaneous structural change.

Together we need to examine and perhaps broaden this catalog of issues. We need to consider the impact of the issues at all systems levels. We need to ask ourselves whether homemakers' interests are represented at each of the various levels and, if not, whether their representation through their other roles—their roles as citizens or employees or family members—is sufficient to achieve their goals as homemakers. Undoubtedly we need to propose some new methods of homemaker representation, particularly at systems levels higher than that of the couple and the nuclear family.

These macrosystems have historically been the province of men. It does not follow, however, that we need to train ourselves to think like men; rather, we need to think more comprehensively about the man-

TABLE 1. SUGGESTED SOLUTIONS BY SYSTEM LEVEL: A SUMMARY OF THE MAJOR STRATEGIES OF FIVE THEORISTS

Level	Oakley	Dalla Costa/James	Bernard	Boulding[a]	Mitchell[a]
International				Use of existing declarations on human rights	Changes in women's relation to production
Societal		Government wages for housework	Increased traditional power for women Use of technology Motherhood income maintenance, insurance Actively political mothering		
Organizational			Flextime in paid work; leaves for both sexes Increased traditional power for women	Influence on early childhood education Continuing education for a variety of skills	Establishment of equal education system for women
Group, including extended family				Creation of extended families Establishment of neighborhood self-help networks	Expansion of socialization functions beyond nuclear family and mother role Establishment of diversified social relationships

Couple and nuclear family	Abolition of the family Abolition of marriage	Demise of the nuclear family	Role-sharing	Redefinition of gender-based social roles	Expanded acceptance of reproduction control Liberalized sexual relationships to revolutionize marriage
Individual	Abolition of the housewife role Abolition of gender roles through consciousness raising	Separate identities from housework		Influence on early childhood training	Work for pay outside the home

aBoth of these authors note that their strategies are pertinent primarily to highly developed, Western societies.

created world. For instance, we need to develop more comprehensive theories about changing homemakers' relationships to the world of paid work. Entering the paid work world may represent a viable solution to individual problems, but, as Dalla Costa and James caution, it is not a solution to the plight of homemakers as an exploitable class. To understand the full implications of this strategy, we need to consider the functioning of our capitalist system. I am proposing a strategy not unlike that suggested by sociologist Rosabeth Moss Kanter, who has recently asserted that, in understanding the causes of occupational segregation, research directed at the nature of organizational structures and the organization of work will be more fruitful than individual or role-related research.[18] Women must get beyond immediate concerns. They must expand their theory and research and action beyond the sphere of domesticity in order to protect and change that sphere. We need to think more about action through such male-dominated areas as unionization, politics, technology, and national and international organizations of all types. For instance, we should become conversant with new methods like technology assessment, a way of estimating the future effect of both social and physical technologies that is still underutilized.

Some of our theorists begin to stretch us in these directions. We need still more exercise—meaning more education and more exploration—while at the same time we must hold onto women's unique sensitivity to and knowledge of the domestic realm. Only by knowing the male-dominated sphere as well as we know the female-dominated one can we make realistic analyses. Only after knowing the universe of areas available for change can we make intelligent decisions about leverage. I am not arguing that we must join the system to change it—only that we must know the system to use it.

Creating a
New Ideology for
Housework

3

We want to call work what is work so that eventually we might discover what is love.

Sylvia Federici

Ask an American homemaker what she does, and she is likely to say she takes care of her children and her husband and her home. Ask her why she does these things, and she is likely to say she does them mostly out of love. Probably she has some idea that there is more to her role. She might mention, if pressed, that as a homemaker she is also a consumer, a community worker, and a citizen.

But that is about as far as she will go. Few homemakers would mention their contribution to national productivity. Few would discuss the importance of homemakers to the national labor supply. And few of them would know, for instance, that outside the home there exists a growing movement to improve the quality of working life—a movement that, not incidentally, is likely to pass them by because homemakers are not considered workers.

Most homemakers simply do not think of themselves in relation to such broad issues; yet they need to recognize that the household does not operate as an entity totally separated from the realm of money and power and "real" work. Failure to recognize the extensive interactions between homemaking and other social institutions will leave homemakers uninformed and powerless.

Women who work outside the home have already had their consciousness raised about some of the important interactions between their jobs and their homelives. They know from experience that the homemaker's job is an indispensable support for the outside worker. Because they may have been full-time homemakers themselves, and probably continue to be part-time homemakers, they can well appreciate the homemaker's value. They know that the human needs filled through homelife do not vanish and may even be intensified when one takes an outside job. They know that people still get sick and need to be cared for, that a well-managed home can be a rejuvenating refuge, and

that someone has to maintain the wage earner's automobile and clothing. Further, because they are the family members who usually shop for
services to replace those of the homemaker, they know that obtaining
these services on the open market can cost a lot of money. Ironically,
full-time homemakers are less likely to see these interactions.

The connections between homemaking and other social roles and
institutions must be clearly understood by homemakers and their advocates. To broaden our perspectives on housework, we need to develop a
dialogue around some key questions. For instance, if housework isn't
"women's work" or merely "shit work," what kind of work is it? If we
want the homemaker's economic and psychological status to change,
what should her new status be? If the home is to be more than "woman's place," what exactly should it be? In short, if actions to change the
status of homemakers are to succeed, we must develop a new ideology
for housework.

The new ideology will emerge in part out of a realization of what the
old way of thinking lacks. And, to begin with, the old ideology suffers
substantially from neglect. Considering their numbers, their problems,
and their potential, the extent to which homemakers have been ignored
over the years is astonishing.

As I have already mentioned, feminists have only very recently begun
a concerted effort to advance the status of the homemaker in the name of
the homemaker. They are certainly not alone in their neglect of the
ideology of housework. Among the social sciences, sociology and
anthropology have conducted research on housework, but even in these
disciplines little research existed before the past few years. Psychology
has constructed the female and created androgyny, but it has paid scant
attention to women's work in the home. Even its consideration of marriage and family life and divorce has rarely led to an analysis of the role
of the homemaker. In economics one hears about households but seldom about the homemaker, and "the new home economics" is not as
broad a concept as we would take it to be—though as a theory of accounting for the time involved in the household use of goods it is
useful, it hardly constitutes a major new emphasis on housework in
economics. Finally, the discipline of home economics has been primarily interested in such things as the scientific analysis of housework and
has generally avoided the sociopolitical issues pertinent to the homemaker herself.

And those institutions that have paid some attention to housework
and homemakers, including government, business, and the media,
have invariably confirmed stereotypical views. Government, for instance, has persistently treated the homemaker as a dependent,

whether for purposes of Social Security or for settlements in the courts. No thrust toward treating homemakers as independent and contributing citizens in their own right has yet emerged in government policy. And why should it? Homemakers have little money and minimal political influence; they are not organized as an interest group.

In the business world we find support of the status quo. The small business supports it by treating the homemaker as if she were truly a homebody, a person for whom housework literally means staying in the house. Thus, even crucial services like telephone installation are often scheduled to satisfy business, not the customer. A company delivering furniture might specify the day of delivery but not the hour or even a rough estimate of it. The homemaker is told, "We'll be there sometime between 7 A.M. and 7 P.M." In such cases the implication is that the homemaker's mobility is clearly less important than the service person's convenience. Employed persons have similar problems, of course, owing in part to this habit of disdaining the homemaker.

Larger firms reinforce the status quo through their advertising, by continuing to represent only women in homemaker positions and to show homemakers in traditionally narrow roles. Such firms are primarily interested in ensuring known markets for their products rather than in changing the nature of these markets.

The media, which can hardly be accused of lack of attention to the homemaker, nevertheless are perhaps the worst culprits when it comes to systematic efforts to maintain the status quo. Obviously it is to their advantage to do so. Advertisers want a predictable market in which to sell their products. In an article in the *New York Times*, Dell Publishing Company reported that, based on the sales of their books in supermarkets, women are much less interested in topics like economical management of the household than they are in topics like beauty and personal care. Of course they do not mention that more money can be made through selling beauty and personal care products than through teaching women how to economize. Millions of dollars are spent to create a market for beauty and personal care products, while little or nothing is spent to interest women in economizing. Thus the Dell results cannot really tell us whether women's interest in beauty and personal care is the chicken or the egg: Did companies manufacture and sell products because women wanted them, or do women want them because companies who can manufacture them and make a profit have encouraged women to want them? We frequently find much the same quandary in today's popular writing for women.

A magazine like *Woman's Day* can include in an article the prohomemaker idea that women are seeking "equality in interdependence" at home, while its advertising endorses old stereotypes by picturing women in the kitchen and by emphasizing youthfulness as the standard of beauty.

A similar argument is made about the wasteland of daytime television. Television executives argue that they produce what women want to see. This statement is questionable and, even if it were true, remains socially irresponsible. A child may want to play all day, but for his own good and for the good of us all, he is gently weaned away from his selfish pursuits. In the same way, television could turn America's daytime viewers away from game shows and passive, irresponsible consuming and toward more socially rewarding activities like community involvement and responsible consuming. Of course, that could mean that the viewers would watch less television and would buy fewer of the products advertised.

Marabel Morgan's books *The Total Woman* and *Total Joy* have sold millions of copies, perhaps because they too are highly supportive of the homemaker's status quo. To understand Morgan's success, it is important to remember that today's thirty-five-year-old homemaker grew up in the fifties and early sixties, at the height of women's indoctrination into a narrow conception of the role of the homemaker. In those years the concept of "housewife" remained unquestioned, and women's accepted role was in the home. For most of today's women, a decade and a half of feminist thinking stands in direct opposition to their twenty years of socialization to the old role. Their transition to the new way of thinking is difficult, or may even be impossible if they are already caught up in the cycle of economic and psychological dependency encouraged—even demanded—by the woman-as-housewife dogma. So when an attractive, happy, and successful woman like Morgan tells these homemakers that they are indeed fulfilling themselves by staying at home, many of today's homemakers are eager to believe her.

Developing a new ideology for housework will involve a reexamination of some of the basic values of our culture. The values associated with housework are complex, encompassing many of the most important standards by which we live, and the discussion here can only be a prelude to the many intradisciplinary and interdisciplinary studies that are needed. I will open the dialogue by considering four areas that are particularly relevant: our individual values about sex roles, work, economics, and homelife.

Housework today is done mostly by one sex and is socialized primarily in one sex, yet both psychologically and economically it supports both sexes. Thus, in creating a new way of thinking about housework, individual values about sex roles will be central. Second, housework consumes time—even whole lifetimes—with physical labor and personal service. In our society such occupations are usually called "work" and usually earn a wage. Clearly, values about work in general have important implications for values about housework. Housework also involves the consumption of goods and services and the expenditure of money. It therefore has a direct relation to individual values about basic economics—about capitalism, consumerism, and money. Finally, housework takes place in the physical and mental space we call "home," and it is intimately related to the important values people hold about the home as a place for satisfying physical and psychological needs.

The reader will realize that my choice of these four areas in itself represents a value decision. In another society the most important values might be associated with rituals, child-rearing, and food-gathering instead of sex roles, economics, and the home. In our society sometime in the future, the most important considerations may be ecology, social contribution, and cultural diversity. Probably our values will evolve with or without our conscious attention. But I believe that by naming them and being aware of them we may be better able to guide them in positive directions.

Beyond Sex-Role Stereotypes

Of all the issues to be examined in creating a new ideology for housework, the problem of sex-role stereotypes has had the most widespread discussion. Thanks to the women's movement, it has also seen the most recent change. Feminism's emphasis on making work outside the home into a feasible alternative for women has had some success. Indeed, consciousness-raising about women's work has gone so far that it has made the dependence and financial insecurity of homemaking seem like a poor alternative to the independence and financial security often afforded by outside employment. The economic and psychological problems of working inside the home become clearer every day.

A recent poll indicates that three-fourths of today's women plan to combine home and job.[2] If nothing else, the women's movement has made possible the *belief* in such choices, and it seems that women are indeed opting for life-styles that maximize their ability to choose. Of course, the choices feminists win for women would also extend to men, though for men the issue of choice has not yet become important. A Yankelovich study shows that, even if they do report that they plan to combine home and job, men's conceptualization of "home" differs radically from women's interpretation. When a man says he "puts the family above everything," he generally means that he will support the family through his paid job, not that he plans to spend a great deal of time in family relationships and home work.[3] Most women still consider full-time homemaking, by which they mean family activities and home work, to be part of their role in life; most men still do not. Women expect to be breadwinners as well as homemakers, while men continue to expect to be only breadwinners.

Does the idea of calling a male a homemaker seem strange? How would you feel telling your boss, or a stranger, that your husband is a homemaker? The uneasiness most people would experience is a measure of just how much our thinking needs to change.

Ultimately, egalitarianism would dictate that family support, whether financial, psychological, or physical, should be shared equitably—fifty-fifty or perhaps by job preference. Roles should be allocated not with regard to sex but by taking into account interests and abilities. In all cases, roles should be allocated with full knowledge of and compensation for the economic and social implications of taking on certain jobs—especially the homemaking jobs—full time. Both men and women should be fully educated about the advantages and the disadvantages of working in the home.

Each man and each woman will have to come to grips with the fact that they were raised with some sex stereotype in mind, so that their interests and abilities may in themselves need reexamination. One hears so often that women like to do housework, and, though we do not have convincing empirical confirmation of this hypothesis, indeed some of them may. Women need to ask themselves whether, given the consequences of housework in their lives today, they want to *continue* to like housework or whether they want to learn to value some other activity more.

As more men become homemakers, we can look forward to seeing the change reflected in our culture. *Woman's Day* might be called *Homemaker's Day*, or some such non-sex-stereotyped title, or we may greet the equivalent homemaking journal for men. Males will be pictured mopping floors and choosing detergents, and perhaps even pleasing their wives by realizing that they'd prefer stuffing to potatoes. Ideas like "women's work" will go the way of the wringer washer, to be replaced simply by "work."

Efforts to change sex-role stereotypes in housework and in paid work are intimately connected. Reasonable arrangements in the home will have to be paralleled by accommodating arrangements on the job, or else changes at home that require significant sacrifices outside are likely to be short-lived. For instance, both men and women need to be eligible for a leave of absence when a child is born, and both need to be able to get flexible hours of paid employment. At this point, equality on the job is hampered by women's domestic responsibilities, so that employers continue to think of them as second-class workers. This vicious circle can be broken only if men are given the right and the responsibility to assume housework and child care. Of course, efforts must continue to end male domination in the best jobs and female domination in the worst, or women will continue to choose homemaking over dead-end jobs, and both men and women will continue to think of women who work in the home as "just housewives."

The Ideology of Work

"Work" is a word with many uses. It can mean activity that is difficult or activity that is paid. As a verb it can describe the functioning of a system—something "works." But, perhaps most important, work is a word that is heavily value-laden. In a society that lives by the Protestant ethic, to label an activity work is to legitimize it. "Work" generally is socially desirable ... unless of course that work is "women's work" or "housework," both of which have connotations of disparagement. One goal of this book is to bring this kind of work into the sphere of legitimate, valued work—to help make "house" work into "real" work.

That the traditional view of the roles of the sexes has been narrow and damaging to both women and men has been repeatedly observed. That our traditional view of the nature of work has also been narrow and damaging is less frequently mentioned but no less important. An improved ideology for housework must reformulate some old notions about work, and it must integrate some new ideas.

To understand our ideas about what work is, it may be useful to review some of their origins. Traditional American views of the nature of work under capitalism, views that have been subscribed to for much of this century, originated when money was scarce and employers generally had more power over their employees' lives than they do today. Thus, traditional views have included the notions that people's motivation to work is primarily to make money—as much money as possible—and to avoid unemployment. Naturally, by this way of thinking, labor like housework, which is unpaid to begin with, has not been considered real work.

Traditionally the increase of production has been the primary goal of work. An early view was that one could increase production by improving the worker's physical environment, usually by upgrading sanitation and lighting and by reducing noise. Later the individual worker became an object of study. Theoretically, at least, his or her ability to produce could be improved through time and motion studies aimed at streamlining each task so it could be done most quickly and accurately.

It is not surprising that people who have held these beliefs about the primacy of production and how to achieve it have found little common ground between traditional work and housework. In today's capitalist industrial society, housework has lost the claim to usefulness that it had clearly established when, for instance, farm wives were essential to a family's survival. Today the homemaker's relationship to production is indirect, and so changing her working conditions or streamlining her job seems relatively unimportant.

Today's average homemaker is probably part of a middle-class family. The full-time homemaker role is best afforded by those who are at least at this income level, though women of the working classes also aspire to it. The middle-class homemaker will have at her disposal a large number of appliances, convenience foods, and services—so many, in fact, that those who believe in traditional means of improving work efficiency have been surprised to find that her workday is as long as ever. Consequently, the traditionalists have been unsympathetic to homemakers, going so far as to characterize housework as primarily time-filling busywork. They have not fully realized that the homemaker's shiny, well-furnished kitchen is primarily a function of her role as consumer, not her role as worker, and thus is not necessarily aimed at helping her improve efficiency. Neither have traditionalists been sympathetic to the fact that over the years many additional time-consuming jobs have become the homemaker's responsibility. Basically, then, our longtime views of the nature of work have been too restrictive to encompass the realities of housework.

Among modern theorists, consensus is by no means common, but at least it can be said that many have adopted a broader perspective on the nature of work. Today, theories about the goals of work and the motivation to work include concepts like the enjoyment of work for its own sake, the pleasure of social interactions at work, the achievement of status, and the desire to contribute to one's society. Improving production is seen as a complicated process involving these kinds of motivation in addition to factors like physical environment and efficiency. Significantly, production itself is no longer viewed as the sole goal of an individual or an organization. These days there is room for goals like worker satisfaction and community impact.

Until the middle of the seventies it was not fashionable to raise questions about the quality of working life, but today such issues are the object of frequent study. More and more workers are dissatisfied with the personal price they pay for having jobs and earning money; they are seeking more autonomy and dignity in their work, and they are refusing to be used by technology or by organizations. Younger workers may be particularly unwilling to put up with highly directive, arbitrary practices, and it may be that over the next fifteen years management will have to make adjustments to cope with their independence. These workers are supported by a growing interest among researchers, professionals, and management.

Generally speaking, such innovations in work ideology have passed housework by. Housework is usually considered a kind of nonwork that is not exactly leisure either. It has been customary to consider housework as a class separate from ordinary work. Thus, even the broadest perspective on work has often failed to encompass it, and housework has often been excluded from studies on the quality of worklife. When it has been professionalized and paid, as among domestics and hotel workers, some attempt has been made to develop housework along the lines of other jobs—to train personnel, to develop promotion paths, and to start professional associations. But, when it has remained unwaged, housework has seldom been treated like other work.

An important force militating against the homemaker's inclusion among the ranks of "real" workers is that she herself has not pushed for inclusion. I have already noted that no one has bothered to push *for* her; but neither has the homemaker herself stepped forward to demand consideration alongside other workers. Certainly her lack of action is not because of her overwhelming contentment. Most waged workers are basically satisfied with their jobs.[4] Few comparable studies have been done on homemaker satisfaction, but some bits of evidence suggest that homemakers are less satisfied than the average worker.[5] There is also an intuitive basis for such a prediction. For instance, standards for housework are vague. Thus any sense of finishing a task and doing it well is lost. Homemakers work in relative isolation, thus also losing the social satisfactions of work. Finally, homemakers exhibit a good deal of ambivalence about the work they do. They are not quite sure whether it is valuable, and whether they should be proud of it in spite of its status or ashamed of it in spite of its necessity.

In the face of dissatisfaction, why has the homemaker remained silent? Why has she not stood up and demanded equal rights with other workers?

To some extent she may have accepted the myth of the happy homemaker and woman's place: She may wish to believe that homemaking is where she is most useful. Any qualms about her own status or security are hushed by her belief that homemaking is a noble cause, a labor of love, and so is not to be associated with baser motivators like personal esteem and money. Some homemakers have bought the domestic double standard.

Another explanation is that the dissatisfied homemaker attributes her problems to herself, believing that she is at fault for not making a better adjustment to homelife. This belief is at least partly the result of her socialization to the idea of a homemaker's narrow sphere. Thus she tries even harder to adapt to her role, instead of trying to change that role and the system that created it. Her actual isolation from other homemakers—physically as a result of the nuclear family and psychologically because of the competitiveness that has been encouraged among women—supports her view that her problem is individual and isolated. Usually she does not see herself as part of a group of dissatisfied workers with a common interest in changing their working conditions. If her attempts to adapt and to be a better homemaker fail to increase her work satisfaction, she generally seeks an individual solution outside the home. Often she takes a paid job that she hopes will meet her needs. If she is lucky, the job does fulfill her expectations and she is happy. If she is less fortunate and finds the paid job is also dissatisfying, she will probably continue to blame herself. In either case homemakers as a group suffer, for they have probably lost an advocate. As an employed woman she no longer thinks of herself as a homemaker, and, though she still has many of the same problems as full-time homemakers, she tends to attribute her problems to her new dual role. Of course, as long as homemakers continue to see their problems as individual rather than as collective, organizing for change will be difficult.

Values and the Definition of Work

Homemakers have also been excluded from studies of working life because of our culture's general understanding of the nature of work. Defining work as "purposeful activity" probably sounds reasonable to most people. The definition is engagingly straightforward, and at first glance it seems to describe an important aspect of the American work ethic—the need to do meaningful work. We shall see, however, that defining work is far from simple.

What is "purposeful," of course, is strictly in the eye of the beholder; what is considered purposeful by one person may be considered wasteful by another. Society's view of what constitutes "purposeful activity," or work, is highly subjective.

It is probably safe to say that, at least in part, a society's most powerful members determine its goals. The goals and values of the powerful will determine the meaning of "purposeful activity" in their society, and this meaning consequently determines what work is considered to be "real"—that is, valuable—in that society. In the United States, as in virtually all of the world, the powerful people have always been men. And, especially in this country, many of the most powerful men have been industrialists, capitalists, and corporation leaders—men who have a strong interest in the production of goods. (One popular theory holds that because men cannot create other human beings, they have co-opted the business of creating things.) Whatever the reason, thanks to these men, production is one of the activities men tend to see as purposeful.

This tendency has had unfortunate consequences for housework. Though the homemaker occasionally bakes bread or makes clothing, she is hardly a producer. She produces relatively few goods for home consumption, and she rarely produces goods for outside use. For decades economists have (erroneously, many now believe) dealt with her as though she were totally outside the means of production. And for decades housework has not been considered valuable work.

The heavy emphasis on the production of goods is today being modified by an increased emphasis on services. Though industry continues to attempt to replace employees with machines, unions are fighting these attempts, a government poicy for full employment seems to be gaining substantial support, and, furthermore, individuals today have a renewed interest in and respect for craftsmanship and handwork. This may be seen as positive progress for homemakers. In a more labor-intensive economy, the distinction between housework and other service work may blur until it becomes obvious to most people that both are socially valuable and should be treated as such.

Our national tendency to value only paid work has also contributed to housework's exclusion from the category of "real" work. While this tendency cannot be attributed solely to the influence of the powerful, it is a result of the capitalism and capitalists that have prospered in this country in the past century. Conventional usage dictates that an activity performed without pay is a hobby or a pastime, while the same activity performed for pay is work. Housework, since it is not paid, is therefore not considered "real" work, even though it meets other criteria and even though it is hard to imagine that anyone would do it strictly for pleasure. The pay model is commonly used for valuing an activity, and it is certainly a flexible and comprehensive model, but it is just as certainly not the only model. Labor can also be valued by the benefit it gives the individual, the pleasure it gives the family, or the service it provides society. Certainly unpaid community work is often purposeful. Housework also serves broad community goals, most conspicuously through promoting effective child care and family well-being, but also through activities like maintaining sanitary and attractive dwellings. This work is valuable and should be appreciated whether or not it earns money.

Another widely held belief, whose origins are obscure, is the idea that physical labor is somehow less valuable than intellectual labor. A parallel belief is that unskilled labor is less valuable than skilled labor. Housework is undervalued on both counts. Whereas effective housekeeping may require all kinds of specific knowledge, from nutrition to nursing, the bare necessities of housework do involve mostly physical labor, and when most people think of housework they first think of things like cooking and cleaning. To be done adequately, these activities require only minimal skills. If unskilled labor is performed in the pursuit of pay or productivity, however, it joins the class of valued work, though at a low level. Yet the same unskilled labor performed in the home for other purposes may actually be ridiculed. Few of us would scoff at the labors of a ditchdigger or a garbage collector, yet people freely poke fun at homemakers, even to the point of popularizing a comic strip based primarily on this kind of mockery.[6] Deriding the homemaker is especially likely when she does more than the bare necessities. Goals that she herself establishes based on her own values, which do not necessarily correspond with the primary social goals of pay and production, are ignored or ridiculed. The homemaker may be accused of "creating useless work" for herself simply because her idea of usefulness does not correspond to the majority view. Even when her work is intellectual, even when it is skilled—as for instance when she becomes a gourmet cook—if the work is not done in pursuit of the goals set by those in power in society, it is not recognized as legitimate.

It is one thing to take a supply-and-demand perspective on unskilled and physicial labor—that is, to say that it is not "worth" much because such laborers are plentiful and can therefore be paid a minimum wage.[7] This of course happens to be true. It is quite another thing to say that the labor done by such workers does not fulfill some legitimate purpose. Clearly this notion is false. Unskilled, manual labor is still needed in our society, and the worker who performs it is providing a valuable service. The unskilled manual labor performed by homemakers is one such service. The fact that there are many people who could do the job does not diminish the importance of the job itself.

In summary, if other values dominated in our society, housework
would receive much wider recognition as a legitimate activity. Improving the status of housework will require that individuals re-
examine assumptions about the nature of work, and that some new
values acquire widespread social acceptance.

The Legitimacy of Housework

Once we see homemakers not as curious female hybrids but as legitimate workers, we begin to discover the relevance of a broad body of
existing knowledge that is pertinent to people's working lives. This
knowledge is available in such academic specialities as industrial and
organizational psychology, sociology, labor relations, and management
theory. By examining existing research in these areas, we may be able
to increase our understanding of homemakers as workers.

A brief foray into this literature follows. Before going any further,
however, let us remind ourselves that the ideology of work remains
largely a male ideology, created out of male socialization, male assumptions, and male motivation. It would be presumptuous to assume that a
woman-created work ethic would be identical to the male-created work
ethic or that, for example, a woman's motivation to work is identical to
a man's. Precious little is known about socialized or innate differences,
or about the possibilities for integration of such differences when they
do occur. As we develop our thinking about homemakers, the male-
created ideology must be examined critically, for the sake of both men
and women whose values about work may already differ from it, and
for the sake of those who may wish to create new values.[8]

Beyond my suggestions for reexamining the values already discussed, I will not attempt to develop a strategy for discovering or creating the female work ethic. I am not certain, indeed, that such a course
would be useful: what we seem to need most is not a male work ethic or
a female work ethic, but a human work ethic. Nevertheless, people who
continue the study of housework and homemaking need to be constantly aware of the male orientation of the current work ethic and of the
domination of male theorists in the disciplines that have studied workers.

Having made this recommendation, let me proceed to an exploration
of the kinds of knowledge the existing literature can provide.

The Quality of Working Life

Of all of the theoretical frameworks one might choose as a guide to
understanding housework, the most immediately interesting and one

of the most encompassing is the research on the quality of working life. The many issues examined in this research begin with one basic question. What *is* the quality of working life? Standards for the quality of working life differ from organization to organization and from individual to individual. One can well imagine that homemakers will have individual differences as well as some group similarities in their ideas of what constitutes quality. The task remains to some enterprising researcher to do an empirical study of how homemakers set their standards and what their standards are.

In *The Quality of Working Life,* an anthology of current research, Richard E. Walton of the Harvard Graduate School of Business Administration suggests some guidelines.[9] The following abbreviated account cannot do justice to Walton's full exposition, but it will give an idea of the usefulness of such a framework in pointing out the kinds of questions homemakers need to ask about the quality of their own working lives. I will not attempt to answer all the questions Walton raises, but rather will show how these quality-of-life issues are pertinent to homemakers. Of the eight criteria he suggests for analyzing the quality of working life, I will examine four in some detail.

Walton's first criterion is that of adequate and fair compensation. The basic questions he considers under this topic are, "Does the income from full-time work meet socially determined standards of sufficiency or the subjective standard of the recipient?" and "Does the pay received for certain work bear an appropriate relation to the pay received for other work?" The first question is posed in a way that instantly clarifies an important assumption homemakers make about the quality of their working life: When housework is unwaged its monetary compensation obviously meets no criterion of sufficiency, and yet being unpaid may meet the homemaker's own standard if she has come to believe that her work is worthless. The second question is useful because it provides an impetus for comparing housework with other kinds of work. How does the wage for housework compare with that paid for domestic service, for example, or with that paid for other labor that has similar characteristics? What justifies any discrepancy, and do we wish to accept that justification?

Walton's first criterion touches on the broad area of financial motivation in work, a crucial factor in understanding the motivations of homemakers. Commonly, views of homemakers' motivations to work have been simplistic, as have been views of all women's financial motivations. The fine distinction that is often made is that women who work for wages more often do so out of necessity, while those who stay at home do so from choice. We need more sophistication in our analyses. For instance, in an effort to legitimize women's entry into the paid work force and partly, it seems, to convince employers that women deserve equal pay, a large number of people have pointed out that many women work for wages because they "have to"—not just for extra money to buy frills. While it is true that a large proportion of women do waged work out of necessity, whether to support themselves or to better provide for their families, it is also true that the American standard of "necessity" is quite different from standards elsewhere in the world. In the United States the motivations of men and women alike are influenced by questionably high standards of consumption. The issue is further complicated because, while many women work for wages because they have to, necessity does not represent the full extent of their motivation to work. While survival is obviously important, so are things like opportunity for increased status, social interaction, and personal growth.

Nor is the homemaker's motivation as narrow as it is often conceived to be. Her motivation to work is widely assumed to be "love" of her family, a formulation that is entirely too simplistic. It is clear that other things are also important to homemakers, including possibilities for social interaction and personal growth, but also the chance for financial security and autonomy.

Often, though especially in the upper and middle classes, what is necessity and what is choice is unclear for both waged and unwaged workers. What is clear is that the human values subsumed under the rubric "love" and the security and independence that are associated with the earning of a wage are both important to waged and to unwaged workers.

The second of Walton's criteria for the quality of working life is the immediate opportunity to use and develop human capacities. For instance, does the job allow for substantial autonomy and self-control relative to external controls? Many homemakers cite independence—mobility and the opportunity to make their own decisions—as a prime motivator for being a homemaker. Yet, while the homemaker may experience autonomy at home, when she tries to deal with external factors such as hiring a repairman or doing the shopping she may find herself frustratingly powerless. Such extremes need to be explored. Walton also asks whether the job permits the learning and exercise of a wide range of skills and abilities, rather than a repetitive application of narrow skills. This question has many implications for housework, since repetitive tasks do consume much of the homemaker's time, and to this extent the quality of her working life may be diminished. On the other hand, a homemaker might improve the quality of her working life by expanding her skills—by learning carpentry and plumbing, for instance, instead of leaving such tasks to her husband.

Social integration in the work organization—the degree to which an individual feels that she or he is an accepted member of an organization—is a third criterion for the quality of working life. A homemaker is in an unusual position in this respect because she has no organizational membership. Because she has no position in a hierarchy, she has virtually no upward mobility. The nature of what would be her supportive primary group—a face-to-face work group in which people help each other and provide socioemotional support—is at best unusual, since each homemaker works in her own remote physical structure. Any sense of a community of workers beyond her immediate neighborhood is strongly influenced by the mass media, especially homemaker-oriented magazines, which have in mind their own best interests. The consumer movement is beginning to speak for the homemaker to some extent, but this is quite different from, for example, a professional association or a profession's trade press. The homemaker's lack of social integration is an important consideration not only for her psychological well-being but also because of the problems of organizing such isolated workers into power groups such as unions.

The final criterion for the quality of working life that I will examine here is a set of issues about constitutionalism in the workplace. Probably most workers would endorse the idea that those freedoms granted by the constitution should be guaranteed not only in one's personal life but in one's worklife as well. This is the popular notion of "industrial democracy" that originated in the early 1900s and is today a part of Sweden's and Norway's efforts to democratize the workplace. The implications for home work, both legally and morally, are extensive. To maintain a decent quality of working life by constitutional standards, the homemaker should have the right to dissent openly from the views of her superiors without fear of reprisal; she should have the right to equitable treatment in all matters, including compensation and job security; and she should have a right to due process—governance by "rule of law" rather than "rule of men." As a citizen in a democratic country, the homemaker deserves these rights. But since courts most often refuse to interfere between husband and wife, even when a man uses physical force against a woman, she is denied them. Thus she cannot dissent without fear of reprisal. She cannot demand equitable compensation or security. And, once married, her main method for renegotiation is divorce. Clearly the homemaker has much to do to make her workplace democratic.

This discussion of Walton's criteria for the quality of working life has raised more questions than it has answered—as it was intended to do. I want to reemphasize that by treating homemakers as workers we can learn a great deal about them. Or at least by tapping existing research we can get an idea of what it would be most useful to find out. Homemakers are indeed workers—they merely happen to be workers who now exist within an alien ideology.

Economic Ideology

I have already noted that most economists have ignored the individual homemaker, concentrating instead on the household as their primary unit of analysis. One explanation for their perspective is that the homemaker usually has a rather indirect relation to money. For example, she does not earn money for work: she is considered by economists to be a dependent of someone who does. She does spend money, but the money she spends is not often considered her own. It is said, rather, that she spends her husband's money, or perhaps the household's money. That the homemaker lacks a direct relation to money is a crucial aspect of her life and her role, affecting her financial security and even the stability of her marriage.

A basic principle of the traditional economic ideology is that the homemaker is her spouse's dependent. This scenario of dependency is played out in various versions ranging from true partnerships to the dictatorship of the wage earner. Some homemakers feel they have an equal say in how the household money is spent; others are on a strict allowance and have to ask for any additional money. From what is known about other social relationships involving money and power, and from what we hear from homemakers themselves, it seems that in most relationships ultimate power rests in the hands of the person who wields the paycheck. If this were *not* true, then why is it that husbands tend to have expensive hobbies like photography, mechanics, hi-fi, and sports, while wives tend to have inexpensive hobbies like crafts and gardening? Why would any homemaker have to talk about her "allowance" or ask her husband for money?

Of course, men alone are not to blame—women often support the unequal division of the household money because they too have believed, at least in part, that in a sense the money belongs to the person whose name is on the check. They may forget that their own work contributes to the wage earner's ability to work and to maintain his chosen style of living, or at least they may find it difficult to support this case in an argument. Often there is just enough doubt in the homemaker's mind about the legitimacy of her contribution and about the money being "really" his that she demurs to the "leadership" of the wage earner.

The economic inequality between homemaker and wage earner often contributes to a lowered self-esteem and social status for the homemaker. It may even threaten the institutions of marriage and the family. As Charlotte Perkins Gilman saw in 1898:

> The long, sure, upward trend of the human race toward monogamous marriage is no longer helped, but hindered by the economic side of the relation. The best marriage is between the best individuals; and the best individuals of both sexes to-day are increasingly injured by the economic basis of marriage, which produces and maintains those qualities in men and women and their resultant industrial conditions which make marriage more difficult and precarious every day.[10]

Today we may be experiencing the fulfillment of Gilman's logic: the economic dependency of women in marriage seems to be an important factor in the dissolution of traditional relationships. Giving homemakers their economic independence, granting them personal power at home, may actually become an important factor in supporting traditional structures of marriage and the family.

Many women are not willing to wait for the changes in policy that might help them solve the problem of economic dependency. Instead, they are attempting to achieve immediate economic equality by entering the paid work force. The new homemaker movement may be one indication of a deepening conviction that for any able-bodied citizen, homemaker or wage earner, dependency is simply not an acceptable status.

The homemaker's role as a consumer has received a great deal of attention. Yet in her role as consumer the homemaker is almost as powerless as in her role as dependent. Some economists would have her believe that as a consumer she has real economic effectiveness. She is told that through judicious consuming she not only improves the quality of her own life and her family's life, but she also contributes to the system of free enterprise in which only the "best" products—the most-consumed ones—survive in the marketplace. In some ways the consumer is truly respected: when economic indexes show that consumer confidence is waning, the economists' optimism also wanes. But this respect for the consumer is based on his or her basic decision to support or not to support consumption *in general,* not on the homemaker's limited power to choose among products. Whether or not one believes that economist John Kenneth Galbraith has successfully debunked the myth of consumer power,[11] his assertion that consumer power is exceedingly small in relation to corporate power—that what cereal gets sold at the local market has a lot more to do with corporate finagling than it does with consumer "voting" through purchase power—cannot be overlooked as a real possibility. Galbraith points out that the housewife role has become "a convenient social virtue"—a role that is convenient mostly for the producers, and inconvenient and uncomfortable for the individual involved. Certainly what power the homemaker does have as a consumer is not power to increase her personal financial worth or her own status, except very indirectly and in minuscule amounts (she can clip coupons for specials); rather, her consumer power is primarily to protect herself against poor products and, to a certain extent, when collective boycotts are undertaken, to have some influence in a circumscribed market situation.

By accepting the consumer role, homemakers are in fact supporting what Galbraith calls the planning system—that system of large corporations whose primary business is manufacturing goods. As it is, most big corporations produce not services but things, and they want homemakers to consume things. Consuming these things requires time and effort—the homemaker's time and effort. Using and maintaining these things requires administration—housework. Naturally manufacturers have a vested interest in keeping consumers in their place, in maintaining what Galbraith calls the homemaker's "crypto-servant" status as administrator of consumption. The repudiation of their role as the nation's consumers can be an important step for homemakers. A better system would be to encourage the use of services—laundries, child care, and the like—all of which would collectivize and thereby reduce the necessary labor of housework. Galbraith goes so far as to argue that as a nation we must move from an emphasis on a planning-production economy, which is inherently unstable, to a service economy, which is more stable. He believes that emancipating homemakers from their role as consumers will foster this change.[12] The advantage to homemakers is clear: as people demand services instead of goods and as the economy responds to their demands, there will be less consumerism, with its associated housework, and there will be less reason for the economy to exert pressure on women to be its unwaged consumer-servants.

The roles of dependent and consumer are the economic functions usually associated with homemakers. Yet the homemaker has other important, albeit inconspicuous, relationships to the nation's economy. Homemakers produce and train future workers, and they physically and psychologically maintain present workers. This is obviously essential service. As Marx wrote, the "maintenance and reproduction of the working class is, and must ever be, a necessary condition to the reproduction of capital."[13]

By taking the lowest-status, least secure of all jobs, homemakers make it possible for other workers, mostly men, to have better jobs and more security. That women do the least desirable work cushions the male from the frustrations and disadvantages of such jobs. Someone has to do society's menial work, and women have even been prepared to do more or less of it as society requires. When more trained labor is needed, as it was during World War II, they do that in addition to housework.

Keeping the homemaker as a backup system for employees is profitable for employers. They get two workers, the waged worker and the homemaker, for the price of one. Just before the turn of the century, an astute Englishwoman pointed out that "if all housewives were to die at once, and the men were forced to buy everything ready for use, wages would have to rise immediately. It is by her unpaid labour that the housewife makes it possible for her husband's wages to be kept so low."[14]

As part of the reserve labor force, homemakers contribute a special segment to that pool of cheap labor that consists mostly of women and racial minorities. Because homemakers are unpaid and are often dissatisfied with their jobs, employers can pay all women who have lower-paid jobs—and that means most women—even less. These women know that there is always someone else waiting at home to take their place. As an Italian woman working toward wages for housework put it:

> But what power have I got to determine the conditions of [housework], what power have I got to get more money, what power have I got to reduce that work, if millions and millions of women at home go on being mothers, wives and maids for nothing? What power have I got to demand social services if millions of women at home go on providing these same services for nothing? What power have I got to demand nurseries while millions of women go on raising children for nothing?[15]

The housework component of women's paid jobs, such as waiting on tables or making coffee for the boss, is relevant to this labor situation. Waged workers, on the one hand, do not want to be associated with people who do similar work for no money; employers, on the other hand, do not want them to forget it.

But, for all her contributions, the homemaker remains outside the mainstream of economic consideration. It has been estimated that homemakers' services are equivalent to one-quarter of the gross national product.[16] Yet their services are not counted by this or similar indexes, since government sees homemakers primarily as dependents and business sees them either as consumers or as cheap and available labor. Though each of these economic conceptualizations of housework has some measure of validity, each is also severely limited and limiting. We need to foster a broader concept of the economics of housework and a more complete image of the homemaker in the economic sphere. In summary, then, a new ideology of housework will include (1) a new consciousness of the exploitation inherent in current economic ideologies and policies and (2) a strategy for encompassing all the contributions that homemakers do make to the economy.

Of Housework, Home, and the Family

The way we think about housework is inextricably tied to the way we think about our personal lives. It is not easy to separate our ideas about housework from our ideas of family, motherhood, and home, and each of these concepts has a highly personal meaning that depends to a large extent on individual upbringing.

The task of understanding our ideology of homelife is obviously important. If one were to take the attitude that housework is merely labor done in the home, without consequences for or influence by the family, one would be open to justified criticism that the new ideology for housework repudiates home and family. I want to emphasize that this is not so: we cannot understand housework if it is removed from home and family life. In fact, for our purposes, it is crucial to begin to explore the pertinent relationships among these ideas.

The home is a place where we eat, sleep, enjoy recreation, display hobby skills, show off our affluence, visit with friends, and take care of our families and ourselves. For most people it is an important place, a place to meet physical and emotional needs. Whether one calls it house or apartment, haven or hole, practically everyone has a home. And someone in that home does the housework.

Housework is home work. It is everyone's work. It is germane to every person's experience because housework is nothing less than the maintenance of an individual's personal environment. How people deal with housework is, among other things, an intimate reflection of their self-image and of the importance they place on various aspects of their lives. Standards for homelife—and therefore for housework—are set emotionally as well as practically. They depend not only on what we know are necessities but on what we *feel* are necessities. Eating is a necessity, but it can range from mere maintenance to gourmet dining; sanitation is important, but cleanliness has become a virtue. The role of the home as a place to satisfy physical needs cannot be separated from the role of the home as a place to satisfy psychological needs.

A commonsense attempt to understand the relationship of home to housework is simply to define the terms so as to differentiate between them. Thus "housework" could be thought of as the physical labor done in and around the home to maintain the home and the family. "Home" could be considered both a physical plant requiring maintenance through housework and a place to which a certain emotional attachment is expected. One problem with these definitions, of course, is that our terms are used to define each other and so are not successfully differentiated.

In 1971 Helena Znaniecki Lopata, author of *Occupation: Housewife,* reported asking 568 women to rank "the most important role of women"; she found the ranking to be mother, wife, and housewife.[17] These women seem to be asserting that their human relationships— relationships to children and husbands—are more important to them than their relationships to their property—their houses. They are using the words "mother" and "wife" to indicate human relationships and the word "housewife" to indicate, at least partially, commitment to the physical maintenance of the family, including the family's property and food. Such distinctions are useful as far as they go. For instance, separating "mothering" and "housework" highlights the fact that a person may have quite different sets of beliefs about these two roles. For the purpose of making such distinctions, "home worker" would actually be a more meaningful term than "homemaker." The former clearly emphasizes work; the latter encompasses all the vague and emotional notions that are associated with home.

The problem with this definitional approach is that the roles of mother and houseworker are not always distinct. Neither can the act of doing housework be totally distinguished from the role of wife or, for that matter, from the role of husband. Cooking dinner can be part of motherhood, wifehood, and housework all at once. These overlapping categories tend to be confusing. One can easily end up uncertain about whether cleaning toilets is a labor of love.

A more pragmatic approach is to ask the general question "Why do we do housework anyway?" Our answer to the numerous spinoffs of this question—Why do we do laundry? Why do we cook?—allow us to begin to clarify and enumerate the needs and values about homelife that go into every act of housework. A compilation of these needs and values will not by itself tell us how to deal with them, but at least it can be a starting point for analysis.

As an example, let us take one simple act that we would call housework and study the many values and interpretations that can be associated with it. Consider a woman cooking dinner for her family.

If we try to place this act in an ideological schema according to commonsense definitions of home and housework and the related terms, we find that it fits practically all of them. The woman is fulfilling her role as homemaker or housewife by preparing dinner for the family; she is fulfilling her role as wife by cooking her husband's steak just the way he likes it and her role as mother by making sure her children have a balanced diet. The physical work and the personal relationships cannot be distinguished by the use of common terms. Thus, using role definitions has helped us very little in our attempt to understand the dynamics of the home and housework.

If, however, we ask "*Why* does the woman cook dinner for her family?" we begin to specify and understand the dynamics of the physical and personal relationships. Why does she cook dinner? One set of reasons may be the following: she cooks because the family has to eat (thus satisfying a need); because the family wants to eat on a regular schedule (thus supporting a family value); because she wants the family to eat together (thus advancing a parental value); because the family and the community believe it is her job to cook for them (thus supporting a family and a cultural value); and because the family appreciates her work (thus meeting her personal need for recognition). Thus, what would be called "homelife" in this family is characterized by regularity, being together, and a traditional view of woman's place. The work done by the homemaker conforms to these values. Using an analysis like this, as opposed to analyses based on role definitions, we can begin to clarify areas where problems may develop. Obviously the values of family members may differ—a child may not wish to eat with the others, a woman may not wish to cook—and deciding whose values will predominate can become a full-fledged power struggle. Another problem area may be balancing the different needs of family members. The cook may need recognition of her work, but the children may need attention, and in a busy dinner hour there may not be time for both.

As we can see, needs-values analysis is likely to be complicated, but it is probably worthwhile because it helps us deal with housework and homelife in terms of people instead of stereotypical roles. It is a task that has yet to be done frequently in individual homes, let alone on a large enough scale to give us a general sense of what happens in most homes.

Analyzing each act of housework in this fashion will clarify existing needs and values, but how will we develop guidelines for finding new purposes or for adopting new values? There is little doubt that the family today is in flux. The evidence is everywhere—in high divorce rates, the increase of single-parent families, the rise in single-person households, the loss of the extended family. Do we dare say anything more than that the future of the family is unpredictable and that, as the family goes, so goes housework?

Perhaps. Some authors have been willing to make predictions or, at least, prescriptions. Arlene Rossen Cardozo, author of *Woman at Home*, predicts that if women buy the success ethic the family will be endangered.[18] Kate Millett avers that the home is the last bastion of human feeling in our society, and that to maintain our sense of humanity there has seemed to be no alternative but to "salvage the private hearth."[19] Oakley writes that the only way to liberate housewives is to abolish the housewife role, gender roles, and the family.[20]

But we do not really know what will happen to the family or, correspondingly, to housework. We can only guess that many people will cling to traditional values and that some of these values will therefore survive.

My own preference would be to salvage the idea of the home as a place of peace—whether for individuals or for families—and as a physical expression of a person's interests and aesthetics, and to reject values that make the home a display area for affluence or for the products of creative consuming. The more we simplify our life-styles, the more drudgery is removed from housework. However, I could not agree with Charlotte Perkins Gilman, who believed that "as cooking becomes dissociated from the home, we shall gradually cease to attach emotions to it; and we shall learn to judge it impersonally upon a scientific and artistic basis."[21] I refuse to give up my strong emotional attachment to my mother's stew.

But as a nation our values are constantly changing, and one can see the benefit of much of this change. Gilman also wrote that, in her day, "There is something repugnant in the idea of food cooked outside the home, even though served within it; still more in the going out of the family to eat, and more yet in the going out of separate individuals to eat."[22] Yet today Americans spend one of every three food dollars in restaurants and fast-food shops,[23] and the work of home cooking is correspondingly reduced.

As each generation is introduced to a revised tradition, we can expect to find more change in our ideology of homelife. What we can assert now is that the goal of such change should be based on an assessment of the effect of homelife on the individuals involved, rather than on some general notion of what homelife or family life ought to be. In other words, if the home situation handicaps a family member—and John Stuart Mill saw the home as a center of "domestic slavery"[24]—the home situation should be changed. No ideology about woman's place or about home being "where the heart is" should be allowed to prevent this transformation.

Conclusion

We are only beginning to create a new ideology for housework, and there is much to be done. Among other things, we need to understand why sex-role stereotyping of home work continues to be ubiquitous and how this can be changed. We need to delve into the existing research on work so we can undertake relevant new research on work in the home. We need to learn more about the dynamics of financial, physical, and social power within families. We need more research on individual homemakers—on their satisfactions, their motivations, and their aspirations. Furthermore, we must disseminate this knowledge not only to the academic community (and to the academics who are also homemakers), but also to the community of homemakers and their advocates—to individuals everywhere who see in the new homemaker movement the potential for the social integration of new and benevolent values.

Homemakers

4

This chapter is devoted to six interviews collected as part of an ongoing research study on the quality of working life for homemakers. They were selected from several dozen open-ended interviews gathered in 1979 by me and three trained undergraduate students. The interview with Douglas Roberts in chapter 7 is also part of this study.

Demographically, the interviews are not a representative sample, but they do show anecdotally both the delightful and the tragic sides of homemaking. They are included here so that at the outset the reader may reflect on what some homemakers themselves have to say about their role and its effect on their lives. The interviews have been edited for organization and repetition but not for grammar, and they are presented without commentary. In the context of the rest of the book, I hope they will be useful for teaching and for consciousness-raising.

"This Is What I Wanted to Be,
with All My Heart"
Helga J. McWhirter

Mrs. McWhirter laughed when she was asked for an interview. "What do I have to tell you that is interesting? I feel like such a fool." As we talked, we had tea and homemade cake in front of a crackling fire.

Years ago I was very busy with the general household: the children would come home for lunch, keeping the house in order, washing and ironing, and the kitchen. And I did extra things, like being available for the children at school for excursions. I was president of the Allen Lake Girl Scout district, which took a great deal of time and effort. This required working with people from all over the area, and that was a big job. I felt very responsible if anything should go wrong, and I found out a great deal about people. I was also a Brownie leader. I was happy to do it. I'm just as busy now as I was then.

Always I have loved home, I have loved being a wife, I have loved being a housekeeper. And when anyone says anything like "I'm just a homemaker" I just look at them, because from my point of view it's the most fulfilling thing I could possibly do. And if my house looks lovely it's because I put a lot of myself into it. I refinish furniture; most everything in here I have refinished. I love to make something out of nothing. I love to make something do. Now, for instance, my carpet that I dearly love—I don't like to change it, but I like to add to it. Instead of changing I take the Rit and go over the worn spots.

When Peter and I were married we both had the same goal. We both wanted togetherness, steadfastness, and just joy in "home." And Peter said he didn't want me working, he wanted me to be at home. I was very happy to hear him say that. This was exactly what I wanted to do. I didn't realize it at the time, but when I was teaching and living with some other girls, it was always I who bought the plant or something. It didn't occur to them to do those kinds of things, but it pleased me to do those things that made the house seem more homey. Peter has been very much the same way.

We planned this house. We went and got all the old doors. Our front door is from old Stone Hall at the university. We went by there and there were these odd doors out on the campus and we stopped and got them. We got the old shutters and everything. We brought plants from his home and the same things from my home, so we had all the lilacs, honeysuckle, and all the different plants that we loved.

One of the basic things is that Peter and I both were brought up on a farm, and we never got it out of our systems, fortunately. When I was a very little girl I had a darling mother and a happy father, and no matter whatever came along, there was always a silver lining. I can remember one summer, during harvest, three horses died. For most farmers this would have been very traumatic, but my father went ahead and bought another horse and he didn't make a great deal of it.

When I was a little girl, I felt like a big part of the farm. I got the eggs, and that was very important in the summertime, because the farmer had to depend on the grain crops and by summer sometimes there was a very lean time. I felt very responsible for finding every egg, because that meant we could take the eggs to the little village and could get what we wanted there. I took the wood in, and did the dishes, and thought about having a riding horse some day.

There was always laughter at the table, always a nice dinner on Sunday, and we always had lots of company because mother was such a good cook. She expected to make a home, expected all the things that went with it. It wasn't until I grew up that I realized that mother never really had a home of her own, with my grandmother living there—not her mother but my father's mother. My grandmother had been a teacher and she felt that my mother was there to do her bidding. I don't know how she ever did it, but my mother made it a very happy home in spite of it. She crocheted in the evenings. If it was pleasant, mother made that pleasantness in our home.

I never thought we were poor. We probably were but I never felt that because we had a nice home. We would go for a ride on Sunday and we'd come home and my father would think his home was the best. The rows of corn were the straightest. If I have made that type of place then I got it from my mother and father. He appreciated it too. I can remember the railroad ran through our farm and he used to bring tiger lilies from the field there to my mother, darling sweet things like that.

My father was hardworking but he had a joy of living. If there was a circus in town, and he had his work done—always the work had to be done first—he would make it a point that we all go to the circus. Out of the blue, maybe on a Sunday he'd say let's pack a lunch, and we'd go over to the riverbank and do it because it was just something fun to do. I remember these special things, that were part of the family, very vividly.

And I think that's what I saw in Peter—that steadfastness, that loyalty. I never felt quite comfortable with boys who weren't that way. Peter would bring me books; I liked to read. And we talked about the world, and earth and things like that. And I never forgot about him.

And these things have carried over into your life and family?

Not as much as I wish they had, really. Peter is very work oriented. There wasn't time, when he was going into business, and he was working at least until Saturday afternoon. He worked five and a half days. And then all the things he wanted to do, like the garden in the summertime. Peter isn't the same as my father. I didn't want to interrupt him in the things he wanted to do.

We've had a marvelous life together. Retirement...I hear other women talking about things...I don't have those feelings about it. Peter has never wanted to go and do the shopping with me—he never did any of that. I have been free to go whenever I wanted to, and he's been capable of taking care of himself. We've gone around the world twice, and driven practically all over Europe together; and we've been to Alaska. And at this age he wants to go to China and walk along the Great Wall. In addition, he can tell me all about these countries...he's given me much more than I could ever give him. I believe that. I think he would say that there would be nothing without each other. And that I'm concerned about.

We went through a very serious operation with Peter. At the time I wondered if I could go through with it, but I did. And the doctor said Peter has a rosy future ahead of him. I think that makes a difference with what we value. I try not to think about [widowhood]. When we were faced with leaving Peter at the hospital there that day, I had to come home and get things together, and I did fairly well. So I have . . . . I could spoil my whole life by anticipating. And I don't know that I could cope any better by anticipating.

I've always felt that I had a great deal in my job; it has been just as important as Peter's job was, in its own way. No different. There was never any doubt in my mind that I was doing an important job. I admire someone who can go out and work and do a splendid job, and I wonder how they can do it. But it's been a full-time thing for me.

I think that I couldn't have any more feeling of gratefulness from anyone than from Peter. He loves what I've done. He tells me that he likes it: everything is just splendid . . . it's "peachy pie." I think that it comes with time with children. It took me a long time to realize just what kind of home my mother and father had and what they did for me. Mary and Carol express these things. They say, "How in the world did you do it all?" I just didn't think anything about it. I really didn't. If Carol called from college and said she was going to bring two or three home for a weekend and have dinner here, I just got in a hurry, went to the store and thoroughly enjoyed it. They were usually darling girls or boys that she brought. And it was fun.

Are there any negatives to homemaking?

Well, I think that cleaning the house is very boring, but I think that's because you're never through. But the alternative is worse. That keeps me going. Peter thinks everything I cook is splendid. He would much rather be at home and eat at home than to go anywhere. But I get into a rut preparing things for him, things I that I know he likes, so that it leads me to very boring things about food preparation, unless we have guests. I dislike shopping for food. It's the same thing—picking up the same things every time. I do all the food shopping, and I'm very glad that Peter doesn't like to go with me. I see other couples going and see the men say "Do you really need that?" or "Don't we already have that?" and that would be very upsetting to me. I'm always on the lady's side when she's explaining "why" to these questions the man asks.

Another thing that bothers me is having company for a long time. I enjoy having people come, but if they stay too long—I'm talking about three or four days—I find that I get very tired of the food preparation. There's something about me that can't take it casually and brush it off. From one meal to the next I'm thinking, "We're done with breakfast, now what about lunch?" I love to have people come, but not for an extended visit.

Do you think there should be more considerations from the government for what homemakers do?

Things like Social Security? Indeed, yes. I think it is very much of a full-time job and it's necessary that there should be some kind of recompense for people. I've thought about what long hours and what complete devotion to life the housewife gives. And if something could be worked out I think it should be, although I can't tell you how. I don't know how to say it.

Do you think homemaking has a purpose in society?

Oh I do, indeed I do. I see it best in my daughters. They saw steadfastness here, and they're carrying on the same thing. They saw their daddy trying his best and being successful: he devoted himself and had a purpose. What more could we ask of Carol than to be first in her class at the university? And Mary to be paid a $2,000 bonus for putting on a World Conference in Philadelphia? I just read recently Christopher Morley saying that some of the ingredients of a good life are learning, earning, and yearning. And I couldn't agree more. I think it's lovely to want something and to have to earn it, to have to do something about it to get it. I think that goes for all of us. I don't think it can be handed to you and get the full fun out of life.

I never would have wanted a career. This is what I wanted to be, with all my heart. This is the ultimate for me, to have a home and have someone with me and that was the whole answer. There was never any other goal in my life. I wouldn't have wanted it early. But if I didn't have it I would be desolate. Anything else would never have been fulfilling to me.

We had a neighbor, very wealthy, with upstairs maids, downstairs maids, a wonderful husband, but no children. And she used to have beautiful paintings—things like that that were way beyond anything that I had experienced—and yet she used to come in here and say "God bless this home." She felt something about this home, about this house, what we had here. If I've created something that is pleasant for people and pleasant for my family, then I feel fulfilled, that's all, for myself.

"Men Think Women Are Machines"
Carol Schaeffer

The interview was held in Carol Schaeffer's bedroom, the only place in her house where we could get away from her family—five teenage children (in-

*cluding three stepchildren from this, her second, marriage) and her husband.
Carol is forty-three and has been a homemaker for twenty-five years.*

What is a typical day like for you?

Typical? Really my days aren't typical. They're not. Well, every day I
straighten up, and twice, maybe three times a week I dust. I wash
clothes every day. I do everybody's wash. And I make dinner, every day
but Friday; that's the day Tommy and I go out together. We don't take
the kids. He always invites them and I always give him this "Don't you
dare."

That's nice, the way you always have that one night a week out.

Not one night—*one hour!* He's not a party person. He's not helpful
around the house. He can do mechanical things, but he doesn't. He
goes to buy a newspaper and peeks around the corner and asks "Is she
done yet? Is she done yet?" But I suppose he's tired too.

But we get tired too. Men don't think women get tired. I mean they
think that we have this constitution that just goes and goes and goes.
He says, "Well, I have to get up at six o'clock in the morning." Well,
that's nice, but he doesn't remember that I'm up in the middle of the
night going to pick up one kid or another from work.

Other than that, that's typical. Run, constantly, doing all the grocery
shopping, the errands, the cooking, the cleaning. Dishes I make the
kids do. I feel I put on all the meals, they can do the dishes. I do make
them change their sheets when I wash sheets, and make their beds
which 98 percent of the time the beds are not made. But I don't go
around every day making them—there are seven beds in this house! I'd
be hunchbacked! They say it's good for your stomach muscles . . . . For
thirty years I kept looking at my stomach muscles!

But I like housework. You know this is a really weird thing. You
know how many people, women, complain about it, because they say
"It's unfulfilling, it's unrewarding, I hate it, it's monotonous." Well so
is typing, and so is running a computer. Any job can be. It's what you
make out of a job. I love housework. When I do a big job, like when I
finished painting this house, it was really *done*. I put the last brush coat
on the kitchen, I sat there, and I said, "Man, it took three years, but it
was nice when I got done."

I think if you're going to do it, do it right. If you're going to be a
homemaker, take pride in it. If you're going to be a career girl take pride
in that. Whatever you want to be, if you don't take pride in it then
you're going to look like a slob.

I used to be really active in a lot of things. I used to manage a club. I
would have liked it if I could have put less of myself into it. What I

would do was I would work there and if we had a party or something we'd close at 2:00, 2:30, or 4:00 in the morning, and I'd come home and throw in a load of clothes. And weekends there was cleaning if there wasn't anything going on, you know. I got to be on the end of this string, where I was just dangling there saying "Oh my God, what do I do next."

What was homemaking like for you when you first got married?

Oh my God, my first dinner. Oh my God. Oh my poor husband—he was new and young and in love and he thought I was wonderful so I made him these stupid pork chops. And I'm cooking them and I'm cooking them and I'm thinking "Well, I know pork's got to be well done. My *mother* told me that." They were so well done the bones jumped off the pan. They were black. Peas were good—I opened a can. Poor guy, he couldn't chew. All those little black things caught between his teeth.

Cooking I didn't like. If I had to pick something I hated in a house, I hate cooking. You plan these meals day after day and then you think what in the world am I going to serve. And you don't know. Out of the five kids—Keith, he loves to eat, God bless him, I like cooking for him—and the others are persnickety.

Do you get a lot out of it when you cook a meal that everybody likes?

No. If the kids would do it I'd just as soon let them handle the cooking and I'd clean up. When I cook I cook in volume. I make like sixteen pork chops, big humongous roasts. I always try to get two dinners out of them—I never do, but I always try. I'd much rather cook for a big gang, two hundred, because it gets so boring. Isn't that awful? And you know what I hate? Holidays. Because I think you're pressured into it. Everybody's got to go to everybody's house. Now why can't they come in, sit down, have snacks? But see, my mom, they're Finnish, and when you walk into their house you have all this food. You can't just have coffee and a piece of cake or a cookie. She's got to bring out the lunches and the pickles and it has to be this big spread. Consequently, she ended up at the end of her life hating company. She detests company. But I don't think I'll be that way. Company comes, they come to see me. I think, if they don't come to see me, if they come to see my house or what I can feed them, well, then they've got the problem, not me.

Is there something else you would like to have done besides being a home-maker?

Oh, yeah, there still is. There's a lot of things. In fact when the kids go—I'll lose two to college this year, but I'll still have two home. But I'm just wondering, that's really got me bothered how that's going to actually work.

I'd like to go back to school. I do and I don't. I'm divided. Well, I was talking with Tommy—we went out and had a cup of coffee and a piece of pie—so we're sitting there. And he's been on my back to go to work since we've been marrried. He'd love for me to work. But, I said, how can I work all day at home, and you never end. You can't say I got up at ten o'clock and I'm going to work till midnight because you can't—you get tired! Well, he said, it would be good for you. Bull crap. It would be good for his pocketbook. And he worries about money, and rightly so, because it's expensive living today. I handle all the money, savings, checking, bill paying. In fact, if you were to go out there right now and ask him what's in the checking or savings he'd say he didn't know.

We had two great years. I mean *really* great. Where we were just so . . . God we were so in love, jeez . . . Oh, we'd have lent each other our toothbrush, you know. Ohhh, wow. And then we had two years that were terrible. In fact I thought we would get divorced. I asked myself why did I do it—all it is is work, work, work. I used to have such pretty hands.

But this year we had a big traumatic experience, and in the past months it's been a complete reversal. I made up my mind that there were going to be some changes made, and I was going to say my piece instead of having my ulcer get the best of me. I hold a lot in—you know, "Keep peace, keep peace"—and I do get ticked off because *nobody* will help me do *anything*. They wouldn't think to pick up a rag and wash the sink and bathtub.

We tried out a point system once. It worked fine when I hung it up. Everybody read it and said, "neat," and then it went right back to the same thing because they'd switch off. "Well, I've got to go to the baseball game so you take my night." Then they'd say "Well, I got stuck two nights in a row—there's two Xs here." The point system, it stunk, for me. Now I don't know about somebody else. Because kids are selfish. You have this chart and they feel that every little X there deserves a reward. Well, life isn't that way. So now I say, "Hey, you live in this house, you're a member of this family, get out and shovel this snow and don't give me a hassle." They'll try and con you. They'll hear dishwater running—my God, you never saw people move so fast in your life.

All this soft, glamourous, beautiful family living . . . you see in on "The Brady Bunch"—"These three little boys and these three little girls they all came together and you have six kids"—well, it's just not like that. "Eight is Enough" and "Family" try and come close to the real little things in life, but they don't even touch the surface. When you have a whole-day fight it's not going to end in an hour with everyone sitting around the table and saying, "Well, you realize we were wrong."

Do you think that more husbands are going to start doing more housework?

They're going to have to. Because more and more women are going to have to supplement today's income, if the prices keep going like they are, if inflation keeps going. I think families are all going to have to contribute—kids are going to have to contribute. I can't feed these kids—I pay a hundred dollars a week for groceries.

I think more men are going to help their wives around the house because they're going to start out younger. See, I spoiled my men. I spoiled my first husband and I'm spoiling this one. I did it myself. If I had to do it over again, I'd make them help. They get to the point where you're depended on for everything. I take the cars in to get them fixed. I walked from here all the way to K-Mart to get a part, and back in the freezing nine-degree weather and the wind was howling and blowing. No, I did that, I did that myself. I could kick my fanny for it, too. I hate it, but.... When I first went with Tommy he did everything. He washed walls, put in light switches, he was terrific! And I kept sending tapes home to Mom and Dad saying "God, I really got me a gem. He makes gravy and everything." He was fantastic. Not that I'd want a man like a little puppet.

I was going to generalize there and say that men get that way, but I don't think so, I really don't. My dad never did. He was always doing something around the house. One of my friends' husbands took a razor blade and took all the plaster off—a razor blade!

I know what I want out of life. I thought I did—I still think I do. A vacation! You know what, I'd give ten bucks for twenty-four hours by myself. Without one soul. No dogs, no cats, no kids, no fish, no husband! I feel cheated sometimes. In fact, I was really on my wagon the other day. I told Tommy. I said I never, day after day, seven days a week, have five minutes to myself. I can never sit and have a cup of coffee. I can never talk on the telephone without someone being here. You're not free. I have never taken a bath that somebody hasn't knocked on the door, I mean never. And this is day after day after day. Tommy says it's stupid to feel that way. No, I said, you have "Tom time," I never have "Carol time." He said, "You have a car." But if I go to a mall I'm still surrounded by activity and people. I can never read a book unless it's three o'clock in the morning. John loves to have me at home. But love isn't the question—*time* is the question.

I like to get away. I like to go shopping. I go to the malls and I have coffee and a cigarette. I'm a people watcher. And I talk to old ladies. I do—they look so bored all the time, so I go talk to them. You don't have to buy to shop.

When you think of your happiest times being a homemaker, what kind of times are they?

The latest thing that was really "happy happy" was New Year's Eve. We had the best New Year's Eve. Really and truly. The kids all had to work. Tommy and I were all alone. You know, when you're a mother and you have a bunch of kids, you wear flannel nightgowns with big clunky bathrobes—I mean you look like the pits because you don't want anyone seeing through your nighty, especially with boys around the house. So I put on this beautiful, flowy gown, and I lit all the candles and had the light really low, and soft music, and then had on the television with what's-his-name, Guy Lombardo. I made tons of hors d'oeuvres, hot ones and cold ones and little tea sandwiches and all this junk. All day I did that. And it was terrific. I mean terrific. We were dancing! And Tommy had his pajamas on. He looked gorgeous. And we're sitting there in the glow, you know, the candlelight. And he said, "You know, did you ever think when we moved in here that this would end up such a cute house?" And I said "It's so cute in here—it really is, it's a cute house—it makes me feel that all the effort was really worthwhile." And of course that night I felt like a queen because he really wanted New Year's with just the two of us. We had really planned this, down to the minute, champagne and everything.

Well, the bosses decided to get generous and let the kids off at eleven o'clock. Four of them! *Balum, balum, balum, balum.* All the lights went on. And it was just...terrible! I called my mom long distance. We didn't even kiss at midnight. Can you really believe it? And he said he wanted this to be so beautiful and so romantic. So then he tells my mother on the phone "Lily, next year we're going to a motel." That was a very happy time.

When I look around, say, after all day I've cleaned and dusted or polished and vacuumed, put all the books and newspapers and everything where they go, then I say it looks nice. I can tell when someone's cleaned. There's a big difference. When you've got a lot of kids and you've let the dogs in and out seven hundred thousand times and wiped their feet when it's wet outside, and then your husband comes in and he has to unwind and you listen to him—and with Keith for dinner on school nights he's got fifteen minutes to eat and get out of here—so it's got to be right on the table—it's not all uphill.

If I had to do it over, I'd probably do it over. I don't know if I'd have even worked.

I told Tommy Friday night, you know, I've been really thinking about work, working outside and working at home. Because I know that you don't feel that being a homemaker is a full-time type job that is time-consuming, energy-consuming, of any value. You feel that I'm just there. I'm taken for granted, is what it is. I said, if I worked outside of the home, in the first place your dinner would never be on the table when you walked in the door, because our hours might or might not coincide. If they didn't that means you'd have to help, and if you had to help with dinner that means you'd have to help with all the other chores. And supposing you wanted that special blue shirt to wear that day and I couldn't get to the washing because I've got a job. All these little things! He can go in his underwear drawer and it's *perfect*, every day. Mind you, it's all my work, and they're in order. He said *"I* did it for nine years." I know he did. But they didn't have any drapes on the windows, and no curtains, it was a mess. When I first came here he was really complimentary. He thought, oh man, I was terrific. That was good for my ego. But now he's gotten used to having a clean house, and his meals prepared and his clothes hanging up. Every shirt in his closet is ironed, and his sweaters are folded in the drawer. He walks around like King *Tut*. I don't think he could adjust; he would hate to think that he would have to pitch in with me, because he's never had to do it.

Men think women are machines. There's this little knob—they're this little robot. Wind them up in the morning and they go "Ch, Ch, I-will-dust-the-furniture...." And when these guys are all lovey and in the mood and want your bod, they're all raring to go and here's this slob saying "You've got to be kidding! I just washed fifteen loads of laundry!" And they think "Now I will push your 'on' button... pant! pant!" [Much laughter.] It's not even funny! But that's the way they think. And I know my dad was the same way with my mother. And I know my uncles do the same thing with their wives, and they feel the same about their husbands. I guess society has placed us in roles: if your're a homemaker you're a homemaker; if you work outside the home, that's fine; if you're a husband you're a husband and you work to bring home the paycheck.

Tommy will say, "Oh, you women got it made. All you women do is bitch about this and bitch about that." Well, it's true, about some things, because we have a right to. We've been underrated all our lives.

Men have felt that we're beneath them in our role as working women, no matter what role they are. If two people are working on a job, and there's a man and a woman on a construction job, the man's going to get the praise even if the woman did a better job because he's *supposed* to be on construction. And they feel homemaking...you know. Tommy says, "Look at the olden days, with the pioneers, when women plowed the fields and they cleared the land." I said, "I'm not a pioneer!"

I wash on the average, say, twenty to thirty loads of clothing a week. That's a lot of steps. That's not only washing—the machine does that— you take them out, put them in the dryer, you fold them, you put them all in the rooms, and you lug them up and down. But does anyone ever think "Gee, she put X amount of hours in this today"? Nobody ever thinks of that.

How would you feel about getting paid for it?

Well, I do because I handle the money. [Laughs.] How would I feel about getting paid for it by someone like the government? For home- making? I don't know, maybe then...Tommy would probably say, "Are you sure you can't find an extra load. You get fifty cents more for that. How much did you get for making that bed? I'll sleep in it again this afternoon." That's a pretty hard question. I mean who's going to run around spying on you, looking over your shoulder? I like it though. The thought's terrific.

There has got to be more effort involved in everything. There's got to be family life in our society. It's a shame that this country, the richest in the world, with so many wonderful things to offer, is so negligent in so many things. Old people are just there. They have no facilities. As far as we feel they've fought whatever wars they're going to fight and their time is over so put them in an old folks' home and let them die. You never see families like "The Waltons," where grandma lives where the mother lives and the kids all live.

There's no family closeness. We get together at Christmas, we get together at New Year's and Easter, but that's not family, that's occa- sions. Family is what you do, day after day. You live through good and bad, you set goals, and moral values and standards of living. And there isn't enough of it. I see kids on the streets, shit, ten years old with cigarettes in their mouths, and drinking—they're drinking at twelve, thirteen, fourteen years old. Where are these parents? How come these parents don't know what their kids are doing?

I think women—I'm not saying all women, because I know a lot of terrific women—have become too involved with "Do I look great?" Society and life today have placed on us goals like "How beautiful am I?

How great's my figure? Oh my God, do I have any cellulite?" Who cares! So what happens is these women—and that's at any age, I'm not specifying any age group—but women with families, basically have become so absorbed in their own personal being and are so selfish about themselves that they can't project far enough. And this will carry over into running a home, it will carry over into how your children turn out. Women have become so wrapped up in glamour and beauty that they're afraid to put their hand in a dirty toilet.

This is why men—now, I'm not using my man, I'm using "men" because I've heard a number of men talk at different gatherings—look down at a woman.

Give of yourself and you get a lot more back. I can look just as nice in blue jeans and a T-shirt as I can in a Christian Dior original.

"I Mangled Nearly Every Night"
Helen Meyers

Helen Meyers was born in 1886, the youngest of three daughters. At the time of the interview she is ninety-two years old. She is interviewed by her granddaughter.

Was your mother a homemaker?

Yes, in a sense. She was a good cook and she was a very clean woman. She made all my clothes.

As a little girl you must have been learning how to cook and clean. Who taught you how to do that?

I only had to scrub down the cellar steps. And I had to scrub those every Friday night.

When she housecleaned we had these deep bowls with the pitcher in and the soap dish and all and I had to wash all of that.

We lived really very nicely at times and people thought, many times, that we were rich because we had a nice furnished house. But many times we didn't have anything to eat. My father inherited three fortunes in his life. And then we'd be on top of the world. We always owned the house, but we couldn't eat it! We had a piano. We had beautiful carpet from wall to wall, and we had everything we wanted.

After my two sisters died, my grandmother took care of me. Then my mother was free, and she worked in the factory and she had her girl friends.

My grandmother was very thrifty and so was my grandfather. They were very very lovely old Christian people. They were thrifty but poor. He just made twelve dollars a week, you know.

We ate mostly jelly bread at my grandparents' house. My grandmother made all her own jelly. And she made her dandelion wine and she did sausage—they'd grind the meat.

I wasn't allowed to have any children in the yard because she had the gate locked and she scrubbed the boardwalk on her hands and knees. And so I couldn't have any company.

I used to save my pennies until I had ten cents and then every Saturday night [my friends the Saylors] had baked beans and then they would invite me and I'd give them the ten cents.

They had a very happy home. My first child was born in their home. I was like one of their children. Lily . . . I always remembered the friends I had when I was poor.

Then I used to visit with my rich grandparents when I got older. That was an entirely different story. They came direct from Germany. They had a beautiful homelife. Oh, and my grandfather was so in love with my grandmother. Oh, she was short and fat and had her hair parted down the middle and real curls. When she put it back in a knot the front was all curls. It was beautiful.

It was a big house, like these brownstone mansions. My grandparents lived with their daughter and her husband and they had three children—Ernie and her two brothers. I visited them every summer, as soon as I could travel on the train alone. They had three sitting rooms, and they had one of those old-fashioned pianos—I don't believe you ever saw one—real flat on top and big thick legs.

Ernie's father was Uncle Abe. My aunt's name was Ernestine. And my grandfather didn't want her to do the work. Her husband was a schoolteacher when she married him, and, oh no, he wasn't to work; he was to stay at home and help her. Her father didn't want her to do the work because they had wood stoves in the summer, you know, and all that, and so Uncle Abe helped with the house, with the kitchen.

And every night they had fried potatoes and meat, you know, and not much else. Not much fancy stuff, but always fried potatoes. They didn't have lettuce in those days, and that kind of stuff, and canned things like we have today. They had cabbage I guess.

My aunt did the cooking but her husband did the cleaning up and the getting ready. And then he cleaned up all the dishes. He always washed up all the dishes.

[*When her first marriage ended, Helen began several years of work as a milliner representing a Philadelphia-based firm. Every selling season she would work in a market outside of the city. She had two daughters to support.*]

Then you see what happened is that I worked in Johnstown. I opened a nice department there. And I took the girls along. We lived with a Mrs. Lubert. Her husband was a banker and died of tuberculosis. She had two girls exactly my girls' age. Somebody found her and she took the two girls in and then I would baby-sit every night. She was a musician and she played at the home of the president of the steel works, accompanied by his two children. He wanted music before dinner every night, and she played the piano and one played the flute or whatever, you know. And so then I stayed at home with the children at night, and she washed and ironed for them and everything.

I took them out the next year but she couldn't take them. I took these children, and they were sick and it was snowing and raining, and when I got there, I stayed with two old maids and an old bachelor and they only had one room for me and the children. And they had nothing to eat for us when we got there, so we had to take the children back in town and get them something to eat again. Well, these two children, mind . . . were sick!

And the success of that department depended on me, and I couldn't sleep at night. One slept with me and they had a cot for the other. When one started to cough . . . . And all day long these poor kids had to stay in this room.

Well, afterward I talked to Mrs. Lubert—I had to send them home to Allentown—and she said, "I wish I had known it—I wouldn't have let you. I would have taken them." Well, my mother then had to find a place for them in Allentown and I didn't know where my children were, see. You can imagine my feeling and yet the success of that department depended on me . . . . So that's why, I guess, I have a brain. And I used it—I had to use it all the time. But you can imagine the heartaches I had alone in strange towns. I'd go to my room at night alone and I used to crochet lace on Turkish towels. Can you imagine that. Any place they'd send me I had to go—to Oxford, or to Virginia someplace.

Now let's talk about something else.

[In 1916 Helen Meyers married a widower. With her two girls and his little boy, they moved into Barren Hollow, a white stucco home set back from the road and framed with trees.]

In the back Barren Hollow was beautiful. I had a rock garden down to the springhouse, and I had a white fence down the side here, and around the front where the stone wall was I didn't have it all covered up like they have now. The stone wall stood there and looked pretty. And then I had the beautiful terrace made, all stone, in the front, you know, and almost as wide as this room. Then around there was a stone wall and I had petunias. It was beautiful.

It must have been hard to keep that big lawn up in those days without mowers.

Yes. And I mowed it one time with a horse. You did it with a horse and some kind of mower. I did it one time—one of the Nehoda girls was with me.

Oh but I worked hard there. When we moved there we had a coal stove heater in the cellar, and I used to take the ashes out every morning, and pick out the black coals—think of that—and then put them in the water heater so they would finish burning up. They hadn't been burned. And that's how I saved.

And every week we started with fourteen sheets and we dripped them like this and threw them through the wringer and rinsed them twice. Then I'd take them over there in the yard. There was the cherry tree there and the wind, and you could. . . . Oh, it was all lovely. The wind would blow the wash you know. And it was lovely. We had a mound in the center of the drive there with a birdcage, with a birdhouse on the top. And it was really lovely.

Dad has said that sometimes it took you three days to do the wash.

And I mangled nearly every night, which was terrible. Dad would sit and read the paper and I'd be down in the cellar doing the mangling. Well, I had a big mangle and I'd do the sheets. Now I didn't care later in life whether I slept on ironed sheets. But the kids all slept on ironed sheets, just think of it. Think of it.

Why did you do it, do you think? Why didn't you just say the heck with it?

But I *didn't* say the heck with it. It wasn't exciting. I worked in the morning. I worked at night. Then I went to bed. And I played cards in the afternoons sometimes. Most of the time.

And we used to give wonderful parties at night. The men all came in tuxedos and no liquor was served and we had wonderful times. I was the one that made the society in the family.

And John always had to be dressed in a white suit every Sunday. Poor kid, he couldn't play because he was all dressed up in case somebody came. The children all had to be dressed up. People came from Allentown. I had a lot of friends. And I made all his suits. I'd sit in that sun porch. And I made all their clothes and their hats to match. And then I'd trim them with black fancy stitches, you know, and they were cute as they could be. Nobody else did that, see.

Did you ever wish, as a young woman, that you had stayed in the business instead of stopping and having your family? You could have had maids to raise your children, to take care of the house, couldn't you?

Oh no. Well then... but I was in business for ten years, till I married again. And supported those children. They were nine and ten when I got married. And you see, I am the oldest—not the oldest, because I don't know that—but the longest depositor in this bank up here in Doylestown. I started when I was seventeen.

Oh, I worked awful hard, Pookie, I worked awful hard in my life.

"You Don't Realize It's a Twenty-four-Hour Job until It's Too Late"
Mary Swiercz

At thirty-one, Mary Swiercz has been a homemaker for eleven years and has three children aged nine, six, and one and a half. She hopes to go to college someday. Mary thinks that her homemaking career will last at least ten more years.

My main purpose in homemaking is the kids—the house isn't that important. I don't think the kids are going to remember when they get older whether or not the house was clean. But I think having a good time and making life interesting for them is important. If you have a happy atmosphere, everybody is happy.

I don't think housework is very important. I have friends who call me up and tell how thrilled they were that they just waxed their floor! To me that's boring. I just couldn't waste my time.

I think now kids need the security of the mother being home. I want to be a homemaker now. If I want to work I think later will be soon enough. If Jim worked during the day, it wouldn't be so bad. But he's only working nights. He works midnights now, but with his job you never know. Maybe next week he could be on afternoons. Sometimes his job changes shifts every other week. That's another thing that kind of throws me. If I did get a job I wouldn't be able to go in every other week and say "I've got to switch." There isn't a job in the world for me that would put up with that kind of a schedule.

I don't think Jim would keep doing his job if it weren't for me and the kids, because he doesn't care for it at all there. In fact I think he hates it. It isn't really what he wanted. I feel bad for him because I really think he feels trapped because of his family and you have so many responsibilities, you can't just pick up and go. He'd like to have his own business, a small sports shop or something like that. But you can't work over there, try to save money, and pay the bills at the same time. And I feel sorry for him because when you don't like what you're doing it's hard to get up every day and go.

Our days start out busy. I hate first thing in the morning. Chris is usually in there screaming; he wakes me up about seven or eight o'clock. The kids get up and I have to get them ready for school—their clothes, breakfasts, and lunches, and get them all packed. Jim gets home about that time. He gets his coffee, talks with the kids, and keeps one busy while I'm working with the others. And then it gets quiet again. Then usually I wash. I wash every day, at least one or two loads a day. We're either one of two things—very clean or very dirty. I haven't figured out which. Every day I take one room, like for instance our room, or the bathroom, you know, one day hit one room. And just straighten up the rest of the house.

It usually takes me most of the morning. I'm not very fast at it. I stop and have a cup of coffee, or I see something else that needs doing, so I'll drop this and go on to that. Then I sometimes end up getting absolutely nothing done. Then about eleven o'clock I put the baby down, then for about an hour, hour and a half it's my time—I do whatever—read, or just watch the news. Just to sit and listen to the quiet. Oh, I just love it!

Then about four o'clock the kids start rolling in again. It's just bang, bang, bang again. Ann's first. She comes in and we look at her papers and she tells me about her day. By the time I'm done with her, someone else rolls in and then we start with her, and on and on. But I figure that's their time, and if they have any major problems we talk them over.

Then it starts all over again—by that time it's the littlest one's bedtime and I get him down. The kids watch TV and I get dinner, they do their homework and I get my dishes done. They go to bed at nine o'clock, and Jim gets up at nine o'clock. That's when we get some of our talking done. Then and in the morning. More or less when we have an opportunity, when it's quiet. We more or less have to catch it when we can. Then he leaves about ten o'clock. I usually sew at that time. I like to sew—I'm making a quilt—or if it's clothes I like to make them while it's quiet. If I know I'm going to be interrupted I just won't attempt anything.

I suppose I feel needed, I really do. I always kid them that if I should die tomorrow they'd be in a heck of a mess. I mean they wouldn't even be able to find their underwear. I know that it's not a big thing, but I fulfill something for them, make a stable life for them. Nothing that's going to go down in history. You're not going to open a history book and find my name in there.

Sometimes I think the government should help the family. Now if I go out to work, and I pay a woman to come in and take care of the children, I can take her as a deduction. I think they should allow me something like a deduction on my income tax because I stay home. And I'm not out there taking a job away from someone who really needs it

and who is supporting a family. We do have only one family breadwinner here. Granted we could use another one. But there are women
who are bringing up children and don't have that, and I would be going
out and taking a job away from them. And she'd end up being on
welfare.

I just think homemakers nowadays are taken for granted. People say
"Oh, you're home taking care of the kids. Oh." They never ask you if
that's what you really want to do. Nowadays you have to be out working being the liberated woman. I feel just as liberated at home.

I get these moods of discontent and then I want to go out and work. I
don't want to be home and be tied down. I think, Why did I get myself
into this? If I was single . . . then I think single's not so great, the grass is
always greener on the other side.

Winter—that's my worst time of year. I get depressed. I think just the
feeling of not having someone dependent upon me. The times when
they all need me for something, that kind of drags me down. I think,
Why me? You can work things out for yourself, too, I tell them. I can't
think everything for you. When I do speak up, at first I feel good that I
got it off my chest. Then I'll be alone here at night and wonder why I
said that, that I didn't mean it the way it sounded. Who else can they
turn to? Then I feel guilty.

To me homemaking is really work. I have to push myself. I'm a hobby
fiend; I wish I could spend the whole day doing sewing or reading. That
would be utopia for me. When I do the housework I think if I hurry up
and do this then I'll have the time for myself. It's sort of an incentive for
me. Jim always laughs when I say this, but sometimes I feel guilty when
I'm doing my hobbies and I know there's something else to do like
cleaning the bathroom. It's really terrible. Don't ask me why I do it.

When I first came home with the baby I had this house spotless. I'd
whip through this house every day. Boy, I cleaned cupboards and
everything. Jim couldn't believe it. And I enjoyed it for some reason. I
was on a super high when I got home with him. I felt the best I'd ever
felt in my life. It didn't seem like work then.

Jim helps me now when he's not working. He cleans, and he cleans
cupboards. I know he'd help me more if I were working. But I don't
expect him to now. He works eight hours a day, comes home and works
on the cars or something, and I can't expect him to. That would be
unfair for me to think he should do housework too. Now if I was
working that's a whole different thing. We could split up the work. But
for me to sit here all day and he's out working, that wouldn't be fair. But
he takes the kids a lot; just keeping them out of my hair helps a lot. He
helps a lot more than a lot of men that I talk to. One girl friend, she has
two kids and her husband doesn't even mow the lawn. He just doesn't

like it. She bought him a snowblower and now she has to use it. He won't even take the garbage out. But she condones it, she lets him do it. He works hard, too. But on the other hand, she goes all the time—hires a babysitter so she's got her free time. They must have a mutual understanding. Jim I suppose does less than some—he's just average. I know that if I say I need help, he won't hesitate.

How did you view marriage at first?

Before I realized, it was just like a storybook. At first things used to just go along. It's more or less what you expected. Then it all starts to come down on you. You don't think about the bills part. The contract that you have between yourselves—you're so used to being one person and you're not anymore. You're two and you have to give and take. Everything is just different.

Nothing against my kids, but I wouldn't have gotten pregnant so early. I was only twenty-one. Now I think I would have waited. One kid having another kid, was all I was. They said you should be able to work it all out, and by the third kid you should be pretty good at it. I think in high school they should have a class about it—not just the economics, that's just one aspect of it—everything else, sex education and the whole route. You don't realize that it's a twenty-four-hour job until you get into it. Then it's too late. Men should be taught too. We were so naive.

After our first child, Jim lost out. He was just in the background. He never said anything, I have to give him credit. He never expressed jealousy. Maybe if he had, I would have realized what I was doing. Then it dawned on me that I was kind of shutting him out.

When the kids are gone—it's like I told Jim—I'll have to go to work. I'm scared now because I've been away from a job for so long. It's been almost ten years. You know I'll get a job, but the thought of going and applying for it really scares me. I think maybe if I do it once or twice you get back into the habit, it probably wouldn't bother me. And, too, to react to people . . . . I'm really away from it. I don't know how to carry on a conversation. You're so used to relating to kids and then to relate to an adult you have to bring out a different personality. It's funny, but it's true. It's just the initial doing it once or twice. Maybe it's a fear of being turned down.

> "The Knight on a White Horse Has Got to
> Be *within* Us"
> Charlotte Tracey

Charlotte Tracey, like her mother before her, was a displaced homemaker decades before the term became fashionable.

In my mother's generation it was a disgrace for a woman to have to work. A woman was to be taken care of, entirely dependent upon the male. A lot of women had married because they needed somebody to take care of them. Maybe some of those marriages were made by matchmakers. It was not the situation where they were getting married to whoever because they loved them and wanted to share their life with them. It was really a gamble.

Many of the men were not professional. Many did not have any real skills. They were expected to go out and work and support their families. The role of the male was a very definite role, which I think in a way is very good.

The woman's role was to be the mother, the homemaker, and also to fulfill her role as a wife whenever her husband needed her. She could never say, "Gee, I'm tired," or be honest about a sexual relationship. She was in a way chatteled to this man. Prostituted herself, in some cases, for years. With a lot of the women from my mother's generation it was an exchange of services. He would go out and supply food for his family and work, and she would in exchange be the homemaker and raise the children, and it was very, very seldom that she had any part in any decision-making process.

My mother baked bread every day. She came from Hungary. She married very, very young. She was a mother at sixteen. But at that time it was not uncommon.

My father died when he was thirty-seven, left her a widow with a teenage son and three very small children. She spoke no English. Here was a woman who was totally dependent upon her husband. I often thought it was a lot of nerve for him to die when he did.

The tremendous struggle for survival began. He left her a very small insurance policy, and she had a great deal of pride and self-respect. She was an aristocratic woman. How difficult for her to be left with these four children.

She made every dollar stretch. She was a very religious person. She had this total belief that God was going to take care of her. I think this belief was the reason she survived. I often wish I had the same type of dedication.

We still don't to this day know how she did it and retained her sanity. Women did not work, so it was a very difficult financial situation. Somehow we managed. Although there were always problems. How were we going to pay the rent? The gas? There was always a fear of the authorities—the police, the church—because in Hungary they had pogroms against the Jews and they were always afraid of anyone in uniforms.

We grew up as decently as we did because the whole neighborhood was involved with each other. We moved into a ghetto but we didn't realize it was a ghetto. We knew it was a struggle, but everyone else was struggling so it was a common denominator. The synagogue was either across the street or around the corner. The butcher was downstairs, the baker was across the street. Everything was within walking distance.

The first job I had was when I was thirteen or fourteen, and I had to lie about my age in order to get it. I didn't have any money for bus fare or transportation, so I walked. There was always the responsibility of taking care of bills or my mother. We assumed it without any question, because we didn't have any choice. Young people today say, "I don't have my head together, give me time, this is not what I like." We didn't have time to think. We just had to get out and do it.

In my first job I made thirty-five cents an hour. I worked for a man who told me dirty jokes all the time. Somehow I knew the right times to laugh at them, although I never really understood them. I was rather naive, dumb. He always wanted me to go to lunch with him. And he'd always manage somehow to subtly put his hand on my rear end or something. He was in his thirties, the first dirty old man that I'd ever met. He used to ask me to model bathing suits for customers. Looking back, I realize that I had this great figure and it was *him* that wanted to see me. And there was always this fear of what would happen if you lost your job, and at the same time you're going to school. But we were always good girls. Being a virgin was an important thing. The whole neighborhood was involved in seeing that all the girls stayed virgins. You were going to get married some day, and you were to be a virgin or else.

For me, everything had to be perfect. I was convinced I must be the best mother in the whole world, the best wife, best homemaker, and the best of everything. I didn't realize that these were my feelings at the time.

It sounds very simple now, but it wasn't. I had this ability to absolutely block out. I hate talking about my marriage because I think it was ugly, ugly. Being raised as an Orthodox Jew, if you were married you stayed married. Being so concerned about what were the neighbors saying, you weren't going to get a divorce. So I was in a marriage that I was very unhappy in for many, many years, and stayed in it much longer than I should have, much longer than people today would stay in an unhappy marriage. You just didn't bring shame on the family.

Divorce has become a part of our lives now. When I separated this was not the case. You were a marked woman. You were a "divorcée." That was a dirty, dirty word, a terrible thing. You were also stereotyped: you were a loose woman. Your friends and family didn't stick or stay with you. Now you became a threat.

With my friends I think I became the "other woman." Some were afraid their husbands would find me attractive or make a play for me. They felt uncomfortable having me around. Some of them were also in very unhappy marriages, and they stayed away in the sidelines and watched me suffer.

This was a very desperate thing for me to do in my life. The reason I separated was that at that particular time in my life, it was a life or death matter. I suffered physically. I had no money. I had three children to support.

Nobody came forth with money or moral support. No support whatsoever. It was something that I was going through all by myself. And at the same time I wanted to be very careful about my children. I didn't want them to know that there might not be enough money. For about a year or two, it was a very learning experience. I learned that I could survive alone, without my friends or family. In a way I'm very thankful that no one helped me. I learned very quickly.

I was very determined that my children would never know what it was like to be without food. I started out with fifteen dollars and bought a makeup kit and sold makeup. I had this tremendous drive and aloneness which made me want to succeed. There was no other choice.

When I separated from my husband the family all wanted me to go back because that was the easiest way for them, and for all concerned. But I couldn't do it because I didn't want to die, I wanted to live. I knew that going back I would one day take my life.

I went out and sold makeup and had a little boutique in a salon. If I had ten or fifteen dollars extra I would run out and buy more and sell that, and so on and so forth. I really thought I was doing well, making seventy-five or eighty dollars a week. I was determined that my children would have a chance in life to be whatever it is that they want to be.

I hate . . . I'm not very comfortable discussing this—how did you do this or how did you do that—I never had time to think about it. Tomorrow is Monday. I just want to go to work and accomplish whatever there is to do.

I enjoyed my children very much. They were never a pain in the neck. I enjoyed being a homemaker; I loved it. When I was forced to leave the home—there's a certain amount of security that you find being in the home—and go out into this cruel world, I thought everyone was nice and kind and helpful. I found out that was true with a great many people but not with all. I learned. But I still have a great deal of faith in people. I will always give everybody a chance to prove themselves. It's been a great learning experience.

When I left home to go to work because it was an absolute necessity, I had these tremendous guilt feelings about my children. I was used to being home when they were home from school. They were used to three-, four-, seven-course dinners. I made everything myself— homemade noodles, cakes, and pies. Then I realized when I started working that I would throw on a steak for dinner. I would think that steak was very expensive, but I didn't have the time to make, say, stew.

There were times when I felt I didn't want to be alone, that I would like it very much if my children were around me. But I realized that this would be a very, very difficult thing for them, that it would cripple them to stay home with dear old mom. When they wanted to go some-place they would ask if it was all right. "Are you afraid to be by your-self?" they'd say. I'd say no, even though sometimes I thought I'd go crazy being alone and all by myself.

I think the most important thing I can say to women, regardless of their age, is that we never feel complete. We're very susceptible people. We have a tendency to look for what we need in another person, to fulfill us and to make us feel whole. I think it's very important for women to try to make themselves whole persons, by themselves and for themselves, and not to feel dependent upon anyone else for support or to fill the gaps in our personality or our being.

I can't say that I'm totally independent. I have a love affair with my business. It's through my business that I can support myself. I fight with my business. Other days I love it. Some days I just tolerate it. It's a tremendous responsibility.

I think we wait for this knight on a white horse to come and rescue us. To feed us, to protect us. I think that this knight has got to be *within* us. I really love men—I think they're great. But I think they like us better when we're not totally dependent upon them.

"The Combination of Homemaking and Abuse Will Catch up with You"
Norma Czernikowski

Thirty-one-year-old Norma has been married for thirteen years. She has three children. During the past two years her husband has beaten her almost every day. Norma was interviewed at a shelter for battered women.

I think a regular homemaker is under a lot of stress. She does have to do a lot of work, and she's never out of the home unless she has to do the shopping, the errands, things for the children if she does have children.

On the other hand, if you're a battered wife you don't even get the chance to be a shopper, see your friends, unless they want to take the initiative to come into your home and help you, which most people don't want to do because they don't want to be involved. Your friends may help on the side for a while, but then they even get fed up when the abuse keeps going on. They're ashamed theirself at what's happening to their friend.

I went through a period where I stayed to myself. I did for a long while. Because I was very ashamed of my black eyes, my beat-up face, my husband's attitude. You can't burden family, because my husband even threatened my family. I was going to stay with a sister when he called up, "I'm going to shoot you and the kids." And he would say this every day, and I believe it.

During that time I didn't go out at all, hardly, because my husband would take my car keys, pull out my car wires, pulled out my telephone if I went out a lot even with the kids. I went out a couple of times.

He would come home. I would be there all day, cooking, cleaning, taking care of Richard, Sammy, and Phyllis; my whole day was nothing but work, from morning until night. There was tension from the time that he came in the door until the time that he left. We couldn't even look at each other. We just knew it, between the two of us, that there was going to be an outbreak of violence. We knew it. I knew it anyway, and I was scared to death for him to come home. Although I don't know at times whether he was just real high . . . he was drunk a few times.

The fighting kept getting worse at home. The more hitting that I seemed to allow, the more worse that it got. Then it really got where I thought that I was losing my self-identification as being a person, a mother, you know, being anybody. I lost my self-respect. I was beat up day after day for two years straight. Policemen were in and out of my home.

One night I was laying there and my husband came home and he told me either you leave or I'm going to kill you, and he had a gun loaded and he put it to my head and I believe he would have done it except for I looked at him and said "Please don't. Leave me alone and I promise to get out." And so he said "All right," and he went back into the living room. In the morning I took the kids and I packed the kids' stuff. I had called the shelter but I never had the courage to leave my home because I was scared: What am I going to do at thirty-one years old with three children aged three, four, and eleven? With no real good education other than working with the young people, no college education to really make a good living. And not having to end up in poverty. But something just told me that you can either stay and end up dead, and the kids end up a mess, or you can leave, start thinking a little bit more highly of yourself, and maybe your children can still have a chance to straighten out. I'd never go back there.

It gets to be a habit, too, to be a homemaker. It really does. I think a woman could be very tired of this after thirteen years. And the combination of the two, of homemaking and abuse, it will finally catch up with you. The abuse will catch up with you mentally and bodily. Physically and healthwise you just can't do it. You can't take care of three kids and be beat up and sore every day and be crying and depressed and good to yourself or your kids.

First thing I would do was get up, make the beds, get the kids dressed, and see that they were washed and cleaned. Well, first I got up with him—I got up at five o'clock because that's when he went to work, and I would make his coffee, make his sandwich or whatever he was going to take to work. Didn't seem like there was much happening in the morning between us. After the beds would be made then I'd make breakfast for the children, vacuum throughout the house, dust. Go downstairs, throw in the wash, come up from doing the wash, watch a little bit of TV, then go outside with the kids, play with them for a while, maybe sometimes I'd clean out the cupboards if they needed to be done or go into the garage, special things that really needed to be gotten after. Most of the time before he came home I'd make sure that my ironing was done, and my closets and my drawers were neat. Then by about quarter to four I'd start to cook supper because he'd come in about four-thirty.

And he'd come in, and most of the time he wouldn't say a word and then all of a sudden he'd start cursing or say that he had a hard day. Things would just start, you know. He'd go, "I hate you, you're no good, you're not worth anything." I'd put supper on, he'd eat supper, then I would do the dishes. All this time bickering, constant bickering. If the dishes weren't done, or if I took time out to take the kids down to the park, if there was one thing out of place he was really angry.

When I first married him he was real shy. He stuttered. He did no calling for himself on the phone. At that time there was a lot of affection between us. He expected his home to be in toptop shape, the bills paid, his friends entertained to the hilt, you know, dinners. Together as a couple we never really went dancing, to the movies, this type of thing. It was always friends into our home or going into their homes. I enjoyed it. Very much. When I did get the break, it was usually on weekends. I'd call up some people. "And you can do the Jello and I can bring some potatoes and we'll all get together and play some cards." We'd take turns.

I can remember a couple of times that he did hit me but I overlooked it because I thought that he'd had a hard day or something and it would go away. I overlooked it. But he did pick me up and throw me against a furnace. And he came looking for me at work one day. He came after me and he did get me and take me home and throw me against a wall and said I wasn't staying home enough, I was gone too much. Then when I did try to give him the attention, he didn't want it, see. I don't understand.

There were four married couples that were always very close. Of course one of the couples . . . the woman is gone today. She was my best girl friend.

She's gone?

She's dead. Her husband killed her. And they were married ten years. She was twenty-seven. And had two kids. She was going through a divorce and trying to make it on her own working out and he came and shot her in the apartment where she was living.

[Here Norma changes the subject.]

There's always going to be expectations of the housewife. Even if she's living alone and she's not a wife she's going to be called a half a house because she's still going to be doing the cooking and she's still going to be doing the cleaning. She's just not going to have the wife end of it. I myself today am glad to see a woman having a good education so that she can get out.

Do you think homemakers deserve more for what they do?

Oh sure. They can't pay a homemaker enough money, they just can't. I don't even think you can put dollar signs on a homemaker. A homemaker is not just being a homemaker, you have to be a whole lot of other things too. If you're a housewife you have to be, if you have children, a psychiatrist, a nurse, a cook, a washer . . . you are everything when you are a housewife. That's really a bad name to put on it . . . you can't have a name for it because she's everything. No, they can't put dollars and cents on it.

I think it could be enjoyable if you're married to the right person and if you both get along real well, and you enjoy working in your home. You have to really have the love of home, I think. It is a job in itself, and it's just like going to work except that you don't get the pay. At the end of the day you're just as tired as if you punched a time clock. The difference is that on Friday you don't get a paycheck except if your husband or your boyfriend says, "Here's some extra money, thanks for all the stuff you've done this week." Which I really think would really help a lot of women want to do that much more in their home if their husband would take the initiative to say that to them, "Gee, sweetheart, the house looks nice today. You changed the living room!" Not come home and say "Guess what happened to me at work today! My boss jumped me," and blah, blah, blah. Which the wife will listen to after having all these other things. Plus I failed to mention that in between all this other stuff she has communicated with the school, taken the kids back and forth to school, and if they get sick she's running them back and forth to the hospital, to the doctor's, she's doing all these things. Just one sentence, sometimes, to the housewife, after being all day working, just saying to her "Gee, you did a nice job today," just the same as you like to hear from your employer. And if you don't hear nothing you get kind of depressed in your work.

I think most women start out real enthusiastic about their marriage and everything else, and I've noticed that in later years it ends up . . . a whole lot of marriages are different.

I'm happiest now when I can achieve goals that I set for myself. I was such a dependent person before, being married. The last two years he wasn't able to be depended on—he was never there when I needed him, let's put it that way—so I finally realized that I could make decisions myself. And I'm happy when I do this, because I say "Gee, I'm not dumb. I can still drive my car, I can still cook, I can still raise my kids." And I found out that there are other people in this world, too, a whole lot of nice people that will help you.

I felt toward the end that I was dependent . . . a whole lot of it was financial. "How am I going to do this? I can't do it! I'm thirty-one years old and I've got three kids. I can't do it!" But you can do it if you're *fifty* provided that you have self-confidence and you like yourself. And if you like yourself other people are going to like you too. I think that I blamed myself because I had a bad marriage. It was a shock to me because I never wanted a bad marriage. My children were having troubles and I never wanted that—I always wanted my children to be happy. I really wanted my husband to be happy. I really don't know what the trouble was.

I think I did everything I could to make him happy. I mean everything. I don't think there's anything I could have done to make him happy. I mean . . . loving him . . . I think sexually. I did everything my husband wanted. I never refused my husband anything that he ever wanted to do, OK? Whenever he wanted something to eat special, I'd make special trips for him.

I really think to have a good marriage if you always put that other per-

son before yourself, and the other person does likewise to you, you're going to have nothing but good communication and a good workable relationship. If you do this for each other. When one partner doesn't do
this for the other, this is where the communication breaks down and
somebody goes, "Hey, look, I'm no fool. I'm not going to keep doing
these things for you, you're doing nothing for me in return." And
there's nothing in the relationship to work toward anymore. You can do
anything you want for a person and it won't make them love you back
once it's over.

I think I was the happiest when I did have a lot of people around and I
was doing a lot of things for a whole lot of people that I knew really
enjoyed it. Like a supper. Or a big holiday, maybe a Thanksgiving meal
for everybody. Christmastime, and I would have liked the whole family
at my house.

Right now I'm an unhappy homemaker because I'm not really a
homemaker, as such. I'm not doing for a lot of people that I would like to
do for—this is really personal—and I'm sure there are a lot of women
who think the same way, though. They like to do things for other
people—if they're cooking a meal or they're planning a picnic for somebody. I'm kind of unhappy because my friends aren't here, and I'm
going to have to make all different friends and a whole new life. So I'm
unhappy about that. But when I do find another home and I do make
different friends, that's when I'll be happy, a happy homemaker, when
my friends will be able to come into my home and enjoy themselves.

Equality
Begins at Home

5

There will be no housewives in the future because no one marries a house; houses make lousy partners; no fun at all. Homemaking will be a part-time occupation for all the people who inhabit a shared domicile.

Wilma Scott Heide

I'm not going to do that shit work!

A young husband

A wide range of people are interested in making the house work. Couples are working out systems for sharing. Small groups of individuals are trying out new ways of living together. Some legislators are concerned about improving the status of all homemakers, and researchers are even interested in homemakers internationally. In between such very personal and such far-reaching strategies are an infinite number of possibilities for effecting change.

A person who becomes interested in improving the status of the homemaker inevitably asks herself or himself which of these various approaches is the most feasible and the most useful. Homemakers in particular want to know what they personally can do to bring about lasting improvement.

Obviously, legislation will have global effects, and individuals can initiate and support pertinent bills. Less obvious, but no less important, is the effort for change that is initiated by homemakers in their own households.

With the onset of a new consciousness about the often sexist division of labor in the home, many couples are working to create new, more equitable arrangements for allocating their household labor. Some are also working out the economics of sharing, developing systems to assure the homemaker of some personal financial security. The problems these people are facing, and their strategies for dealing with them, are at the crux of the movement to improve the status of the homemaker.

Sharing the Housework

Many homemakers do not think their family work arrangements are equitable. They object to bearing most of the burden of the housework. and they are lobbying within their families to get some changes. Of course, theoretically, the problem is not theirs alone; it is a problem that a couple or family should face together.

Evidence is beginning to accumulate that sharing the housework has an important relationship to overall marital satisfaction. Ann Oakley's work with homemakers in London indicates that, among women who report a moderate or high level of housework help from their husbands, marital satisfaction is higher.[1] A study done in the United States in 1960 shows that in general wives report greater marital satisfaction when husbands do more housework.[2] And another done ten years later in Britain indicates that, when a man finds more satisfaction in his family than in his work, the marriage is more satisfying to both husband and wife:[3] presumably, this home-oriented husband does more housework than his company-oriented contemporary, though we cannot be certain of this. A great deal more research needs to be done before we can make many definite statements.

We do know that many homemakers are uncomfortable about some important aspects of their role, and that this is sometimes a cause of dissension between spouses. In Laura Lein's recent sociological study of sixteen American families—mostly young, middle-income families in which both spouses work outside the home—half of the wives reported dissatisfaction with the distribution of household work. One of these women put it this way: "When a man comes home from work, he comes home and his meal's cooked. For a woman working there's always another job to do around the house. I come home and I'm tired . . . and I really honestly feel that if I can come home and cook supper, he can at least clean the kitchen and the two boys can help." Her husband, on the other hand, feels that women "can work [outside the home] and take care of the house, and the man can work and kind of help the woman when she comes home."[4]

Increasing separation of husband and wife roles over the years leads to increased marital unhappiness and impermanence.[5] Most couples begin their relationship with relatively less role separation than they develop later; at first they share both outside and home work relatively equitably. A young couple considers doing the housework together fun; a young woman works outside the home until she has children. But men become increasingly involved at work and women become increasingly involved at home, and as roles diverge couples are more and more likely to argue over family decisions, to be less happy, and to consider separation or divorce. Thus it may be that, in many households, moving from a sex-stereotyped model for housework to a more equitable sharing relationship will have an important positive effect on the marriage.

Couples who are dealing with such transitions and who are creating new systems for sharing are essentially pioneering. It is difficult to determine how much outside help these couples seek as they attempt to create their new patterns of work allocation. Even though housework disputes undoubtedly contribute in some way to the marital discord seen by therapists, there is almost nothing in the psychological literature about the process of housework allocation, and it is seldom made the focus in marital counseling. Little theory has been generated about the psychology of sharing housework and about the best ways of effecting the transition from one method of labor distribution in the home to another. At this point the most I can do to fill the gap is present some tentative ideas about strategies that seem to show promise. What information we have is based on information from a limited number of studies drawn primarily from intensive interviews with a few families.

What motivates a couple to seek an egalitarian housework arrangement? Ideally, a relationship between two people living together starts out equitably. A new couple may apply "the roommate test" to their situation: Are they treating each other as if they were roommates, dividing all work and all responsibilities equally, or have they permitted some vestige of self-role stereotyping in their relationship? At least some women are actively pursuing men who will maintain their half of the bargain. Listen to one woman extolling the virtues of a man who cooks:

> I married John to save myself from a life of soup, cereal and TV dinners. He's a beautiful cook. He has his own garden, a sort of gourmet garden. He grows a lot of the things he cooks, everything from beans . . . to tomatoes. Usually when he's done cooking, he cleans up the kitchen, too. I wouldn't trade him for any other man or machine in the world.[6]

One hopes the basis for sharing housework equitably will be established early in a relationship. Today many young couples live together before they are married, when both are working or going to school, and this seems to be an appropriate environment for fostering equality. On the other hand, most research has been done on marriages that began a decade or more ago, and these relationships tended to start out with a traditional division of labor by sex. Usually some major life-style change has precipitated a change in housework allocation.

Taking on outside work is sometimes the impetus for significant change
in the division of labor at home; it is often the cause of changing expectations by the woman, who is suddenly burdened with two jobs. Sharing the housework in these circumstances seems more reasonable than
when the homemaker was at home full time. Or perhaps the employment hours of one or both of the spouses change, making sharing
housework and child care a necessity.

Sometimes a spouse becomes discontented with stereotyped roles
because she or he realizes the implications of these roles for all men and
women. One young man, a student who does the ironing, cooking, and
cleaning while his wife works outside the home, asserts that, "Every
week when I clean the house, I feel like I'm striking a blow for women's
liberation."[7] Alas, such men are rare! Meanwhile, the attitudes of
women who remain in the home full time may also be changing as their
awareness of their role grows and as the possibilities for improving
their job seem more realistic. Why, for instance, should homemakers
work longer hours than wage earners?

Support Systems

Whatever the precipitating factor, finding moral support for the change
is crucial to making it work. The homemaker who is trying to
initiate change will have to find or create enough conviction within herself to sustain her through initial setbacks. After six months of working
full time and coming home to find her husband reading the paper and
waiting for her to start dinner, one woman I know confronted her
spouse and got the spontaneous reply, "But I'm not going to do that
shit work!" Fortunately for her, the words were no sooner out of his
mouth than he realized the sexism inherent in his reaction, and they
were soon on their way to a change.

Other homemakers are not so lucky and will need all the support they
can muster to face a battery of spouse, relatives, and children who
oppose them. Sociologist Jane Hood has interviewed a number of such
cases. One woman, a thirty-four-year-old working mother of two, tells
this seemingly typical story: "Daniel had a birthday in February, and I
made cupcakes for school and cupcakes for here and took his friends to
the show on Saturday, and from there to Farrell's and celebrated his
birthday. I really think he had a bang-up birthday. Well, a week later
we went to see my parents and my mother made him a birthday cake
because she was afraid he might not have even had a birthday cake for
his birthday."[8] The husband of an editor with three children also seems
fairly typical in his attitude:

I think I do my share. I still feel that she has certain responsibilities to the home. I don't feel, for instance, that I should have to cook the meals. But there are a lot of things I'll help her with. When it comes down to whose responsibility it is for some of those things, I feel that it's hers. This equality thing goes only so far. Everybody has to have responsibilities that are theirs. . . . I understand what Joan is trying to do and sometimes I wish she didn't have that drive. It's somewhat selfish in a way . . . wishing that she would be satisfied to stay at home.[9]

Of course spouses do deserve some commiseration. When the homemaking is shared, they do, after all, experience a loss of important services and an increase in their personal burden of work. They may even lose what they consider to be their dignity, and their special status in the family.

Like their wives, men who defy the sex-role stereotypes in home-making need support for their new roles. And they are even less likely than the women to get it. Even so comprehensive a book as Jack Nichols's *Men's Liberation* fails to lend dignity to work done in the home, let alone suggest that men might reasonably do more of it. Nichols goes so far as to suggest that tasks done in the home have become so "simple and swift" that they are hardly work at all, implying that the homemaker role is minimally useful. He does deplore "dominant chauvinist husbands" who thoughtlessly dump "family 'duties'" on working wives.[10] However, when such a man as Nichols, who has devoted a great deal of careful thought to men's roles, has not come up with a more sensitive approach to housework, men can hardly expect to find much support among their less sensitive peers.

In fact, men who do more housework than average for their sex are likely to face derision and even dislike. As one husband puts it, at parties with his fellow workers, when his wife describes what he does around the house, "The guys want to kill me. They say, 'You're getting us in trouble.' Their wives say, 'Does he really?' and the men get really mad." This man obviously has a problem: He wants to help some at home, and his wife wants him to help even more, but he faces censure from other men because he jeopardizes their accustomed style of living.[11] It would be interesting to know more about those men who are courageous enough to share housework even in the face of such criticism.

Who Is Going to Change?

The question that faces each household is "What kind of change is desired?" First of all, who is going to change? Tolstoy once said, "Everybody thinks of changing humanity and nobody thinks of changing himself." It seems to be generally true that the person who has been doing the housework, the person who has accepted the title of "homemaker," is most likely to initiate change. After all, it is usually she who feels burdened. And the thrust of change is usually directed at the other people in the household, those who are going to ease her burden by taking on some of the work themselves.

However, before homemakers assume that it is only the others who need to change, it may be wise for them to take a realistic look at themselves. We know very little about homemakers as a group—we have many anecdotes and unfounded beliefs but very little hard information about homemakers' job training, skills, and values. Thus, at this point homemakers are pretty much on their own when it comes to figuring out the most fruitful areas for self-reexamination. And they may, in fact, totally balk at the idea of self-change, especially when they strongly believe the system is at fault.

Nevertheless, before plunging into the fray, the homemaker who is anticipating a change in household work allocation may wish to consider a few of the following ideas. For instance, as I have already mentioned, it *may* be true that because of the ways in which they are socialized, women in this country have higher standards for cleanliness and tidiness than men do. In Laura Lein's study of couples, one pair reported that they had discussed problems about sharing housework with their friends, and had decided it seemed that women "took on this ability to notice dirt." Both husbands and wives thought it was neurotic of the women to notice the dirt. They said that when the husband did half of the household work, "[He] wouldn't mess around with the margins of things, like dusting and stuff."[12]

One woman found that she is very "dirt conscious," and that having things lying around the house "bothers me a lot and it doesn't bother a man at all."[13] Her sex-based generalization may be warranted, but of course other explanations are possible. It may be that the husbands, though doing more work, simply have not taken on the responsibility for it: they may still believe that the housework is really, ultimately, their wives' responsibility. The notion that having the responsibility for a job increases a person's attention to it is supported by one homemaker's observation:

> When I was home I paid the bills. I'd walk around and shut the heat and lights off to make money. But after I'd gone back to work and we'd made a few major purchases—furniture, etc.—we were worried about how we were going to pay for these things. So he took over the payment of the bills and after about a month he began walking around the house turning the lights off.[14]

At any rate, a homemaker anticipating change in family housework allocation may wish to examine her own standards for housekeeping to see whether they can realistically be altered. Obviously she is not a "neurotic" for holding high standards; she is merely the product of a social indoctrination that dictates that girls be especially tidy and detail-oriented, and that asserts that the household is her responsibility. A reassessment of what housework realistically needs to be done may be useful to her. In doing this reassessment she may wish to take a second look at the views of the males in her household, views that may be useful precisely because of their presumable socialization toward expedience in housework. She needs to be wary, of course; because of this same socialization, the males may also believe that housework is not their responsibility anyway. In the final analysis, both sexes will need to examine their values about the desired state of the household.

The homemaker may have other ideas that significantly affect her plans for sharing the housework. Angela Barron McBride, author of *The Growth and Development of Mothers*, asserts that women are chained to present roles by their belief that they have the ability to "keep everybody 'happy,' to charm away aggressive feelings with a lullaby, to soothe tired souls, pointing out the joy of everyday living."[15] If the homemaker has the feeling that she and only she can keep her family happy, she will feel guilty when she asks others to assume part of "her" role. Homemakers will do themselves and their families a favor by coming to terms with this myth about their abilities and by placing responsibility for the family happiness where it belongs—on every individual concerned.

Along the same lines, it may well be true that the homemaker can do the housework better than any other member of her family. After all, she was probably trained for the role as a child, and she has had years of experience. It may be difficult for other members of the household to admit they cannot cook or do not know how to do the wash—after all "everyone knows" that "anybody can do housework." The homemaker herself is likely to take her skills for granted and to overlook the necessity of teaching these skills to other members of the family.

Tact and Tactics

Which brings us to the next question: Assuming that she has her own house in order, so to speak, how does the homemaker proceed to change the beliefs and behavior of her spouse and family?

Let us remind ourselves in the beginning that psychologists have shown that a change in attitude does not have to precede a change in behavior. Too many homemakers see their husbands' negative at-titudes toward sharing as an insuperable obstacle. "He'll never change—he doesn't believe in helping out," they say. And yet it is the blue-collar worker, the man who is the most outspoken against doing housework, who helps out most around the home. And, in general, psychological studies show that when a behavior changes, attitude changes may follow. Thus, changing a chauvinist pig into a household democrat may be less a matter for discussion than for action. Get him to do the dishes and sooner or later (though, alas, probably later) he'll believe he ought to be doing them.

Many strategies have been suggested for encouraging family partici-pation in the housework. I will discuss two basics here: first, simply asking family members to do more housework; second, "resigning" the role of chief homemaker.

Requesting

In the best of all worlds, the most reasonable way to initiate change is simply to ask for it. Assertiveness training may be useful here. Learning to make a request assertively rather than aggressively may do wonders for the discussions that will, one hopes, follow. Paula Reade (a pseudonym) is a forty-five-year-old mother of three who returned to outside employment after seventeen years as a full-time homemaker. Her tactful request for help has been at least moderately successful.

> "I never was a great housekeeper," she says, and "when I discussed [going back to work] with my husband, I said, 'Well, you know that the housework will not suffer because I never did it anyway.'...But it has suffered.... My boys do their own rooms, and it looks like they do their own rooms, but I close my eyes to it, and that's their re-sponsibility.... My fourteen-year-old does a significant job when he wants to...and the 11-year-old doesn't do such a great job, but he's trying. And...so I said to my husband, 'Let's see, I've got two of the bedrooms taken care of. And I obviously have to do the kitchen I suppose, so what room would you like to do?' and he said 'How about the bathroom?'...And I said, 'Oh, would you?' Even though it's the smallest room, I hate to do bathrooms. His reasoning was it was the smallest room and you get it done the quickest. Well, he does the bathroom.... Poor man, known as the 'bathroom cleaner.'"[16]

Clearly, Mrs. Reade has made reasonable requests of her family, and, though they still seem not to be shouldering their full share of the housework, at least they have responded positively to her need for help.

In other not so fortunate circumstances a homemaker's requests fall on deaf ears. And when she gets no response, or an uncaring one, the frequency and anger of her requests are likely to escalate. Eventually she is accused of nagging, a behavior that is probably as unpleasant for her as for her spouse or children. She does not want to create dissension in her family. Indeed, she probably feels guilty for doing so. But the alternative is increasing frustration and powerlessness and perhaps a severe loss of self-esteem, which is equally aversive.

In the extreme cases of noncommunication, when a spouse or family refuses to listen or for some reason cannot comprehend the home-maker's frustration, a professional therapist should probably be consulted by all concerned. At first it may seen ludicrous to consult a therapist on a problem stemming from housework. We tend to believe we should consult a mental health professional when the problem has something to do with sex or depression or marital discord—things society labels as serious. Yet how often are homemakers belittling themselves and swallowing their anger and pride because their problem is "just housework"? The idea of taking housework seriously is new. But we know that the homemaker's frustration is real, and that her problem is important not only to her but to her whole family. If they cannot solve the problem alone, they should get help. The problem is not "just housework"—it is human suffering.

Before we move on to discuss other change tactics, one more point should be made about nagging—that unpleasant escalation of simple requesting. It is unfortunate, but true, that people sometimes respond better to unpleasant requests than to pleasant ones. In short, sometimes nagging works. It may not be the method of choice; we would all rather be able to sit down and pleasantly work out rational agreements. And it can become a nasty habit when it is used in situations where it is inappropriate and unnecessary. Certainly just because nagging has been successful does not mean that once in a while one shouldn't try something more positive. But, when worse comes to worst, it can get the job done.

Resigning

In her charming and insightful story "I Hereby Resign as Keeper of This House," Stephanie Roberts describes a tactic that falls somewhere between simple requests and outright noncooperation. She suggests that the homemaker simply resign as chief houseworker. In her story the homemaker leaves this letter of resignation on the refrigerator:

LETTER OF RESIGNATION

Dear Jack, Thane, Stephanie, Michele and Kevin:
    This is to inform you that I am no longer running this household. The cupboards, the Lysol, the linoleum, the washer, the dryer, the

marketing—they're all yours. I HEREBY RESIGN AS KEEPER OF THIS
HOUSE, AS YOUR LIVE-IN MAID/COOK/MENTOR/NURSEMAID.
You can fend for yourselves. Best of luck.
                                                        Mom[17]

In the story, the resulting chaos motivates her spouse and family to
develop a system for doing their share. It should be pointed out that the
letter was backed up with action; the ex-keeper of the house, an artist,
moved her studio out of the house and refused to do customary jobs like
cooking.

Refusing to do the housework is the ultimate tactic. Surely the idea of
taking a vacation from the housework may not turn out to be as pleasant
as it sounds. To be effective, resigning must not be merely a threat;
plans must be made for carrying through. One has to be prepared for a
standoff: perhaps no one else will do the housework, and waiting for
other members of the family to reach their tolerance level on various
chores may be unpleasant, to say nothing of unsanitary. In the end,
refusing to do the housework may be intolerable unless one actually
moves out and establishes a separate, personally amenable place to wait
them out. If family communication gets so bogged down that leaving
home for a time seems the only resort, then again it may be wise to get
professional counseling.

Designing a Work-Sharing System

All the strategies I have mentioned have a common aim: to enlist the
cooperation of family members in designing and implementing a new
household work-sharing system. It is important that everyone cooper-
ate in both the creation and the administration of the system. People are
most likely to support a system they themselves have helped create,
and, furthermore, part of the point of sharing the housework is to allow
homemakers to give up total responsibility for decision-making.

Having family meetings to discuss a new work-sharing system is
obviously crucial, and anything that will encourage openness within
these meetings is welcome. Three kinds of information need to come
out of the meetings. First, the present state of the housework allocation
must be clarified. Then people must come to an agreement on exactly
what housework actually needs to be done. Finally, a strategy must be
devised for assigning specific jobs to individuals. Readers familiar with
the psychology of behavior modification or management by objectives
will recognize here the basic processes of collecting baseline data, setting goals, and establishing a reward system. Another pertinent con-

cept is the recognition of policymaking as a component in home management.[18]

The present state of housework allocation in a given household may be obvious to everyone concerned, or it may be hotly disputed. One useful way to clarify specific points of agreement and disagreement is to have each person fill out a checklist of present housework responsibilities as she or he sees them. The checklist should be as specific as possible in referring to jobs. For example, it should list "feed the cat" and "give the dogs fresh water" rather than "take care of the pets." Usually, the more specific the list is, the easier it will be later to determine the cost of each chore in time or inconvenience. (See table 2 for an example of some basic categories of housework.)

The checklist should be filled out by every family member who is capable of doing so; it should not represent the viewpoint of one person, or even of two parents. Again, participation of all members at this stage will make implementation easier.

Completed checklists in hand, the family should meet to compare views. Perhaps twelve-year-old Johnny and his father each feel that bathing the dog ends up as his job most of the time. Maybe both husband and wife feel they make most of the beds. One family member may feel that she does more than her share overall; the family checklists will confirm whether others see things the same way.

This one-time survey, getting people's impressions of what they have done, may be adequate for analyzing the situation, especially when there are no really substantial differences of opinion to begin with. But if it indicates that there are major differences of opinion among family members, it may be necessary to gather more specific information in the form of an ongoing log of jobs completed. This technique is effective for finding out exactly who does what: A summary of jobs completed is kept up daily for two weeks to a month, at the end of which time opinions will have to be judged by the facts.

A phenomenon to be aware of here is what behavioral psychologists call the intervention effect—merely intervening to gather information may change the behaviors you are trying to measure. Thus any person in the household who realizes that his performance is now being measured is likely to improve that performance, which is, of course, a step in the right direction. Still, the main purpose of the log is not to change behavior, but to measure it. Once the log has been kept there will be no room for generalized protests like, "But I *do* take care of my room!" when no work on the room has been logged during the specified period.

TABLE 2.   Housework Checklist

Family member: (Jane)

Job	Person Who Does the Job Most of the Time				
	Jane	Tom	Daughter	Son	Outside Help
Meal preparation					
Menu planning					
Grocery shopping					
Putting groceries away					
Washing dishes					
Setting table					
Clearing table					
Cooking breakfast					
Cooking lunch					
Cooking dinner					
Cleaning oven and refrigerator					
Laundry					
Washing					
Ironing					
Taking clothes to cleaners					
Cleaning					
Vacuuming					
Dusting					
Mopping floors					
Washing windows					
Cleaning bathrooms					
Repairs					
Home and contents					
Automobile					
Clothing					
Yard work					
Lawn mowing					
Gardening					
Pet care					
Watering and feeding					
Bathing dog					
Miscellaneous					
Taking out garbage					
Changing sheets					
Paying bills					
Straightening up					

Whether a family uses a housework checklist or a log, or both, once they reach some agreement on the way things actually are, the next step is to decide how things ought to be: What housework will be done? This is a difficult part of the design process because it attempts to synthesize all the different values about housework held by the various family members. One member may insist that dishes be done right after a meal; another may want the sheets changed every three weeks instead of every week. Many compromises must be reached.

It will be useful for each family member to bring to this discussion a sense of his or her own values about housework. Using the housework checklist as a guide, one can begin to analyze how one feels about various housework chores. For each chore, each person should determine how frequently she or he believes it should be done, and how well. Why does that frequency make sense? That standard? This analysis requires careful thought. Is a certain way of doing things merely habit? Is it an attempt to please someone in particular? Is it a matter of aesthetics? Sanitation? Everyone should write down his or her reasons. Some may also want to work through the values analysis questionnaire on work in the home (table 3) in order to review their ideas on housework in general.

Here the point is that everyone in the household should know why he or she is doing a given task. He himself may not feel the task is worthwhile. Doing it may represent a compromise—a tidy living room in exchange for paying the bills—but fulfilling the compromise is in itself a valid reason for doing the work. In the end each person will be getting

TABLE 3.   VALUES ANALYSIS OF WORK IN THE HOME
---

1. Do you think housework is important work? Why or why not?
2. How many hours a week do you spend on housework?
3. What is the minimum number of hours per week in which you can accomplish the housework that *really* needs to be done?
4. If there is a difference between the number of hours a week you spend on housework (question 2) and the number of hours you think you ought to spend (question 3), explain why this difference exists.
5. What would important people in your life (your mother, father, in-laws, boss, or friends) say about the state of your house right now?
6. What do *you* say about the state of your house right now?
7. What are the important differences between how you feel and how important others feel about the state of your home? Do you sometimes find yourself trying to live up to their standards rather than your own?
8. What do you want most out of your life at home?
9. What do you like most about doing housework? Least?

something in return for his or her efforts, instead of doing something he doesn't want to do merely because he was told or otherwise coerced to do it.

Finally we come to the question of who will do which jobs. Should the distribution of labor be based on sex, skill, preference, convenience? Should outside help be hired for some of the work? Once again it will be useful for each family member to think about these issues before having a family discussion. And, once again, where values differ, compromise will obviously be in order.

Work-Sharing Systems: Examples

"And so," writes Stephanie Roberts, "THE CHART was born." And what is THE CHART? It is one family's work-sharing system, a fairly typical system established after much discussion and subjected to continual revision. THE CHART is not for everyone, but it or something similar may be useful for those families who decide that labor should be distributed equally, without regard for age, sex, or sometimes even skill.

Roberts's chart consists of a color-coded acetate board with her children's names on it and seven squares representing days of the week next to each name. In a family conference, household jobs are assigned points depending on their desirability and the time it takes to do them. The family decides that, to complete all necessary housework, each person must accumulate nine points a week. Work that needs scheduling, such as meal preparation, is distributed via a signup sheet. Otherwise, people work when they want to or do whatever jobs they want to do.

Table 4 is a sample of a work chart, established by month for a couple without children. The couple has already analyzed their housework values and has agreed on point allocations for all the relevant chores. They have agreed that some chores should be regularly scheduled, while others will be scheduled as necessary. For those chores scheduled as necessary, the couple has decided that both persons must agree to the necessity of the task before its points can be added to the individual monthly point totals and to the total monthly goal.

The couple has also decided that they want to be about even in points earned at the end of the month. If toward the end of the month it appears that their point totals will be heavily unbalanced, the person with fewer points is given an opportunity to catch up. If he or she does not catch up, he pays a penalty of ten dollars per point differential.

Thus, if Jane has earned two points more than Dick, Dick pays Jane twenty dollars.

The monetary penalty was chosen because in this particular case the couple maintains totally separate funds and sees the exchange of money between them as real rather than as a token redistribution of common money. Both find ten dollars to be a significant sum. Other penalties, such as extra work or loss of personal privilege, may be more effective in other situations. Families may prefer the system of giving substantial rewards to people who do meet their point quotas, or they may wish to experiment with a system that uses both rewards and punishments.

TABLE 4.   SAMPLE WORK ALLOCATION CHART FOR A COUPLE

	Points	Frequency	Maximum Monthly Points
Regular chores			
Clean bathroom	4	Monthly	4
Dust living room	1	Monthly	1
Change sheets	1	Monthly	1
Pay bills, including penalty points	1	Monthly	1
Clean kitchen	4	Bimonthly	2
Launder sheets/rugs	2	Bimonthly	1
Clean bedroom	2	Bimonthly	1
Vacuum living room	.25	Weekly	1
Chores to be done as necessary			
Cook dinner	2	(As needed—by agreement)	
Set up/help with dinner	.5		
Wash dishes	2		
Help with dishes	.5		
Do grocery shopping	3		
Do minor grocery or other shopping	1.5		
Take out all trash	1		
Take out some trash	.25		
Put groceries away	1		

Goal: to have an even number of points at the end of the month
Penalty: underdog pays $10 for every point he or she is behind
Ground rules: Points will not accumulate from month to month; the slate is
         wiped clean at the end of each month.

         Partner who is ahead near the end of the month must make
         a reasonable effort to allow the other partner to catch up.

Whether a work-sharing system is as simple as "I'll do this; will you do that?" or as elaborate as these point systems, it is an indication that people's needs and values are being considered. Obviously, there is no one best system—any system that works is a good one.

A final word about these work-sharing systems. Often things that seem important within the household are considered by men and women alike to be too trivial to mention to outsiders. I have already noted that people are unlikely to seek psychological counseling because of housework problems. Arguments over the failure to dust or to wash the dinner dishes are not often cited as grounds for divorce: such arguments have to be called "irreconcilable differences" before they seem important enough to be discussed in public. And yet, let me reiterate, the arena for change is the arena of these very actions; "irreconcilable differences" may very well mean disputes over the details of everyday living.

Social scientists who study housework have so far been more able to gather information about beliefs and philosophies of housework than about actual family disputes over who is going to change the sheets. Yet it is in large part through the changes made in thousands of such actions that homemakers will receive a measure of improved status.

When I first told a colleague that this chapter would include some very specific ideas on how to evaluate and share housework, including details like drawing up work charts and keeping track of who does what, he remarked that this struck him as ridiculous. His response reminded me of the comment Pat Mainardi's husband made when she had just finished writing *The Politics of Housework*. When he came in and asked what she was doing, she replied, "Writing a paper on housework." "Housework?" he said. *"Housework?* Oh my God, how trivial can you get. A paper on housework."[19]

The point is that, if housework were any other job, it would be taken seriously right down to who scrubs the pots. With any other job, knowing who does what is considered a rational management technique. With any other job, time spent and measures of production are considered crucial factors. Part of taking housework seriously is taking the details of the job seriously.

The Economics of Sharing

In their studies on marital power, Blood and Wolfe have found that wives who work outside the home make significantly more "really important decisions than wives who don't."[20] In addition to the increased

social and psychological power a woman gets when she works outside
the home, she gains important economic power. It has been
hypothesized that she feels a new sense of independence that can come
only through having her own financial security.

This feeling of independence is equally important for the woman who
works inside the home. There are several specific things the individual
homemaker can do to maximize her sense of independence and self-
worth.

One thing is simply to realize that all individuals should have the
rights and responsibilites of economic autonomy. A 1968 report to the
United Nations sums up this way of thinking:

> No decisive change in the distributions of function and status as
> between the sexes can be achieved if the duties of the male in society
> are assumed a priori to be unaltered. The goal for a long-range pro-
> gram of "women's rights" must be that every individual, regardless
> of sex, shall have the same practical opportunities not only for educa-
> tion and employment, but also fundamentally *the same responsibility
> for his or her own financial support as well as shared responsibility for
> child upbringing and housework.* [Italics added.][21]

Realizing this, the homemaker should also be aware of her worth in
dollars.

I have already noted that judging the value of work by the money it
earns is not the only possibility, and that indeed this may not be the
most desirable valuation. We can and should try to expand our ways of
thinking about the value of work. But such ideological change is likely
to be slow. Given that, at present, earning money is virtually the only
path to physical security, if not to status, realistically we must also work
within our present economic system.

For the homemaker today this means creating for herself a more direct
relation to the system. The homemaker needs to have money of her own
(if not in actual dollars, then in credits), earned for her own labor, with
which she can buy at least the basics of security and independence.
There are essentially two strategies that have been suggested for
bringing homemakers into the economic mainstream: giving homemakers credits for housework or paying them actual wages.

The idea of credits for housework is straightforward: for some legal
and social purposes, home work should be evaluated and a dollar value
should be assigned to it. Although the homemaker never directly receives any money for her work, she does get some credit for what she
has done. This idea is gradually being introduced into our legal system
(see chap. 10).

Giving the homemaker actual wages for her work is an interesting alternative to the credit system that would bring her into the mainstream of economic reality. The homemaker role would then fit conventional economic models of wage earners, and with both immediate security and a wage history to build upon, homemakers would be better able to defy inequities related to their work roles. Further, if homemakers received wages, their work could be relatively easily integrated into such evaluative strategies as the gross national product, and their contributions could easily be quantified for purposes of Social Security. Homemakers would immediately gain a greater sense of contribution to their society and more security for themselves.

According to one recent survey, one in four Americans believes that homemakers should be paid. Strong support for wages for housework is found among women eighteen to twenty-nine and among female college graduates. White-collar workers support the idea more strongly than do blue-collar workers. (Men thirty to thirty-four are among the groups most opposed.)[22]

However, wages for housework is an idea that may be very difficult to implement. It raises complicated value issues. Who will pay the homemaker? Should the husband pay her out of his salary, since he has the most direct benefit of her services? Should the government pay out of general funds, since homemakers are essential to the nation's economy and, indeed, as the mothers of its children, to the country's very survival? Further, who will qualify as a homemaker? Will any person who stays at home, out of the "regular" work force, qualify? And which of the homemaker's services will be paid? Presumably a new work ideology would value some of her services but not others; society might become willing to pay for her work in child care, but what about her services as a household decorator? The wages-for-housework issue is stirring some interesting debate in these areas but as yet has reached few resolutions on these difficult problems.

At this point the most likely strategy for increasing the homemaker's financial independence seems to be to combine credits for homemaking in such programs as Social Security, retirement, private pensions, and disability plans with individually established financial protection within the marriage contract. Marital agreements could be a reasonable alternative to government wages for homemakers; a legal contract between marital partners could provide for equitable distribution of income and property between wage earner and homemaker.

It is important, therefore, for the individual homemaker to know what she is worth, in financial terms, to her family system. The first thing she needs to do is to figure the cost of being out of the paid work market. For instance, suppose that to stay home full time she quits an outside job worth $10,000 a year in salary and benefits. A reasonable estimate of the cost to her of each successive year in the home would be that $10,000 plus a 5 to 15 percent yearly increase. Thus a homemaker who earned $10,000 in salary before quitting, estimating a 5 percent annual increase in pay, would be losing approximately $12,760 after five years in the home. A woman who had made $6,000 a year would be losing approximately $7,600, and one who had made $15,000 would be losing approximately $19,250.

These costs represent what her labor would have been worth had she stayed in the job market—but of course she did not. With each successive year out of paid work, she becomes less employable. Thus an added cost of being out of the paid work market is the cost of retraining, which may range anywhere from a few hundred dollars to the expense of a college degree.

The years of experience that were never gained would be difficult to measure in dollar terms. Perhaps the homemaker would have advanced rapidly, earning considerably higher raises than we have estimated here. Perhaps an employer who hires her after her absence from the waged labor force will consider her recent retraining an adequate substitute for her lack of experience; but perhaps not. Even though she may not be able to estimate their financial cost, the homemaker needs to remember these possibilities. Probably her lack of experience is costing her something.

Having figured the cost to her of staying home (and this can be analyzed in terms of part-time as well as full-time homemaking), the homemaker should calculate the dollar value of her household labor. One reasonable way to do this is, first, to figure out how many hours a week she spends in various tasks, second, to research the wages for these or similar jobs when done outside the home in her area of the country, and, third, to estimate her worth based on this replacement cost. The chart in table 5 from the New York State College of Human Ecology is based on such an analysis, though the figures for it were assembled in the region of Syracuse, New York, and would thus need to be adjusted for regional differences.

Knowing both the family value and the personal cost of staying at home will help a homemaker judge her job realistically. If she has been feeling relatively useless, seeing how much she is worth to the family may give her a new sense of self-esteem. However, if she is worth $15,000 in work outside the home and only $8,000 inside the home, the

TABLE 5. Average Annual Dollar Value of Time Contributed by Various Members in all Household Work (All Values Expressed to Nearest $100)

Number of Children	Age in Years	Employed-Wife Households			Nonemployed-Wife Households		
		Wife	Husband		Wife	Husband	
None	under 25	$ 4,700	$1,800		$ 7,000	$1,100	
	25–39	5,000	1,900		8,000	1,600	
	40–54	5,900	1,100		8,400	2,100	
	55 and over	6,000	1,500		7,400	2,700	
	Youngest Child	Wife	Husband	12–17-Year-Olds	Wife	Husband	12–17-Year-Olds
1	12–17	$ 6,700	$2,400	$1,400	$ 9,600	$2,700	$1,200
	6–11	8,000	1,500	—	9,400	2,000	—
	2–5	6,200	2,000	—	9,100	2,400	—
	1	8,300	600	—	9,900	2,300	—
	under 1	*	*	—	10,900	2,100	—
2	12–17	6,300	2,100	1,000	10,000	2,200	1,100
	6–11	7,200	2,000	1,100	9,900	2,100	1,100
	2–5	8,300	2,400	1,500	11,000	2,200	900
	1	8,400	5,000	*	11,700	2,200	*
	under 1	10,200	2,100	*	12,600	2,000	*
3	12–17	5,000	2,100	1,100	9,000	1,400	1,000
	6–11	8,600	2,000	1,700	9,900	2,200	1,600
	2–5	10,200	2,800	*	10,700	1,900	1,000
	1	11,500	3,200	*	11,600	2,200	1,400

	under 1	8,700	2,800	*	13,300	2,000	*
4	12–17	8,700	1,900	1,700	8,400	1,400	1,000
	6–11	7,200	1,400	1,100	10,700	1,900	1,100
	2–5	*	*	*	12,000	2,000	1,100
	1	*	*	*	11,800	2,600	800
	under 1	*	*	*	13,700	2,600	*
5–6	12–17	*	*	*	—	—	—
	6–11	*	*	*	11,500	2,800	1,700
	2–5	*	*	*	12,000	2,100	900
	1	*	*	*	9,900	700	*
	under 1	*	*	*	13,600	2,600	1,000
7–9	6–11	—	—	*	*	*	*
	2–5	*	*	—	11,900	2,900	1,400
	under 1	—	—	—	15,200	2,600	*

Source: Kathryn E. Walker and William H. Gauger, The Dollar Value of Household Work, Information Bulletin 60, Consumer Economics and Public Policy no. 5 (Ithaca: New York State College of Human Ecology, Cornell University, 1980).
*Averages not calculated because there were fewer than four cases.
—No cases.

same dollar comparison may encourage her to reappraise her situation. At the very least it will force her to confront the idea of using dollars to gauge the worth of her work; it may also prompt her to recognize that she is not living up to her salary potential.

Perhaps most important, the homemaker who knows her dollar value can begin to judge the personal costs to her of staying at home. She has lost a certain amount of money in salary and benefits. She has contributed a certain amount to the upkeep and well-being of her family. What has she gotten in return?

Usually, as I have noted, she has gotten nothing tangible. The homemaker who understands this, and who knows her personal value both inside and outside the home, is in the best position to ask for her fair share of the household's money and security.

Once we have established a system of credits and legal protections for the homemaker, she can have real security in her role. Her increased confidence and self-esteem are likely to improve the quality of life in the family. Because she is more satisfied with her work, less eager to take on an outside job, she will be less of a threat to workers already in conventional jobs. All women will thus be less exploitable.

Furthermore, once given a reasonable assessment of the economic value of her work, she can either accept her job as it is or seek to upgrade it based on a realistic assessment of its value. The new homemakers will be economically independent individuals who choose their work because it is reasonable and pleasant to do so, not because it is in their "nature" or is their duty or is their only economic alternative.

Attempts should be made to make all benefits to family members as equivalent as possible. If the family's outside worker has a pension, the homemaker should have a pension. If the waged worker has disability insurance, the homemaker should also have it. If the waged worker has a credit rating, so should the homemaker.

All these things are possible even though law or institutions today do not endorse them. Where a homemaker is not eligible for an Independent Retirement Account or cannot purchase disability insurance, she should have a personal savings account (or stocks or bonds) that would be reasonably equivalent. The account would obviously have to be large, as any account used for self-insurance must be.

Where she has no income for purposes of establishing a credit rating, she should try to get credit as a household manager, or contrive to get an income from her husband, to make regular deposits into her own account, and to pay bills in her own name.

Independence Insurance

Above all, she should have a nest egg—call it independence insurance—of her own. This should be a personal savings account equivalent to the current costs of supporting and retraining herself for as long as would be necessary to allow her to reenter her former career or its equivalent, taking into account that had she spent her home years in outside work, her employment position today would be better than the one she left years ago. Thus the woman who was formerly a secretary may deserve enough money to retrain herself to be a supervisor; the woman who was a teacher may deserve the opportunity to return to school for her Ph.D. in education; the woman who quit college to support her husband may deserve that college education plus additional training to compensate for lost experience.

To many families, independence insurance will seem expensive at first. Even $100 a month in such an account will amount to only $4,800 (not including interest) after four years, barely enough to accomplish the objectives of the insurance. It may seem like a great deal of money to save, especially if the saving is not for the whole family but for the sole use of one member.

But the cost of housework *is* large. It is expensive for women to work in the home. And to date the burden of that cost has fallen squarely on women alone. The women are the only ones who are left without pensions or disability insurance or credit or decent jobs. They are the ones who are supporting their families now by risking their personal security and health and happiness later.

In the age of affluence, the risk has become unbearable. We do not really need that color television, that expensive furniture, or that new car. What we do need is the conviction that homemakers deserve to share in the basic economic benefits available to all workers in our society, and we need the individual actions that support that conviction.

Psychology Looks at Homemaking

6

There is nothing so practical as a good theory.
                                        Kurt Lewin

In the spring of 1978 I attended the annual conference of the Association for Women in Psychology to give a paper entitled "Needed Research on a Neglected Worker: The Homemaker." Among four days of presentations, mine was the only paper that directly addressed the concerns of homemakers.

Because it did not readily fall into a category with other papers, the talk was scheduled as a separate conversation hour. About thirty-five persons crowded into a small room. The audience consisted of a few established psychologists, many graduate students in psychology, and others who were just generally interested. The group seemed slightly older than the overall conference crowd. My impression was that the women who attended were very interested in homemakers; in that short time we began a lively discussion. Naturally I hoped to spark enough interest so that in future years the amount of research on homemakers would grow.

As the session was breaking up, a small white-haired woman approached me and introduced herself. She was the mother of a young woman who is one of the country's most distinguished feminist psychologists. She said she had enjoyed my presentation and sympathized deeply; then she added, "You know, I've raised three fine daughters, all very successful, but where might they be today without the efforts of their homemaking mother?"

Where indeed? The question is of course unanswerable, but her sentiment was important. (I would guess that the older women in the group may have understood the strength of her feelings a bit better than did the younger ones.) And for me her personal affirmation of the perceived need for research on homemakers was the high point of the presentation.

The conference had many presentations on employed women—
fifteen to twenty, depending on one's criteria for selection. The ratio of
fifteen or twenty to one is obviously not a scientific estimate of psychologists' relative interest in paid work roles and in homemaking, but in
my experience it is not all that bad an estimate either. The point is that
to date psychologists' concern with homemakers has been slight.

I should note that the conference did have many presentations on
topics related to the homemaker role—topics like childbearing, divorce,
motherhood and mental depression, love and separation, power and
interpersonal relationships, battered women, and social and sexual adjustments in marriage. Given this scope of interests, one may well ask
what difference it makes for research and theory whether the homemaker herself is addressed directly.

The answer lies, I believe, in an examination of the current psychological theories that encompass the home and its inhabitants, because
the psychology that has studied homemaker-relevant issues has been
largely a psychology of interpersonal relationships rather than a
psychology of individuals. Thus, at the conference of the Association
for Women in Psychology, as elsewhere, we find research on homemakers (mothers) in relation to their children, and on homemakers
(wives) in relation to their husbands, but very little research on homemakers (people, workers) in relation simply to themselves. In the
psychology literature, the journal that probably publishes more housework articles than any other is the *Journal of Marriage and the Family,* a
title that suggests a theoretical emphasis on relationships—husband
and wife, parents and children—rather than on individuals.

By emphasizing the homemaker's relationships, psychologists have
neglected the individual homemaker and her or his life goals and satisfactions. One can easily make too much of this issue, but isn't it possible that psychologists, like many others in our culture, have put the
needs of children and husband before the needs of mothers and wives?
And isn't it time, then, to reaffirm the importance of the individual,
human needs of homemakers?

Some social scientists are trying to do just that. Those psychologists
and sociologists who have begun to do research in this area are akin to
those forward-looking economists who have pointed out the in-
adequacy of current economic measures for describing society's productive activity. They are telling us there is another way to study
society—that the psychological satisfactions of corporations and the
employed, or even of children and husbands, do not have to take pre-
cedence over the psychological satisfactions of people whose primary

role is homemaking. They are telling us this simply by using their own resources to do research with homemakers, some of which I am pleased to present in the following pages.

Of Homemakers and Happiness

Asking if homemakers are happy is rather like asking if office workers or high-school students or men over seventy are happy. The question is so general, and the individuals are so varied, that the answers are extremely difficult to interpret. Yet, while it is perhaps not the most useful approach to understanding homemakers, or other individuals for that matter, asking questions about general satisfaction has frequently been employed as a research technique, and it will probably be employed many times over in the future.[1]

Answers indicate that homemakers' reported satisfaction may be fairly high. One study was done by the University of Chicago in 1972 and 1973 with a sample of people representative of the total population of the United States. It found that 53 percent of white females whose full-time activity was keeping house reported being very satisfied with their work.[2] Another study, published in 1972, found that 71 percent of homemakers expressed high satisfaction with the job as a whole.[3]

Some researchers, though too few, have tried to discover which subgroups of homemakers show extreme satisfaction or dissatisfaction. For instance, Carol Tavris and Toby Epstein Jayaratne found in their survey of 75,000 *Redbook* readers that the happiest married women are those whose marriage includes egalitarian attitudes and behaviors: both spouses share in the housework and child care.[4] Elsewhere, evidence shows that mothers who hold contemporary views endorsing equality in the sharing of domestic, child-rearing, and financial responsibilities are more than twice as likely as more traditional thinkers to be satisfied with their homemaker role.[5]

If we take a problem-solving approach to these and other studies, we will also want to know as much as possible about which homemakers are dissatisfied. After all, the numbers are compelling: if even 10 percent of all homemakers are dissatisfied, this represents 3.5 million persons. Further, we will want to know more about how homemakers may have adjusted to their role. The psychological theory of cognitive dissonance would predict that dissatisfied but powerless homemakers may adjust to their role and even come to affirm it when asked, whether or not the role is, in some objective sense, good for them.

In other words, reports of high homemaker satisfaction should not lead the researcher—or the public—to complacency. There are good reasons to look into and beyond measures of overall satisfaction to ferret out homemakers' problems. Intuitively we suspect that such problems exist. We all know couples—maybe even several couples—who squabble over housework. We have all experienced or heard of the loneliness described so poignantly by humorist Erma Bombeck:

> No one talked about it a lot, but everyone knew what it was. It was the day you alphabetized your spices on the spice rack. Then you dressed all the naked dolls in the house and arranged them on the bed according to size. You talked to your plants and they fell asleep on you. It was a condition, and it came with the territory.[6]

Yet we must use our intuition with caution. Many of our intuitive notions about the pitfalls of homemaking have been labeled homemaker "syndromes" and, after investigation, have become part of the psychology literature. Among these are the "empty nest syndrome," the "trapped housewife syndrome," and the idea of an inclusive "housewife syndrome."

Just how serious are these and other homemaker problems? The terms used for them tend to be rather too cute, a fact that is in all likelihood related to our culture's general lack of seriousness about homemakers. The problems themselves may nevertheless be significant. On the other hand, new evidence indicates that the syndromes may not really exist at all: another tendency of our culture is to stereotype homemakers as weak individuals particularly prone to "syndromes."

For instance, a very popular concept in homemaker-related research has been the "empty nest syndrome," a term indicating the series of problems faced by homemakers whose children leave home. Sociologist Lillian Rubin believes that this "package of depressive pathology" is a myth perpetuated by clinicians until recently, and she credits reevaluation of the myth to women's new self-awareness about life problems and to the fact that more women researchers are moving into the social sciences.

Of 160 middle-aged employed and homemaking women in her study, only one exhibited classical symptoms of the empty nest syndrome. "Almost all, even those most committed to the traditional homemaker role, responded to the departure of their children—whether actual or impending—with a decided sense of relief. . . . They cope quite well with whatever feeling they're experiencing—fright, sadness, whatever—for alongside those exists another, at least equally powerful hunger to turn attention to their own lives—and the relief that, finally, this may be possible."[7] Rubin's findings are supported by Elizabeth

Bates Harkins of the Battelle Human Affairs Research Centers, who concludes that empty nest effects on well-being are small and have largely disappeared two years after the event. Further, the transition has no effect on physicial well-being, and there is a positive effect on psychological satisfaction.[8]

So things may not be what they seem. Understanding homemakers' areas of dissatisfaction, as well as satisfaction, will not simply be a matter of doing more studies in established directions, but will require reevaluation of current terminology and practice. It will involve rejection of some of the simplistic and normative theories that have developed out of our intuitions (or our prejudices) and commitment to helping homemakers express their own values and their own issues.

Relationships

Because of the nature of the existing research, much that we know about homemakers' satisfaction concerns their satisfaction within various relationships, particularly marriage. Other primary relationships that homemakers frequently experience are the parent-child relationship, which has also been frequently studied, and the relationship to other homemakers, which has received much less attention. This by no means exhausts the possibilities, of course—homemakers also interact with their relatives and their in-laws, with friends, and with tradespeople of all kinds both within and outside the home. For those homemakers who are also part-time workers or part-time students, the list of relationships becomes even more complex.

Obviously, if we are to fully understand homemakers, we need to understand their various relationships—their "support networks." Indeed, I believe we need to better understand the support networks of all people. It has been demonstrated that the quality and structure of these networks is associated with mental health, and that the effect of stress upon a person's mental health is moderated by the quality and structure of the social support he or she receives.[9] And it may well be that at this point the most fruitful research on homemakers will attempt to encompass the effects of all of an individual's relationships rather than to concentrate on one or two of them. To choose to study the marital or parental relationship assumes the importance of that relationship; a more objective approach would derive the relative importance of various relationships from what homemakers themselves tell us.

Unfortunately, much of this kind of research falls into the category of "needed research" rather than actual research. Here we will have to

limit ourselves to information gained in studies of particular relationships.

Women's satisfaction in marriage has been studied frequently, if not
adequately.[10] More recently, researchers have paid particular attention
to the marital satisfaction of homemakers.

The older view of homemakers' marital satisfaction is represented by
a 1963 study indicating that marital satisfaction is lowest when a wife
works full time and highest when she works part-time. Families in
which the wife is a full-time homemaker fall in between.[11] This information may well have been accurate in the era when it was
gathered—before Friedan, before the women's movement, and before
women's increased participation in full-time employment.

More recent studies show a different picture. Lenore Radloff's
1971–73 study confirmed previous findings that marriage is more satisfying for men than for women.[12] In her sample, groups of homemakers
and employed wives both showed more depression than did groups of
employed husbands. (The study, which involved 2,829 households,
found no homemaking husbands.) Although she explored several factors that might explain the difference between husbands and wives—
factors such as age, education, income, happiness with job and marriage, reported amount of housework, and status of parents—Radloff
found none that accounted for the men's advantage. She concluded that
it may be women's socialization, especially their lack of experience in
being assertive, in being "actively in control of their lives," that handicaps them in dealing with life problems. Basically, too, Radloff found
that homemakers are not more depressed than employed wives, and
that the relationship between satisfaction in marriage and work is much
the same for both homemakers and employed women.

Determining which homemakers are happy with their marriages, and
why, has not been an easy task. Many things are said to account for a
homemaker's satisfaction in marriage, among them her own satisfaction with her role, the amount of housework help she gets from her
husband, and the husband's attitude toward women in general.

One study that has examined these variables found that homemakers
who were relatively satisfied or dissatisfied with their job did not differ
much in marital satisfaction.[13] The finding was similar for employed
women. Marital satisfaction for homemakers was not affected by the
degree of husband's participation in homemaking tasks either, though
this finding was questioned because the study showed that husband
and wife often disagree about how much the husband does and the
researchers had simply taken people's word about the work they did.

Wives of husbands with liberal attitudes toward women were in general less satisfied with the homemaker job than wives of more conservative husbands. The authors surmise that this may reflect the more liberal husbands' expectations that their wives will work outside the home as well as inside, or that it may reflect a disparity between the amount of housework support homemakers expect from such husbands and the amount they actually get.

As this study shows—and I have reported only a small part of it—the relationships are far from simple. Either our attempts to understand the marital relationship and its effect on homemakers are becoming more sophisticated or the social situation itself is becoming more complicated—or, probably, both.

Homemakers and Employed Women: Is One Group More Satisfied?

One of the developing areas of research into homemaker satisfaction compares the satisfaction of homemakers and employed women. With the entry of large numbers of women into paid employment, this comparison has been made ever more frequently, but the question is not really new. In 1958 researchers reported that most employed women cited their jobs rather than home or family as the chief source of their feelings of usefulness and importance.[14] However, in their classic 1960 study Blood and Wolfe compared the marital satisfaction of "working" and "nonworking" wives and found no significant differences.[15] This confirmed a 1958–59 report by Nye,[16] but another study by Nye (1963) determined that, while homemakers' marriages were "better adjusted" than those of employed women, women employed full time were more satisfied with their work than were full-time homemakers.[17]

The national opinion survey taken by the University of Chicago National Opinion Research Center in 1972 and 1973 examined twenty-two demographic and attitudinal variables, looking for differences between employed women and homemaker women and tapping such characteristics as age, marital status, satisfaction with present financial situation, education, social class, and number of children. The survey found that among white women who believed their income of $6,000 was below the income level of the average American family, homemakers were more likely to be satisfied with their work than women who had full-time jobs. However, this distinction borders on the esoteric, and otherwise the study found no differences in work satisfaction between homemakers and employed women.[18]

The alert reader will note that the issues on which these comparisons have been made have not always been consistent: they have included marital satisfaction and adjustment, in which homemakers seem to have a slight edge, and work satisfaction, in which employed women seem to have an edge. Furthermore, feelings about work have been conceptualized not only in terms of "satisfaction" with work but also in terms of the "usefulness and importance" of the work.

Enter onto this confused scene Myra Marx Ferree, who studied women's attitudes and employment experiences for her Harvard doctoral dissertation. Ferree collected her data in late 1974 in a predominantly working-class community and concluded that full-time housewives are definitely more dissatisfied and feel themselves to be worse off than women with jobs. Full-time housewives were more likely to be dissatisfied with the way they are spending their lives (26 percent versus 14 percent of the employed women), to feel that they have not had a fair opportunity in life (47 percent versus 38 percent), and to want their daughters to be "mostly different" from themselves (35 percent to 22 percent). Ferree also asked the two groups of women to compare themselves in terms of who they thought was "better off," and employed women came out ahead both from their own viewpoint and from the homemakers'. Ferree did not find any difference between the groups in terms of marital satisfaction, however.[19]

Ferree's work, interesting in itself, becomes especially important because she is taken rather severely to task by James D. Wright of the University of Massachusetts, who concludes, "National survey data for the period 1971 to 1976 do not reveal significant differences between working women and housewives in regard to life in general or to the measurable components thereof: work, marriage, family and so on . . . there is no substantial basis for concluding . . . that 'housewives appear to be comparatively dissatisfied with their lives.'" Wright's opinion is based on data taken from six national surveys: the Quality of American life survey conducted at the University of Michigan in 1971 and the five General Social Surveys conducted by the National Opinion Research Center between 1972 and 1976.[20]

The reader may wish to consult Wright's reports and others' before making up her or his own mind. But at least two points should be mentioned here. First of all, Wright's data, like Ferree's, add to the long list of separate and not quite comparable questions that are being used to describe satisfaction. The 1971 Quality of Life survey asks, "How happy are you these days?" with seven possible responses ranging from "completely satisfied" to "completely dissatisfied." The General Social Surveys ask, "Taken all together, how would you say things are these days—would you say you are very happy, pretty happy, or not too happy?" Social scientists in general need to ask more similar questions if we are to make good comparisons.

Second, the data Wright presents from the General Social Surveys show a trend over the years that he does not mention. Among working-class women who said they were generally "very happy" in 1972 and 1973, there are more homemakers than employed women. In 1974, the same year Ferree's data were collected, a shift occurs: now there is a higher percentage of employed women in the category. In 1974 the difference in percentage of housewives and employed women who are "very happy" is 4.6 points; in 1975 it is 5.8 points; in 1976 it is 12.8 points (34.8 for housewives, 47.6 for women in the labor force). It may be that Ferree's data tapped the beginning of this trend, and that, though the difference between husbands and employed women in 1976 is not statistically significant, if this trend continues the difference will reach significant levels.

Who is right? The argument is unsettled. There is no conclusive evidence in either direction—and there may never be.

Then who cares? I'm not so sure. The researchers involved undoubtedly care, probably enough so that soon people will attempt accurate replications of former studies, using identical questions and matching methods of survey administration. But what effect does this kind of comparative research have upon theories of the psychology of homemakers, and what relevance does it have for individuals? If we decide that as a group homemakers do not differ from employed women in overall satisfaction, does it mean that we should therefore abandon our efforts to understand that subgroup of homemakers who are dissatisfied? Certainly not. If homemakers are more dissatisfied, does it mean they deserve more of our attention? Not necessarily. Does knowing that one group is more or less satisfied than the other help individual people to make decisions about their lives? Perhaps. It may be that our attempts to compare homemakers and employed women derive primarily from the current cultural self-consciousness of these two roles rather than from any theoretical and practical need. A resolution of the issue is beyond me here, but it is something psychologists should think more about.

Changing Values

The keynote in the psychology of homemaking is change. Women are changing, psychology is changing, and psychologists' ideas about homemakers are changing. Basic to all of this are changing values.

The impact of feminist values cannot be underestimated. As psychologist Helen Weinreich has stated:

> The women's movement is probably the social movement with the most extensive implications for social change of the present time. It has highlighted in political debate some criticisms that were, in fact, extant in the scientific literature a decade or more earlier . . . and generated through this debate new scientific, as well as social, issues . . . . As in the issue of race, this is an area in which there is a conjunction and interaction of political and scientific argument, and where neither aspect can ignore the other; both have contributed to a prevailing examination of interpretation, methodology, and the nature of evidence.[21]

According to Weinreich, personal changes attributed to the movement have come about largely as a result of consciousness-raising—the process of self-examination and self-redefinition, of value change, that has characterized the movement since its inception.

Researchers' values have also changed. Psychologist Judith Long Laws points out:

> When a feminist approaches the research literature on marriage and the family, she comes prepared. Her primary interest is in women, in their potentialities, their experiences, and the institutions that shape these. She has no vested interest in marriage as such: indeed she brings with her a feminist critique of that institution.[22]

The feminist view has been partly responsible for encouraging a return to the study of the individual, to the study of homemakers as persons in contrast to the study of the homemaker role.

One does not need a social scientist to inform one that women's values have changed, but it is interesting to find our intuitions confirmed and elaborated in the research. Furthermore, in research by sociologist Ann P. Parelius, it is fascinating to see how quickly and definitively values have altered.[23] Parelius studied the attitudes of female college students in 1969 and 1973. In 1973, 83 percent of the women expected that they would not do all the household tasks themselves, compared with 56 percent in 1969. In 1973, 77 percent expected their future husbands to help with housework, compared with only 47 percent in 1969. The percentages of women expecting their husbands to do 50 percent of all household and child-rearing tasks, however, dropped from 17 percent in 1969 to 13 percent in 1973. So, although these women's values did not switch fully to expectations of egalitarianism, many did move away from a traditional sex-role orientation.

At the same time, a few major changes occurred in the women's perceptions of men's attitudes: women in both 1969 and 1973 tended to view men as basically traditional in their sex-role orientations.

Of course feminism is not the only recent movement that could reasonably have been expected to affect values relating to the household. Whereas feminism may have most strongly influenced values about the conduct of homemakers' personal interactions, the ecology and anti-consumerism movements have undoubtedly shaped values about the household as a physical environment. Thus more people are reported to be choosing simpler lives; standards for household elaborateness, neatness, and even cleanliness have relaxed. At the same time, an increased consciousness about foods has affected some people's habits of meal preparation. Naturally psychologists tend to emphasize changes in interpersonal interactions—to the neglect, so far, of people's values about their physical environment. I suspect that as we delve further into the interpersonal dynamics of the household we will find that the changes in standards for the household as a physical environment will be seen as increasingly relevant to interpersonal relations. The argument that women care more about having a pleasant environment (and that therefore they should do more housework) has been mentioned elsewhere in this book. It is an issue that may be worth investigating further, both in terms of sex differences and in terms of changing cultural values.

But let us return to what psychologists have studied—to what they can tell us about the values homemakers and other relevant persons hold about the social interactions in the home.

Jean Lipman-Blumen's 1972 *Scientific American* article summarizes women's attitudes toward homemaking and presents evidence to support the hypothesis that sex-role ideology—a person's concept of what kinds of behavior are appropriate to her or his sex—shapes women's lives.[24] (Of course sex-role ideology also shapes men's lives, but this was not the author's focus.)

Lipman-Blumen's data were collected in 1968 among the college-educated wives of 1,012 graduate students in the Boston area. The women were grouped into two categories. Those who espoused "traditional" values believed that under ordinary conditions women belong in the home, caring for children and doing the housework, whereas men are responsible for the financial support of the family. Women who espoused a "contemporary" ideology felt that the relationships between men and women are, ideally, egalitarian and that husbands and wives may share domestic, child-rearing, and financial responsibilities.

Twenty-seven percent of the women studied held the traditional view, whereas 73 percent held the contemporary view.

Lipman-Blumen did not ask whether these differing ideologies had had a direct effect on the actual housekeeping behaviors of husbands and wives. She did explore the origins and some ramifications of the two different views, however. For instance, she noted that a mother's attitude toward homemaking influences her daughter's attitude: mothers who were dissatisfied with homemaking had a greater tendency to raise daughters with the contemporary view. Also, women with the contemporary ideology tended to have challenged their family values more strongly in adolescence than did women with the traditional ideology; the former tended to achieve a certain psychological distance from their families—to evolve a sense of separateness as individuals. The author suggests that, while the traditional viewpoint may ensure continuity and security, it may also result in less ability to cope with life problems that require individual flexibility. On the other hand, the data showed that women of both ideologies were equally happy in their current lives.

In 1973 a study by Betty Yorburg and Ibtihaj Arafat comparing women's and men's values found that the responses of women were "consistently and significantly" less traditional than those of the male respondents.[25] Although the study was done with 1,048 men and women residing in New York City and therefore is not representative of the total population of the United States, the authors anticipated that discrepancies in belief and expectation of the men and women in their sample would spread to other segments of the population. Women were more likely than men to believe in most of the goals of the women's movement (24.6 percent compared with 14.4 percent of the men). When asked whether household chores should be shared equally, approximately two-thirds of the men and four-fifths of the women agreed. There were also significant differences between the sexes on the questions "Do you think total equality should exist in our society?" and "Do you think total equality will exist someday?" The authors found that 47.3 percent of the men and 52.5 percent of the women believed in total equality; 23.1 percent of the men and 30.6 percent of the women believed total equality could be achieved.

However, in a research project done the same year in the Seattle area, sociologist Sharon K. Araji of Washington State University found that both sexes tend to express egalitarian or role-sharing attitudes toward family roles in general.[26] Other researchers have found that the percentage of both males and females who believe both husband and wife

should do the same amount of housekeeping is less than 4 percent.[27]
Clearly there is more than one side to this issue.

Women do seem well aware that, though they may espouse equality,
their values may not be shared by men. In the Parelius study mentioned
above, a minority of women believed that men would want to marry a
feminist. In 1973, for example, 77 percent expected husbands to help
with the housework, but only 28 percent believed men would want to
marry a feminist (who, presumably, would want help with the housework).

The crucial question, of course, is whether men's and women's
changing values—aside from the fact that they may not be changing at
similar rates—will change their behaviors. Is equality in housework an
unlikely dream or a potential reality?

Generally, people expect that a change in attitude will precede and, at
least partly cause, a change in behavior. However, psychology has
shown that the relationship between changes in attitude and changes in
behavior is a great deal more complicated than our intuitions might
predict. Some theorists believe that, to avoid inconsistency, which is
perceived as an aversive cognitive state, individuals will try to match
their values with their behaviors. Other research indicates that situational influences such as group pressure may affect behavior much
more strongly than attitudes (values) do. It is very difficult, in any case,
to predict whether behavior change will follow attitude change, and in
some cases behavior must change before attitudes change.

Araji's data indicate a clear discrepancy between values and behavior
in her sample. Of those few husbands who said housekeeping should
be shared equally, only 2 percent actually performed most of the tasks.
Among the women who said that housekeeping should be shared
equally, 36.6 percent said they actually performed most of the tasks.
About as many men as women reported these discrepancies in their
households.

What is going to happen to individuals and to marriages in which
such discrepancies exist? One can anticipate a certain amount of conflict. The obvious conflict will be between husbands and wives (or other
partners) with differing values. Through discussion these differences of
opinion are at least likely to become overt, and then people can begin to
make choices about how to deal with them.

But there will also be another kind of conflict—the conflict for those
who come to realize the discrepancies between their own values and
behaviors. As Carol Tavris predicted in 1972, "The strongest barriers to
women's liberation will come not so much from the stereotyped male

chauvinist, but from the well-intentioned fellow who supports women's liberation—as long as it stays outside the home. These men support equality in housekeeping and childrearing—but only 15 percent of those who are married actually share these responsibilities . . . they are overwhelmingly content with the traditional division of labor."[28]

The women's movement continues to raise the consciousness of such men, and also of many women. Employed women trying to juggle paid work and the housework and child care as well are realizing more and more that they are not superwomen and that this is not equality. And now we may hope that homemakers, realizing some of the disadvantages of their job but some of its benefits as well, will begin standing up for their beliefs and demanding that behaviors follow—whether they are demanding equal time for their own education, or decent benefits, or an equitable sharing of the housework. The process of realizing and changing the discrepancies between what we believe and what we do is seldom easy, but it is always growth.

Power

Before we can fully evaluate possibilities for change, we need to understand how power works within the family. Many studies have attempted to describe power relationships, particularly the power relationship between husband and wife. The portrait they paint is not particularly rosy, nor is it particularly uncharacteristic of human beings in general.

In their 1970 paper "The Myth of the Egalitarian Family: Familial Roles and the Professionally Employed Wife," Margaret M. Poloma and T. Neal Garland assert, "The existence of the egalitarian family in American society has been assumed by family researchers and writers—an assumption that remains to be verified and may well be an erroneous one . . . . While we are indeed approaching the day when the average married woman has some kind of a job, we are *not* witnessing any dramatic increase in the prestige of the feminine role nor any reversal of male-female roles in the family."[29] In their study of what they called neotraditional couples, couples in which the husband and wife have equal or close to equal professional status, these researchers found a clear lack of a sense of sharing. They concluded that wives are constrained by their own idea of ideal feminine roles and that they are concerned about infringing on their husbands' provider role.

There is evidence, however, that earlier in a marriage the relationship between husband and wife is more egalitarian.[30] This is especially true before children enter the scene (and therefore before the woman becomes a full-time homemaker). Particularly when the wife is working, a couple shares household tasks and decision-making more equally, though of course the pattern of putting the husband's career before the wife's is well known. Such evidence points to the idea that employed women have more power than homemakers do. The notion that the power relationship changes over time also points to the idea that equality in the family is a result of power—that it is a result of the particular characteristics of the situation rather than of some innate and immutable characteristics of males and females. When it comes to inequality, human culture, not human nature, is the culprit.

Almost invariably, the husband emerges as the more powerful partner. One researcher even suggests that marital success is based not on any interaction between the personalities of husband and wife but, rather, on the stability of the male identity alone: the higher the husband's income and education the happier the marriage; the more stable and nonneurotic the husband is, the happier the marriage; the higher the wife rates him on emotional maturity and on fulfilling his role according to cultural expectations, the happier the marriage. And, *the more closely the wife comes to resemble her husband in attitude and personality inventories over time, the happier the marriage.*[31]

Data gathered from 1972 through 1974 indicate that, the more important a decision is considered to be, the more likely it is that the husband makes it.[32] Husbands and wives were asked who made the following decisions and how important each decision was: (1) who pays the bills; (2) how their home is decorated; (3) whether they will have (or do have) children; (4) how much money is spent on food; (5) how much money is spent on clothes; (6) whether the wife works; (7) what job the husband takes; (8) whom they invite to their home; (9) what they do with extra money (after essentials are taken care of); and (10) where they live. Husbands more often make decisions dealing with events outside the home: work (for both spouses), money, friends, and where the couple lives. Husbands also tended to exercise control over more decisions. Spouses generally indicated that they were jointly involved in all decisions, but not equally.

A homemaker's very status is dependent on her husband's occupation.[33] If the husband is in a high-status job, the homemaker's status also is seen by others as high—though not as high as his. A homemaker married to a physician is rated similarly to a woman who is an artist or a registered nurse, while a homemaker married to a civil engineer is rated slightly higher than a woman in a clerical job.

Why do husbands have this kind of power—the power to determine the happiness of a marriage, to make the most important decisions, and even to determine another person's status?

The idea that men should rule in the home is related to the more general notion that men should dominate women, a notion only recently—historically speaking—being questioned. A strong cultural factor strengthening the power of patriarchy is of course the Judeo-Christian concept of the superiority of the husband. But we will not assume here that anatomy is destiny—or that historical trends need determine what happens between husbands and wives today. What other clues do we have to what determines the balance of power in the household?

We have already mentioned that couples tend to be more egalitarian early in marriage, particularly when the wife is employed, and before children come onto the scene. A number of factors, most unexplored by psychologists, may account for the success and also for the termination of this early egalitarianism.

For one thing, both spouses may have recently been living with other persons, probably roommates of the same sex, and may therefore be in the habit of sharing housework equally (or at least of attempting equality). One might hypothesize that these habits and ideology would transfer to a marital relationship. Certainly the transition from living with roommates to living with a spouse would be interesting to study.

The psychology of the male's transition is particularly interesting. One can perhaps understand why a person would work hard to please someone she or he is so newly in love with, and that this labor of love would include various homemaking duties. This expression of love is, however, more strongly the female's. It is less clear why an individual would choose to withhold this expression of love—the choice made by many men. It is not clear why men would move from an egalitarian housework situation with roommates, in which equality of housework is a symbol of respect for those one is living with—to a nonegalitarian situation with a woman they "love."

But, to return to our exploration of those couples that do have an egalitarian relationship, a primary factor in the termination of this relationship is parenthood. The interaction of parenthood with other factors in the spouses' lives is complex. Strong and largely unchallenged cultural sanctions about the importance of mothering come into play. Psychological support for fathering, especially full-time fathering, is growing, but it hardly competes with the injunction to motherhood. Generally the woman of the household is significantly better educated in how to maintain a nurturing home, and a couple tends to set a high priority on giving the best possible care to their children.

Probably the single most important factor in the balance of power is the spouses' present and potential ability to earn money. We have seen that early in marriage equality is especially likely when both spouses are employed. When children arrive, the likelihood of employment, especially for the wife, goes down drastically. This situation is often said to happen by choice, though it would perhaps be enlightening to see what would happen if more part-time jobs were available for both women and men.

It makes sense, however, that the ability to earn money would be important to the balance of power at any point in a relationship. Money is a basis for power in many realms—in business, in politics, in government. More money means increased control of resources, and more ability to reward other people for behavior one finds appropriate or useful. In these contexts these things appear self-evident. It seems foolhardy, then, to underestimate the importance of money in balancing power in a marriage—which is what most women have been trained to do. Whereas money is esteemed as an important contribution to any group, including the family, women have been taught to give love. Whereas money is essential to individual independence, and therefore the ability to defend one's rights in *any* relationship, women have been taught to value love—and dependency.

One would predict that homemakers who have money, or the skills with which to earn money, may have more egalitarian relationships than homemakers who are currently and potentially financially dependent. Certainly employed wives are demonstrating a new sense of independence. Those whose earnings are about the same as their husbands' are more likely than others to leave a marriage.[34] Employed wives are also substantially more likely than homemakers to express the wish that they had married someone else and to report having considered divorce.[35] These latter findings are not explained by role overload (having the double job of employee and homemaker) or by the wives' or their husbands' belief that "a woman's place is in the home."

Of course we are dealing here with a chicken-or-egg problem: Have these women sought employment because they are dissatisfied, or does the independence gained through employment give them the courage to challenge a mediocre marriage? Only studies done over time can tell us. But the independence these women are demonstrating lets us reasonably hypothesize that income, or perhaps some combination of income and specialized contact with the world outside the home, may increase the power of homemakers within a marital relationship. Even potential income—the possession of a marketable skill—may be a factor.

Transitional Processes

For convenience, I have been talking about the balance of power and about the egalitarian marriage as though they were easily recognized. Not so, unfortunately. It is one thing to assert that housework should be equally shared and quite another to decide what an equal division of the labor would look like. It is one thing to say that decision-making should be equally shared and quite another to determine it: Should each decision be made by voting, thus creating equality for couples but also leading to the need for tie-breaker votes? Should individuals make decisions about the spheres with which they are most familiar, thus perpetuating the sexism that has raised women to be better home-makers and men to be better providers? One might assert that it is not egalitarian relationships we are after but rather happy relationships, but then we have to deal with the argument that compares homemakers to slaves who are content with their lot because they know of nothing better and cannot change their lives in any case. The direction of change and the exact characterization of the resulting relationship are best left to individuals, though of course I would not have written this book if I did not think change should increase homemakers' personal options, dignity, and satisfaction. Let us turn now briefly to the transitional process itself—to the psychology of changing relationships.

Volumes have been written on human change in every sphere from the marital dyad, to organizations, to societies. Since I cannot possibly cover this literature here, let me set two modest goals: first, to detail some of the issues that need to be raised about change processes affecting homemakers and, second, to describe one type of change process that seems particularly promising.

I have already mentioned that establishing the end product of a change project is not a simple matter. Goal-setting will involve an attempt to match values and behaviors, and when two or more persons are involved this process may be complex and time-consuming. Add to this the fact that cultural values about the home are in constant flux, and the project becomes even more complicated. Yet goal-setting is basic to any change effort.

Another important concern is the volatility of the process. Employed women, having gained some power, sometimes use that power to break up their relationships. While such changes sometimes are positive, perhaps we need to reconsider the technology of change in order to develop processes that can equalize power without destroying the relationship. In this respect relationships between individuals are quite unlike relationships between large organizations such as nations: in

many cases nations are forced to maintain a relationship and are therefore motivated to improve it, whereas, in our society at least, individuals can almost always leave one relationship and establish another.

A third issue is the question of personal change because of a discrepancy in values versus personal change because of environmental rewards and sanctions. Change via values comes about when an individual realizes a discrepancy between his or her own values and behaviors:
the realization alone can be enough to encourage a behavior change.
Change via rewards and sanctions emphasizes the role of others in the
change process: an individual's behavior is rewarded or punished by
others in the environment, therefore tending to increase or decrease the
behavior.

Of course there are psychological interactions between the two systems. But I think a case could be made that the commonly held romantic
view of love emphasizes the first process largely to the exclusion of the
second. How often one hears, "If you really loved your husband . . . you
wouldn't refuse to do anything for him" (not even something like sex
and certainly not a little thing like his laundry). The result of the
romantic view is that homemakers' power to effect change is depleted.
Homemakers should take a long, hard look at their cultural assumptions
about what are reasonable and effective processes toward their goals.

A type of change project that seems particularly promising in its
ability to mitigate marital discord, and to advance theory as well, is the
behavioral approach described by University of Iowa researcher Neil
Jacobson.[36] Jacobson points out that, while the behavioral approach is
not the definitive approach to marital therapy, a number of findings
warrant optimism about its usefulness. Particularly promising change
techniques are training in communication and problem-solving skills,
along with contracting between partners for specific behaviors and rewards.

Jacobson set up an experimental treatment program to determine
which kinds of couple contracts are most useful. He compared two
contracting programs. In the "quid pro quo" type of contracting program, each partner agrees to make a change that the other wants. The
fact that the pair has a deal—"if you do it I'll do it"—is hypothesized to
be sufficient reward for changing their behavior. In "good faith" contracting programs each spouse agrees to make a change desired by the
partner, but the reward is not the behavior of the other spouse. Instead,
things outside the problem area—like a night at the movies or new
clothing—are used as rewards. Jacobson had used the good faith contracts in previous research and noted that they have the disadvantage of
being cumbersome to implement. On the other hand, he pointed out

that quid pro quo contracting creates a "who goes first" problem, and that if one spouse fails to hold up her or his part of the bargain, the other is likely to retaliate by stopping the new behavior too.

The behavioral counseling also included teaching problem-solving and communication through modeling and role-playing. Couples had homework assignments consisting of problem-solving practice sessions at home between therapy sessions, and they kept notebooks on their progress.

To summarize this research: Jacobson studied groups using the different types of contracting as well as other groups used as scientific controls. The groups using the behavioral methods improved significantly more than did the control groups: their negative behaviors toward each other went down and their positive behaviors went up.

However, there was very little difference in effectiveness between the two types of contracting. Jacobson makes the important point that, nevertheless, the good faith contracts may be preferable for severely distressed couples, given the deep lack of trust and the resulting likelihood that a quid pro quo contract will break down.

It would be interesting to conceptualize severe distress in terms of power to see if an imbalance of power will also indicate the need for good faith contracts. It may be, of course, that an imbalance may exclude contracts altogether: an extremely powerful person may not be willing to give up any power whatever, in which case change, even though engineered by a skilled therapist, will be impossible.

Jacobson's behavioral approach is promising. Not only does it give us measureable ways of improving relationships, it also provides additional information about contracting, which is an important method of conflict resolution. On the road to achieving equality of housework, and egalitarian home relationships in general, it is a reasonable direction to take.

Trends in the Psychology of Homemaking

The work of sociologists Berk and Berheide warns us that much of the homemaker research done to date must be taken with a grain of salt. Much of this research is based on data gathered by questionnaires and thus is limited (as all such research is) by such facts as people's tendency to color and filter their perceptions and by the way questions are inflexibly grounded in the researchers' theories.

Even beyond such common problems, however, are others specifically related to homemaking. Berk and Berheide write:

Our earliest finding was the great extent of pluralistic ignorance

surrounding household work; people were not only unclear about
what the term meant, but also ignorant about "normative" standards
and the actual content of household work done by their friends and
neighbors. Possibly the most cogent illustration of these confusions
comes from our survey data where some respondents were unable to
clearly specify how many hours a day they did household work, and
were almost incapable of separating hours of household work from
child care.[37]

While the authors have here overlooked the quite reasonable problems
inherent in separating housework from child care conceptually, the result is the same whatever the reason: questionnaire data are suspect
partly because such answers tend to gloss over real-life complexities,
especially with forced-choice (multiple-choice) questions. When a
homemaker is asked how satisfied she is with her housework role, for
example, and is given the alternatives "very satisfied," "somewhat
satisfied," "somewhat dissatisfied," and "very dissatisfied," she is
likely to pick some answer even though her idea of what housework is
may be vague. Berk and Berheide go on to explore the possibilities for
doing on-site, observational research in the home—a much needed
method, and, I hope, the beginning of a trend in the psychology of
homemaking.

Action research in which the goals of data collection and the advancement of theory are combined with the goals of immediate or
long-term individual or social change is also a technique that may be
increasingly employed in the psychology of homemaking. Weinreich
notes that recently there has been an emphasis on determining how
employed women actually cope with "role conflicts" rather than merely
on identifying the conflicts.[38] We may anticipate a similar pattern in the
study of homemakers, and, in addition to the usual problems in action
research design (most often problems about mixing objective science
with subjective values), the research that is generated will pose special
ideological challenges. For instance, in attempting to improve homemakers' job satisfaction, researchers need to be wary of the seemingly
simple solution of merely socializing people to the job as it currently
exists—and thus perpetuating a larger system based on a sexist division
of labor and on dependency relationships. To state this more theoretically, researchers will need to encompass both the short-term and the
long-term reinforcements, both the immediate and the wide consequences associated with change.

Let me suggest just a few areas in which action research may be
appropriate. Researchers might want to consider the psychological implications of financial dependency, or the psychological effect of various plans to improve homemakers' economic status. They may want to

pay more attention to influencing the process of becoming a home-maker, emphasizing childhood socialization and career counseling for both boys and girls in the high-school years.

One especially favorable trend in the homemaking research is the expansion of theory beyond narrow concepts like "family" and "role" and even "homemaker." An example of this is work by Joseph Pleck analyzing male and female work and family roles.[39] Pleck's "work-family role system" involves specifying how various roles interact and how variations within a role tend to affect the system as a whole. The attempt to integrate family and other environments is notable.

The more general model, toward which Pleck and others seem to be moving, is open-systems theory. This theory conceptualizes a family group as an open system—a group that has a certain unity and cohesion but that is also open to input from the environment. It considers that family members may belong to more than one system at a time. (Probably the most influential second system in most families is the organizations in which people are employed; individuals' conflicting allegiances to the two systems are a topic of concern.) The notion of boundaries is also important in open-systems theory: Pleck, for example, discusses the differences for the sexes between boundaries of work roles and family roles. To my knowledge, the definitive article reconceptualizing the family in terms of open-systems theory has yet to be written. I look forward to reading it when it is.

Psychologists' relative neglect of homemakers as individuals has left us in the unfortunate position of having seen the forest but not the trees. Continued research on homemakers' relationships is warranted, but the pressing need now is to pay more attention to homemakers themselves. We need a deeper understanding of who the homemaker is, of what she does every day and how she feels about it and about herself, in order to help homemakers deal with their demonstrated personal problems and as a prerequisite to understanding homemakers' relationships with others.

A corollary of the need to emphasize individuals is the need to conceptualize homemaking more as an occupation held by real, complex people and less as a role relationship. The fullest possible understanding of homemakers will include an understanding of the dynamics of their relationships with others, and these relationships may best be defined in terms of individual motivations rather than of roles. When theory deals adequately with the circumstance that baking a cake, for example, may involve both housework and child care, that it may involve at least two constellations of motives for a single individual, then we will have forged a useful merger of the now mostly separated ideas of housework roles and child-care roles. The point is that the scientific study of the psychology of homemaking will best be advanced by understanding individual homemakers and their motivations and actions. Pursuit of concepts like the "housework role" and the "child-care role" will be useful only after theorists deal adequately with the issue of how individuals encompass both of these—and other—roles.

By the same token, the study of human behavior in the home will be enhanced by emphasizing the study of individuals in relation to the numerous and various environments in which they operate. For research purposes, the household itself is best viewed not as an entity unto itself, but as an open system—as a group of individuals who, while important to each other, also have important relationships with other persons and other groups in the larger environment.

Alternative Life-Styles for Couples and Communities

7

Whatever his background, personality, or previous occupation, the homemaker-father usually encounters doubt, skepticism, and some rejection from all but close friends. While the privacy of individual family life is well respected . . . a nontraditional family structure presents by its very existence a questioning of the norm, and provokes strong feelings.

James A. Levine[1]

We don't believe that collective living is an alternative to the traditional family, but we see it rather as a complement which can help us to be richer and have a more human coexistence. An alternative which is not based only on the strong and efficient people in our society, but which counts every possibility of every human being.

Gunilla and Goran Hallberg[2]

For various reasons, the pursuit of alternative life-styles is not for everyone. People's lives fall into patterns that, like all habits, are hard to break. Models of alternative life-styles that have been successful are encountered infrequently, and seldom close to home; the utopian community described in a book is real to its residents but a dream to readers. Still, even for those who cling most tenaciously to tradition, and perhaps especially for them, confronting the dream can be fascinating, a glimpse into what might be. And this is my purpose in this chapter: to take a look at some alternative futures for homemaking.

However, before discussing alternatives, it may be useful to clarify the patterns that are currently in use. What are the alternative life-styles alternatives to? Basically here I will be discussing alternatives to two prevalent models of the family. The first is the traditional model, in which the wife is the full-time homemaker and the husband is the full-time wage earner. Two of the typical assumptions on which this kind of family is founded are, first, that husband and wife should play separate and complementary roles rather than similar and competitive roles—lest the foundations of the marriage be disrupted—and, second, that sex differences in roles originate in the woman's biological role as mother. This role differentiation is believed to lead naturally to a family

141

in which the woman is responsible for the members' emotional well-being, while the father is responsible for the members' financial well-being.[3] Of course, alternatives to this life-style challenge these assumptions.

A second current model is the neotraditional model in which both husband and wife work for wages, though the husband is still considered the primary breadwinner and the wife continues to do most or all of the housework. I term this the neotraditional model because, though it does assimilate a recent factor, the wife's paid work, other changes in family life have been minimal. Partners are still operating under the primary assumptions of the traditional model, possibly rationalizing that the woman's paid work role is assumed only out of financial necessity or only temporarily.

The possible alternative relationships are many, as Jessie Bernard has pointed out in *The Future of Marriage*.[4] Bernard characterizes the possibilities by two factors. The nature of the personal commitment is one factor: Is the commitment to the other(s) in the relationship exclusive? Is it permanent? The other factor involves the number of people in the relationship and the issue of private versus communal properties. The forms of marriage that Bernard envisions range from informal, limited-commitment relationships in private homes (people "living together") to group marriage in communal households.

Here we are going to look at three alternative life-styles, all of which have been carried out somewhat successfully. While two of these are not generally termed marriage, they all deal with important aspects of marriage—namely, establishing a home and emotional support—and they would all fit into Bernard's schema. I have not used Bernard's interesting but rather elaborate classification system here, but rather have classified models simply by the number of persons involved: first we will examine an alternative life-style for couples, exploring the possibilities for changing men's roles in the family; then we will discuss an individual household involving a number of adults living together, without children; finally, we will look at two larger alternative communities.

The three models have several things in common. For one thing, the function of any family, be it a couple with children or a commune, continues to be the psychological and physical nurturing of its members. As Jessie Bernard describes it:

> The concept of a "home," which can serve as a firm, permanent, solid, stable base from which one can sally forth, confident that there is a secure place to return to, has always been salient in the discussion

of the future of marriage. In a world of increasing mobility and flux, the need for such an anchored base becomes even greater than in the past. The individual can tolerate a great deal of rootless movement if he knows that there is a place to return to.[5]

Some alternative life-styles are based on political motives as well, but the idea of home as a refuge remains central to most. (Perhaps the concept deserves examination—perhaps wider networks of support would be more beneficial to both individuals and society—but to date no serious challenge to this function of the family has been forthcoming.)

Other things the alternative life-styles have in common are their problems, and frequently these problems are internal. For instance, research indicates that in the demise of communes, as in the demise of couple marriages, personal conflicts are more frequently a factor than are external economic-related factors such as jobs.[6] Furthermore, housework frequently is specifically mentioned when communal living arrangements fail within a year or two of their inception, and it may be a major factor in such failures.[7] Housework-related problems common to all the alternative life-styles include issues of inequality in the division of labor (and especially sexual equality), related power issues, and differing standards for housework. Each of the alternative life-styles is evolving new ways to deal with these issues.

Nuclear Families: Men's Changing Roles

I have argued that the future of the nuclear family should include an improved status for homemakers, who are usually women. This change in itself represents a sort of alternative life-style, though perhaps we should reserve the term "alternative" for even more unusual changes. At any rate, the term "alternative" seems to fit the changing life-style of the growing but still small number of families in which the men of the household are taking over major portions of the homemaking.

In the last decade the percentage of such households has doubled, moving to one-half of one percent nationally.[8] In 1974, 211,000 men were out of the paid labor force because they were housekeeping; by October 1975 their numbers had grown to 219,000.[9]

Though I have no evidence to prove it, I strongly suspect that, barring unusual circumstances, feminism has been largely responsible for the existence of these male homemakers. Once the women's movement gained momentum and was obviously here to stay, some men saw that there was something in it for them, too—the possibility for personal choice. Women were growing and changing, and challenging their roles, so why not men?

Out of this male consciousness-raising was born the men's liberation movement, which now has its own literature and workshops and politics. For example, a National Conference on Men and Masculinity is held annually and explores such issues as the Equal Rights Amendment, abortion, and gay civil rights. A sampling of conference workshops in a given year may include rape, battered women, child abuse, violence between men, celebrating changing men, power, and intimacy.

Despite some ideological support, however, in general the male homemaker seems to be pretty much the odd man out—literally and figuratively. He has to cope with many unusual situations like being the only male in a group of "mothers" or explaining his motives to other men. Reaction to this role can be downright hostile. As one middle-aged man said of male homemakers:

> Men should do one thing and women another . . . a man isn't really
> built to take the time and understanding to take care of the children
> and make the food. And I think a man who stays home while his
> wife works is the same as, if you'll excuse me for saying it, a pimp.
> He puts his wife on the street to work for him.[10]

The best writing I have seen on the male homemaker is in James Levine's 1976 book *Who Will Raise the Children: New Options for Fathers (and Mothers)*. Levine includes several interviews with male homemakers. In these it is especially fascinating to see how the role has molded these men just as surely as it has molded millions of female homemakers before them. For instance, people worry about the male homemaker's future: "Sometimes I say to him, just joking, 'When are you going back to work?' He doesn't answer and he knows I'm only teasing, but sometimes I do wonder if he'll be able."[11] Their wives enjoy having someone else take care of all their housework needs.[12] And the men themselves have many familiar problems:

> I had to get used to the idea of a disjointed appetite situation,—not
> just food, but for activity . . . . I resigned myself to spending the
> mornings mopping up. The most complex thing of my own work that
> I'd get done would be a letter—that was a major triumph!
> . . . I really had to examine my whole liberal role-reversal and
> libertarian posture. I didn't take into account that women's work as
> traditionally defined wasn't a gratifying thing . . . that it was
> drudgery. It wasn't hard, even with my limited experience as a
> househusband, to understand what the real issue of the women's
> movement was, to understand the nature of the trap.[13]

Mostly you start feeling sorry for yourself. "Why am I staying in all
day?" It's your responsibility to change it . . . .
It's easy to be lazy, to kind of get into sitting around at home.[14]

The interview that follows is yet another example illustrating the
similarities (and some of the differences) between male and female
homemakers. Douglas Roberts, thirty-six, is a homemaker we met
during the course of a research project on the homemaker's quality of
working life. On a tour of his home, he pointed with particular pride to
the things he has made by hand: a plant rack, an island in the kitchen, a
knife rack, lamps. He also pointed jokingly to a plaque on the front door
that says "Kathy Roberts and Husband." Doug does about 70 percent of
the housework for his family, which includes two children aged three
and five. He mixes homemaking with occasional consulting. At the time
of the interview his wife is out working and the children are in school
and day care. This is his story:

I just sort of fell into staying home. I was a student and Kathy was
working full time, so the obligation just naturally fell on me. I lived
alone for several years, and that gives you a sense of self-reliance. Plus,
when I was in college I worked in the kitchen so I certainly learned to do
pots and pans and dishes. For my whole life I've cooked my own
breakfasts, but one does not live on pancakes alone. I think I really got
into cooking regular meals after I got married, but I did some cooking
before when I spent two years in the Peace Corps.
    Do my kids like my cooking? Well, it depends on what I fix. Some-
times they like it and other times they'd like to fire me.
    Personally, I'm glad they can see me doing the housework. I would
like to see them grow up with a great deal more role variation than
people generally get. My own standard is irrespective of whether a role
is stereotyped masculine or feminine: the more that a person knows
how to do, the better off a person is going to be in this very complex
society.
    When I do woodworking downstairs, and my daughter says "Can I
help with the drill and hammer?" I go get it for her. I want her to know
as much about everything as she can. The children are not ready to
grasp the role concept—the best I can do is to provide the various
models.
    A variety of things make me happy to be a homemaker. The kids are a
great thing. I think I generally learn more from them than they do from
me. There's. a great deal of satisfaction watching them grow and develop, answering their questions, watching them develop a sense of

humor. And repairing things, making things in the home—we're re-doing a room upstairs right now, that kind of thing. Making some of the furniture.

Is there anything that you just despise doing?

I despise it, I yell about it, I grumble about and even sometimes I can make a joke about it: and that's windows. I cannot stand doing win-dows. That would be number one on my list of things I hate to do.

I think my wife would say I don't have that cutthroat instinct at the grocery store that she developed—such things as going to the back of the shelves for things that are lower priced from last week. I do have that but I think it takes constant shopping to appreciate that lettuce at $1.03 a head is a crummy price to pay. I'm constantly comparing prices. I blunder sometimes, but not really that much.

I think I'm probably more active in what's going on around the house than most men I know, but I don't perceive it as being all that abnormal. I have a brother-in-law who does essentially the same thing I do. I think the real contrast comes from the type of people where my wife works, which is a blue-collar community, where you are much more cast in with stereotypes. I guess I know intellectually that there are men that it would absolutely destroy their masculinity to make soup or something. Like the men in *The Women's Room*, Marilyn French's book. I know these people exist, but it's out of my frame of reference that someone in this day and age could be that idiotic.

Actually we first decided to share responsibilities even before we got married. Kathy had a party. She was working and I was a student, so I said I'd take care of it—fix hors d'oeuvres and everything. So I fixed the hors d'oeuvres and she came in with a group of people and she started complaining about something. So I retorted, "What do you think I am, your bloody servant?" It cracked up one of the other people, and I always remember that.

We each have our specialties. My specialties are when someone's coming—guests for dinner—and the other is when the classical phrase comes up, "There's nothing in the house to eat."

I have a couple of things I like to do. One is to take a bad cut of meat and make it into something good. And the other one is, occasionally, the scratch and dent sale. The cans are all right as long as the seal isn't broken. Then there are the "5-cent can" sales. You gamble: the original price is on the can, which is unlabeled, so you have a pretty good idea what price range you're talking about. I bought one for $1.19 and one for $1.29 at five cents each. I fixed a chicken dish and decided to gamble and open the $1.29 one—six artichoke hearts! And the other was cherry pie filling, but I made cherries jubilee out of it.

I don't like paying a lot of money for some of these things, but I don't really like starches either. The trade-off is really hard. We generally don't eat potatoes. Rice is in my very tolerable range, and noodles I use in stroganoff or beef burgundy. Usually I cook a main dish, a vegetable, and a salad. I tend to cater a lot to my wife's tastes: she has a nose like something I've never seen before in terms of what's good and what's not. She can also tell the difference between cuts of beef by taste. Some meat will taste very good to her, and other meat won't. That's another reason for going into sauces—to disguise the taste of it.

One of the other interesting areas about my wife and me is that when I get upset about something, she will be the calming influence. And when she gets upset, I'm the calming influence. Absolutely a beautiful balance! I don't know what would happen if we ever had something we both should have gotten upset about.

Do you ever argue about chores?

No, no. It may be a topic of conversation for several conversations. Like the dog taking a bath—it's been on the agenda for about a week. My wife asked when the last time I changed the sheets on the bed was, so I'll change the sheets. The schedule isn't strict and it's recognized as not being strict, so no one ever gets yelled at.

Who shovels the snow around here?

We both do; it's a trade-off.

Since I stay home and my wife works, I get to meet and take over the relationship with my wife's boyfriend (facetiously), the mailman. We have a lot of fun over that. I visit with some of the wives across the street for coffee occasionally, or maybe I'll take their kids for a while.

I think there's quite a conflict now about whether a person who stays in the home has as much economic value as the partner in a marriage who goes out and works. I don't see any difference at all, after having done both. If there is a difference, I think the advantage really goes to the person who has a paying job. The more difficult job is the one at home: when the kids drive you up the wall, there's no place you can go. In other kinds of work, sometimes you can defer things, and things in the house often cannot be deferred. The decisions that you have to make in working in a house are things that reflect more immediately upon you or your family unit than the kinds of decisions you might make at work. I've never kidded myself about which was the hardest. That's my soapbox.

My wife knows more medically. She can look at one of the kids and say "She has a fever and it's in her ear." I can't do that. If I'm going to be the complete homemaker, I'd better get my act together and learn how.

A lot of people say it's unnatural for the father to play the mother role—that it's defying the laws of nature.

The institution of marriage has a good historical-social basis. The role of a homemaker has a good historical basis. The man has been the hunter, the one that went out; the woman has carried the child and nurtured the child. Although certainly the woman is more agile and probably would have been a much better hunter. But we come to points where we don't have to carry on some of the history we've carried before. In the end it comes down to what's expedient and practical. Yet people are afraid of change.

My wife certainly has more of the role of getting the children's clothes than I do. When I do go, to see if there's something special the kids want or need, I get instructions not to buy the place out.

Homemaking to me is seen from two perspectives. One is a maintenance thing. One doesn't do it for the sake of homemaking, one does it because you need a semblance of a healthy environment in which to live. I am not a great one for cleaning a place up when people come over. It's not creative. I have a friend who strives for the "lived in" look, and I agree with that. As for the second perspective: it's a challenge to make homemaking as easy as possible. For example, when I get on a cooking jag, I have five main courses going at once. I freeze four and eat one.

There are people, for instance a person we know, who can only talk about three things—about her cooking, her Cuisinart, and her kids. I get hungry for someone to talk to about other things—like Iran. That's one of the things that's very depressing about homemaking, I think. You're cut off from other people that you used to talk to. I sometimes turn on the news on TV or the radio just to hear something on a little higher level.

I think I view homemaking more as a necessity than as something that one gains concrete rewards from. I think if homemaking is a chosen role, then you can talk about looking for a reward out of it. I guess the only satisfaction I would really get out of it is getting stuff done so that my wife doesn't have to do it. The reward I get out of it, is trying to figure out a more efficient way of doing something.

There are some people we know who would really freak if they knew the amount of housework I do. There are some people, but not a lot. The real problem comes for a man who is in a very stereotyped masculine role: when he cannot characterize the man who is a homemaker as being nonmasculine, then he's forced to confront something.

Does a person like this give you a feeling that what you're doing is unnatural?

Oh no. I think it's scaring him. That's his problem, not mine.

One thing remains clear: that the logical extension of the feminist ideal of choice means choice for men as well as for women. The fact that in recent years homemaking has not been a particularly reasonable role to choose affects both sexes. If female homemakers are economically dependent, psychologically isolated, and politically ignored, so to some extent are male homemakers.

Also important is the positive side of homemaking. I don't think it is unreasonable to assert that men who avoid homemaking are men who are missing out. Obviously they are missing a lot of the pleasure of their children. They are also missing the psychological and physical pleasures of creating a home, pleasures that women have known for centuries. The effect of male homemakers on children, especially male children, may be beneficial. Having males as primary nurturers may have significant effects on males' training in aggression. As homemaker and writer Kenneth Pitchford has written so movingly:

> Our child Blake is now in fourth grade. One of the most touching things about him is that he "instinctively" loves to take care of younger children. This isn't for approval or even for show. It's because his earliest memories include not solely his mother but, as far back and just as often, this grumpy lovable old shoe of a person who snored sometimes when cuddling his baby asleep. It's what a Real Man does. Like his father. There's my reward. He will become a young man, swimming through his own Technicolor dream. But I know one thing: a child's crying will pierce his sleep as much as mine. Inherent? Instinctual? On the contrary, it's something that men can do in learning the work of love. And because of that lesson, my baby, I've come to love you far more than I could have in any other way.[15]

And the influence of male homemakers on women and on feminism, and ultimately on our culture, should be favorable. Choice itself is an important ideal, but the fact that men make the choice to leave paid work may turn out to be especially significant. When people who are already accepted by the system challenge it, those who are still outside trying to get in will sit up and take notice. The example of male home-makers can help women avoid the error of embracing the male paid work as currently defined; it can lead both sexes to continue their search for alternatives.

An Empirical "Household"

"Household" has been defined by Shulamith Firestone as "a large grouping of people living together for an unspecified time, and with no specified set of interpersonal relations."[16] I have chosen to look at this kind of group here because, while it represents a new alternative, it is also a relatively simple one. Households are not the same thing as extended families. Thus, in studying them one can observe simple cases uncomplicated by novel marital arrangements and by children. Fur-thermore, as Firestone feels, "The word *family* implies biological re-production and some degree of division of labor by sex, and thus the traditional dependencies and resulting power relations, extending over generations."[17] Households, she thinks, may have significant advan-tages over families, including increased housework efficiency.

At the outset we should be careful not to get swept away by some utopian vision of life in a large group. Groups, just like couples, have their housework problems, and these problems are crucial to their suc-cess or failure. In his article "Two Communal Houses and Why (I Think) They Failed," Matthew Israel notes the following irritations that one household has experienced:

> Betty believed that one should show beautifying behaviors in a house—for example, one should open or close the window curtains in the living room, straighten up furniture as needed, and so forth. Sally did not show these behaviors.
>
> Communally prepared meals seemed to take a long time to prepare, eat, and clean up after—often several hours. I often wished that I could just eat quickly and run, as I had been accustomed to doing at my apartment or at a restaurant....
>
> Jim and Elaine, poorer than the others, wanted to spend little on food; Randy, Alice and I didn't mind spending a little more to get variety and quality. Jim and Elaine were vegetarians; the rest of us all enjoyed meat....
>
> Betty, brought up in Holland, liked the temperature in the house to be about 68. I preferred 71 or 72. Betty and I sometimes played little games with the thermostat.[18]

Clearly the differences in preferences experienced between the members of a couple are compounded when several people are involved. Yet it seems that these differences can be resolved. Cooperative houses, many of which are on university campuses, do succeed—of course, some more than others. Let us look at one of the successes.

The Center for Intentional Living

The Center for Intentional Living, a co-ed house for students attending the University of Kansas, is one project that has recognized the problems of housework allocation and has been determined to surmount them.[19] The project is important for a number of reasons, not the least of which is that it recognizes housework as a crucial variable in a shared living arrangement. The project directors, social scientists at the University of Kansas, have hypothesized that, when housework systems break down, people tend to become more aggressive toward each other. Thus, one of the first major social designs for the project was a work-sharing system.

The social systems being used in the house have been based on behavioral technology, and they have been monitored and recorded by social scientists so that others can readily learn from them and copy them. When the principles on which they are based is unclear, such alternative life-styles can only be curiosities. However, the Center for Intentional Living is nothing but intentional: desirable behaviors are specified and specific rewards are given for these behaviors, provisions are agreed to by the members, and the program is written down.

The center is in a large three-story frame house near the university campus. Owned by a nonprofit corporation called the University of Kansas Student Housing Association, the house was purchased in 1969 and, as I understand it, has been used for the center ever since. It includes twenty-nine single rooms plus common areas including a dining/meeting room, a lounge, a large kitchen, a small snack kitchen, a game room, a shop, bathrooms, and storage areas.

Up to thirty students ranging in age from eighteen to twenty-eight live in the house at any one time. About 80 percent are undergraduates and 20 percent are graduate students, with about equal numbers of women and men. Their fields of study vary and have included business, psychology, social work, chemistry, and fine arts. The designers of the project feel that these students represent a reasonable cross section of the campus population.

The overall purpose of the project has been to apply scientific behavior principles to group living in an effort to determine how group living can be improved. The project has confirmed, for instance, that group members are more likely to do assigned jobs when they earn credits toward a monthly rent reduction based on the percentage of the cleaning task completed. (Members are much less likely to do housework if the credits are merely posted rather than being posted *and* tied to a rent reduction.)

Three explicit project goals have been established, all of which—not incidentally—would be reasonable goals for any household relationship, including nuclear families. The first goal has been to design an egalitarian, efficient work-sharing system. A main thrust of this goal is to ensure that all persons do their equal shares of the housework and that no one member gains an unequal share of power: the directors had observed that, in many successful communes, one or a few members have taken over "managerial" responsibility even though equality of power had been a goal of those groups.

A second goal has been to develop what the social scientists call a "behavioral culture." At several points in the book I have touched on this idea without making it explicit, partly because to do so would require far more space than I want to allot. Basically, the design of a behavioral culture involves using the rewards and punishments available in any environment to encourage those behaviors the culture finds desirable and to discourage those it finds undesirable. B. F. Skinner's book *Walden Two* describes a utopia that uses such methods. However, Skinner's utopia was managed by a group of planners. As a matter of principle, the Center for Intentional Living has adopted a more democratic framework to monitor the culture. I discussed behavioral principles elsewhere in the book when I described Neil Jacobson's approach to transitions in marriage (chap. 6) and when I proposed work-sharing systems for couples (chap. 5).

The third goal of the project has been to develop a "positive verbal community." Though straightforward, the idea is far from trivial. Achieving a sense of togetherness is often one of the primary goals of an alternative living arrangement. To do this—again, whether in groups or with couples—it is important that members engage in frequent positive interactions (praising each other and taking an interest in each other, for example) and that they attempt to minimize negative interactions (criticizing each other and ignoring each other).

How Thirty Persons Share Housework

The work-sharing system at the center is complex. It is set forth as a contract in an eighty-page handbook given to each new member of the house, and members are required to pass a quiz on the rationale for the system as explained in the handbook. Each member is also required to post a forty-dollar bond to ensure that he or she will live up to the terms of the contract.

The necessary work in the house has been broken down into about a hundred jobs in cleaning, food, and repair programs. Each Thursday a list of these jobs is posted, and members sign up for an assortment for the next week. Each job is defined in terms of five to fifteen measurable criteria. (For example, a sink would not merely be "cleaned," but would have "all hair and other materials removed" and would be "scoured with detergent.") Based on these criteria, jobs are inspected each evening by a trained house member.

All members earn credits for their work. Each job is assigned a credit value according to the amount of time it takes and its desirability as work. Thus, while fifteen credits per hour is the base rate for a job, jobs that seldom attract volunteers are allotted more points. A two-hour job that is popular, like cooking the evening meal, may be worth thirty points, while an unpopular one-hour job like cleaning the oven also earns thirty points. The value of any job can be adjusted by a majority vote of the members as long as inflation is avoided: increases in one job must be balanced by decreases in one or more other jobs.

Members can earn any number of credits per week, but they can use only up to one hundred credits per week toward rent reduction. Since each credit is worth ten cents, the total possible rent reduction for a month is forty dollars. Average rent is about one hundred dollars, so the forty-dollar reduction is significant.

Credits can be saved from week to week, and they can be borrowed from friends, adding to the flexibility of the system. Actually, about a third of the time members use credits earned in previous weeks to fill the needed one hundred credits per week. One problem that developed was that members with credit savings tended to skip jobs they had signed up for. Since this greatly inconvenienced other members of the house—dinner, for example, would have to be made by others at the last minute—it was decided to impose a two-dollar fine for any job signed up for and not done. The program researchers report that this has virtually eliminated failure to do jobs.

When members sign up to do a specific job they are awarded full credits if the inspection indicates that at least 90 percent of the criteria set for the job are met. If more than 50 percent of the criteria are met, they receive proportional credits, but if fewer than half are met they earn no credits and are also fined the two dollars for not doing the job.

Each of the essential housework programs—cleaning, food, and repair—is carefully coordinated.

The goal of the cleaning program is to maintain the common areas—bathrooms, hallways, the common rooms, and the exterior of the house. (Individual rooms are exempt from the common behavioral contract.) A coordinator for this program maintains the equipment and supplies required to do the jobs. His or her role is essential if the day-to-day chores other members sign up for are to be completed. Because of this central and responsible position, the coordinator is required to sign a special contract outlining her or his duties and providing for special contingencies if they are not adequately performed.

Similarly, the food program is highly organized. Menus are planned for three months. Then, each morning, a menu coordinator places the daily menu plus the pertinent recipes in the kitchen. At the same time another member checks the pantry to make sure the proper foods are available and puts them out for the cooks. If items are missing, it is the menu coordinator's responsibility to purchase them before cooking time. At four o'clock the two cooks begin their job. Later a server sets the places and brings the food to the table, while others clear the table and clean up.

Coordination of the repair program depends heavily on a member who is skilled in fixing things. This member identifies problems and works out step-by-step checklists indicating how the repairs are to be done. The jobs are then posted and, when completed, are inspected by the coordinator according to the checklist. Currently, as one can readily see, the repair coordinator has considerable power to create and reward jobs. The program is dealing with this inequity by developing standard job descriptions for common repairs and by developing in-house training programs to teach skills in fixing things.

Success?

How well has each of these essential housework programs worked? Very well, according to most house members. The results of the daily inspections of cleaning jobs indicate that an average of about 95 percent of the criteria for cleaning jobs are satisfactorily met, and members report that the house is kept about as clean as a dormitory. The average percentage of food jobs completed is also 95 percent, and the members rate the quality of the food as very high. Finally, members felt that needed repairs were being made about as quickly as in a dormitory.

It seems clear that the project has designed an efficient housework-sharing system for a large household. Is it also, as the founders hoped, egalitarian? I have noted that the skills of the repair person give that member a disproportionate share of power, and that attempts are being

made to remedy this. The researchers also report, though without supporting data, that "one of the results of the worksharing system is that it
has a remarkable leveling effect on the sexes: Men do half the cooking;
cleaning tasks are equally shared; and a high proportion of the repair
work is done by women. Also, as many women as men hold super-
visory and coordinating jobs."[20]

The project also continues to move toward the goals of designing a
particular behavioral culture and encouraging a positive verbal community. The behavioral culture now includes three primary strategies:
(1) a self-government process in which any change in the behavioral
system requires a majority vote of 75 percent, and in which members
are paid fifteen credits for attending weekly meetings; (2) the handbook
describing the work-sharing system, and also social guidelines such as
rules about stealing; (3) an educational program including an in-
troductory course on the behavioral principles used in the project.

A method for creating the positive verbal community is now being
developed and will also involve training. Members will learn such techniques as how to praise others sincerely, how to enhance this praise
with follow-up questions, and how to accept a compliment by re-
inforcing the person who gave it. It is hoped that the ability to develop
and maintain a positive community will be valued in its own right, but
also that this ability will be a powerful tool for social change—that
unwanted behavior patterns will be reduced, and even eliminated,
through reinforcement of alternative behaviors.

The Center for Intentional Living is proof that households can become a reasonable alternative life-style for single young adults. The
designers of the project are careful to point out that the project must be
considered within the larger social environment. The housework system might not have been so successful if the project as a whole were not
relatively inexpensive and satisfying to its members. Furthermore, in a
university town such living experiments are more acceptable than they
might be elsewhere. But the designers of the project are eager to deal
with these issues and to extend the models to groups of married couples
and eventually to groups of married couples with children.

Experimental Communities

It is interesting to see how housework issues have been handled in still
larger groups. In the experimental communities we will explore next,
the issue of work is central to the social design. Often such communities
attempt to equalize the division of labor between the sexes and to

improve the status of housework. Studying the housework arrangements in experimental communities can be particularly revealing because the communities exist for relatively long periods of time. Interpersonal commitment tends to be strong. People in the communities make long-term commitments to change, and they often reevaluate a community in light of its established goals. Thus we can examine the fate of housework ideology and practice over time and can make some inferences relevant to more traditional communities.

I will briefly describe here two particularly relevant experimental communities, the Israeli kibbutz and the Twin Oaks community of Louisa, Virginia.

Housework in the Kibbutz

Rae Lesser Blumberg cogently sums up the fate of women in the Israeli kibbutz in the title of her article, "Kibbutz Women: From the Fields of Revolution to the Laundries of Discontent."[21] As an experimental community the kibbutz is particularly noteworthy because of its failure to maintain equality of the sexes in spite of an initial desire and continuing commitment to do so.

In 1958 Martin Buber called the kibbutz "an experiment that did not fail."[22] I think most feminists today would disagree. Although the kibbutz has continued as a viable organization, it has not met many of the social goals that have been important to women.

In addition to political motivations, the kibbutz movement held idealistic social goals that included rejection of the traditional family in favor of equality between the sexes and the abolition of traditional sex roles in work. The kibbutz movement has always been a minority movement within its own society: today the kibbutz population constitutes less than 3 percent of Israel's total population.[23]

Because life on the kibbutz has undergone many changes through the years, it is inaccurate to speak of the movement as though it represents a single set of conditions or even a single philosophy. Some authors suggest that we should speak of the "classical" or "historical" kibbutz as contrasted with the modern kibbutz.[24] Others describe several stages—the pioneering days, a second stage representing a second generation, and the industrialized stage that began in the fifties.[25]

Blumberg uses the latter model convincingly as she explains the evolution of women's role from relative equality to relative inequality, and finally to a renewed hope for egalitarianism. She suggests that in the pioneering days equality in work was an important goal of the kibbutz community. Members were young and childless, and both sexes labored to improve agricultural production.

It is important to note that, in the kibbutz, production jobs like farming have always been more highly esteemed than service jobs like cooking. Ideally, from the beginning, the low-esteemed service work was to be shared equally by both sexes. However, diaries of some pioneer members indicate that the larger share of these tasks fell to the women, and that they complained to no avail. There is no evidence that men ever worked in the nurseries. As Blumberg puts it, "Basically, sexual equality was seen as a one-way street: women were to be integrated into 'male' economic and political roles, but there was no systematic attempt to integrate kibbutz men into 'female' domestic roles."[26]

In terms of housework then, the kibbutz ideology was flawed. (The parallel in today's American family is striking in that women are gaining a foothold in so-called men's work, but men are taking over little of the housework.)

The result was that the second stage of the kibbutz movement has been characterized by an extreme division of work by sex. Women are found primarily in service jobs. Fewer than 10 percent of them today work in the highly esteemed agricultural jobs, and few participate on the economic committees that are so important to kibbutz government.[27] Naturally, ideology was not the only factor in this change. Lack of recognition of the importance of service work interacted with changing social necessities such as the need for women to bear and nurse children. However, the sex segregation in work went far beyond these necessities. Women and services began to be equated. "A downward spiral was created. It affected not only women's occupations but also their voice in economic control, political participation, prestige, self-esteem, personality characteristics deemed typical, and roles deemed appropriate."[28]

In the fifties the kibbutz entered what may be a new phase for women: the beginning of industrialization, in which the possibilities for improving women's status increased. More labor was needed for manufacturing, and the kibbutz began to invest in domestic labor-saving devices that would free women for the new positions. Thus, as Blumberg argues, women have the opportunity to rejoin the status- and income-generating production force, and to gain the political and economic power that may eventually lead them to full equality.

In the kibbutz, we have a portrait of an experimental community that has so far failed for women. Perhaps if housework had been accorded more importance from the beginning of the experiment, stage two could have been avoided. Certainly the introduction of children and child-rearing represents a difficult stage in any experimental community.

This is witnessed by the fact that both the Center for Intentional Living and the Twin Oaks community (discussed below) have seen the introduction of children as a situation to tackle only after other less complicated situations are understood. To enter this stage without a clear idea about equality in housework has proved hazardous for women in experimental communities as well as for women in traditional marriages.

Further, I would argue that this housework ideology should have included the assertion that women do not need to enter what has been called "productive labor" in order to gain equality. My assertion in this book has been that homemakers' psychological, legal, and economic status can be improved to the point where one can reasonably assert that they have achieved equality with other workers. Blumberg argues that direct female contributions to production of goods and capital seems to be a precondition for equality.[29] I agree that this often has been true, but not that it needs to be true.

The history of the kibbutz as briefly examined here illustrates clearly that the social importance of housework must be recognized, and that the predominantly male ideology of the supreme importance of production needs to be tempered. At least one other experimental community is working to prove these things can be accomplished.

Twin Oaks

Twin Oaks is the Virginia community patterned after principles set forth in B. F. Skinner's utopian novel *Walden Two*. Since its founding in 1967, Twin Oaks has evolved a distinctive philosophy of work sharing. Kathleen Kinkade, an original member of the community and author of *A Walden Two Experiment* (1973), has described that philosophy at several points in her book:

> In the book *Walden Two* there is a labor system hinted at but not described. The basic theme of it is that, while all work is equally honorable, not all is equally desirable, and that those who do the nastiest jobs should get the shortest hours.
>
> There is no such thing as unstructured division of labor. If a commune survives at all, the work is divided somehow. Somebody does it. An "unstructured" situation will quickly evolve into a structured one where certain people accept a role as workers and do the bulk of the work, while others do very little or avoid it entirely. This is not only obvious on the face of it; it has been painfully demonstrated in commune after commune.

We come from a society that values brain above brawn. Recognizing this as a prejudice which is detrimental to an egalitarian
society, we are determined to do away with it, if possible in one
generation. Brain may at times be more needed than brawn is, in
which case intelligence is a useful thing. If some people are more
useful than others, then let them serve more. We want a society that
rejoices in the useful and enjoyable talents of its members without
according to anyone prestige or honor on account of them.

We try to make it obvious that leaving one's work undone is equivalent to asking other members to do it for you, and not many people
are so lacking in conscience that they are willing to do that on a
regular basis.

There are still problems to be worked out, and we will undoubtedly
find that fundamental changes in the labor system will be necessary
from time to time. We may even lose our resistance to specialization
and find some of our members preferring and requesting role-
assignment jobs. There is already evidence of this. What will probably not change is the basic idea of the labor credit—all work is
equally honorable.[30]

Even though the original Twin Oaks members were idealistic, their
work-sharing system was not initiated until one of the women in the
original group wanted to know why another woman wasn't helping
with the housework. Having read Skinner, the members recognized
that here was an issue they would have to deal with. In the ensuing
discussions they decided to formalize a system for sharing work, and
originally only the most disliked work—the housework—was included.
As the novelty of other tasks wore off they were added to the system,
and within a month it was decided that all work useful to the group
belonged on the labor credit system. "Useful work" included labor that
did not produce income as well as labor that did.

Today at Twin Oaks the labor system changes from time to time, but
the basics as Kinkade describes them are as follows. Since the community is fairly large (forty members in 1973), it has been possible to do
away with the random assignment of tasks that are unpleasant: someone always finds one job or another to be less unpleasant than other
people do. So periodically each member ranks the currently available
jobs in order of preference. Members earn more work credits for those
jobs they find least preferable. Thus two people doing the same job may
earn different credits—the person enjoying the work more earns fewer
credits than the person enjoying it less. The assignment of tasks and the
accounting of credits is handled by clerks, who work for two days and
are paid credits for it. The community is willing to pay this cost in

clerks' time because "the alternative is role assignment. No serious community of our size and complexity can just let the work go from day to day on the assumption that someone will do it."[31]

Just as important, the community members do not want role assignment. They want week-to-week, even day-to-day choice of what work they will do. Usually they work about forty hours a week in jobs ranging from farming to businesses to housework. Some members work outside the community to bring in cash. Kinkade's book itself was written under the labor credit system, earning her a standard one credit per hour for her writing time, with the profit from sales going to the community.

The reader will readily observe that the Twin Oaks system is similar to the system at the Center for Intentional Living. Both are based on behavioral psychology, and both use a fairly complex system of work allocation and rewards.

Although the systems are basically more alike than different, some differences are notable. For instance, Twin Oaks does not use an inspection system to monitor completion of tasks. Instead, they have adopted a less formalized approach to change. Individuals who have been criticized for not doing their work well, or for adding to others' work by being particularly sloppy, may try to change their own behavior. Or such self-control projects may involve more than one member. Several may band together in a kind of friendly game to remind each other to improve. Perhaps this less formalized technology works more efficiently than inspections for this larger group with a longer-term commitment; or perhaps the people of Twin Oaks will simply not tolerate the regimen of inspections. But there are problems with Twin Oak's reliance on the individual conscience. As Kinkade so succinctly puts it, "What if the sloppiest people won't play?"[32]

Another difference between Twin Oaks and the Center for Intentional Living is the method for allocating more points for undesirable jobs, thus ensuring that those jobs get done. The center's method is group-based: jobs that do not attract sign-ups are given more points. Twin Oak's method of having individuals rank desired jobs reflects a strong dependence on individual responsibility, and their system is open to abuse. After all, individuals could shirk by putting their favorite jobs low on the list. Perhaps this emphasis on individual responsibility and trust is in some way necessary for maintaining the culture of a large group committed to living together for an extended time. On the other hand, one could reasonably hypothesize that group size and commitment are irrelevant, that individual demands for self-control are inevitable, and that only a household based in the rules-oriented setting of university housing would tolerate an inspection system. These interesting issues remain unstudied.

Some of the goals of Twin Oaks are similar to those of the Center for Intentional Living. Eventually the community wants to extend its program. For one thing, it wants to include more children. To date this has been difficult for both economic and social reasons; at present Twin Oaks does not accept children into the community from outside.

Twin Oaks has also attempted to establish what the center has called a positive verbal community. Among other things, it has an antigossip rule: talk that does damage, such as disparaging remarks about others, is frowned upon. If people hear such talk they are likely to get up and leave the room. And channels for complaints have been established that temper their impact. A kind of ombudsperson called the bitch manager receives a written complaint—and passes on a gentle hint to the person deemed at fault.

Like the center, Twin Oaks has sought to eliminate sex-stereotyping in the division of labor. Kinkade has said that at Twin Oaks:

> We have no sex roles in our work. Both men and women cook and clean and wash dishes; both women and men drive trucks and tractors, repair fences, load hay, slaughter cattle. Managerial responsibility is divided almost exactly equally—this in spite of the fact that our women are on the average two or three years younger than our men.[33]

But her statement is perhaps too reassuring. In the August 1976 issue of the Twin Oaks newsletter, member Susan says, "I see many fewer women in decision making positions now. I see a male-energy system forming as the female energy retreats to traditional female areas of concern, (children, kitchen, etc.). I fear that in this respect, we will move closer and closer to the male-dominated system on the outside."[34]

I received Susan's article enclosed in a letter from member Glo, who explained:

> My personal opinion about this subject is that our main problem here is that we don't have, maybe don't take, the time to teach women or any unskilled people skills. Not that women never learn any new skills here. They do, Susan is just one example. But those women tend to be more persistent and luckier. Some other women find it easier to stay in "women's" areas, like cleaning and watching the kids, and don't learn many new skills (except for hammock making, our main industry). As for men doing housework—every day I see men doing dishes, taking care of children, and cleaning up. Some

even seem to enjoy these things. But I also see more men than women operating machines and being community planners . . . . I just noticed the article [among those I sent] "Ye olde gold bolt award." All the people on the auto crew a year ago, when this was written, were men. We now have two women on the auto crew. I wonder if there are more or less gold bolt awards [given for goofs] given now?

Thus, while Twin Oaks experimental community has survived and even, some would say, flourished, it has not yet settled this most basic housework issue.

The Twin Oaks people would probably assert that the next generation—the children they will raise in a behavioral culture free of sex stereotyping—will be the answer to many of their unsolved problems. Perhaps they are right. Parents in traditional life-styles have found that avoiding cultural sex stereotyping for their children is nearly impossible, but the children of Twin Oaks community will grow up in a different environment.

These, then, are a few of the new directions, a sampling of the alternative life-styles, that people are exploring. They are options in themselves, but they are also sources of ideas for improving traditional relationships. Whether they involve reversing old roles or creating new ones, they all have in common the need for careful thought and planning. Especially for systems involving households or communities, but also to some extent for nuclear families, a certain degree of structure and a moderate investment of time and energy seem to be necessary to keep the systems operating smoothly.

Let us not overlook the fact that all the systems also share one common goal: to make the necessary work in our most intimate surroundings as pleasant as possible for both men and women, both immediately and over the long term. In pursuit of this goal we are well reminded of Henry David Thoreau, a homemaker whose simple alternative life-style may put some of our current complexities into perspective. Of his life on Walden Pond Thoreau wrote:

I had three pieces of limestone on my desk, but I was terrified to find that they required to be dusted daily, when the furniture of my mind was all undusted still, and I threw them out the window in disgust. How, then, could I have a furnished house? I would rather sit in the open air, for no dust gathers on the grass, unless where man has broken ground.

. . . Follow your genius closely enough, and it will not fail to show you a fresh prospect every hour. Housework was a pleasant pastime. When my floor was dirty, I rose early, and, setting all my furniture out of doors on the grass, bed and bedstead making but one budget, dashed water on the floor, and sprinkled white sand from the pond on it, and then with a broom scrubbed it clean and white; and by the time the villagers had broken their fast the morning sun had dried my house sufficiently to allow me to move in again, and my meditations were almost uninterrupted. It was pleasant to see my whole household effects on the grass, making a little pile like a gypsy's pack, and my three-legged table, from which I did not remove the books and pen and ink, standing amid the pines and hickories.[35]

Homemakers
and Organization

8

I have three kids. I keep reading in magazines and elsewhere about women doing these great things—jobs, tennis clubs, classes and just every kind of activity. Even in the TV commercials they're all busy having fun. Well, all that, or any of that, takes three things—money, a car and a sitter. I don't have them. My big weekly outing is going to the grocery store. I play coupon games. Where are all the support groups for people like me?

A homemaker who is a college graduate[1]

There are societies in which the domestic role works, but in these societies the housewife is not isolated. She is either part of a large extended family household in which domestic activities are a communal effort, or participates in a tightly knit village community, or both . . . . In our society the housewife may move about freely, but since she has nowhere to go and is not a part of anything anyway her prison needs no walls.

Philip Slater[2]

One of the greatest problems in the homemaker movement is organization. How can homemakers organize to combat the isolation so many of them feel? How can they organize to gain economic and political power? A corollary of the organizational issue is the problem of linkages with other interest groups. What are homemakers' most promising links with the women's movement? With labor? What other contacts might they explore?

It has been said that, if men bore children, abortion not only would be legal, it would be free. Maybe if men did the housework, homemakers would have unions. At any rate, it is likely that if homemakers were organized in some way we would have heard a lot more from them than we have to date.

As it is, most homemakers are isolated from each other. Collective life-styles have had little impact on the nuclear family with its separate dwelling, separate meals, and separate appliances. Organizations of homemakers to share child care are gaining popularity but are still the exception rather than the rule, and cooperating to do mundane house-work is even more unusual.

The primary organization of which the homemaker is a member is the family. It used to be that a person's family network was fairly large; several branches and generations lived near each other, if not in the same household. Close ties were maintained: the individual family unit was a subunit of the larger family organization. Through her family, the homemaker had access to a wider social and financial support system. Female relatives helped each other with child care and housework; perhaps even more important was the availability of emotional and financial support for the homemaker whose husband did not meet these needs. Today, however, for all practical purposes the family unit is a subunit of nothing. Physical and financial mobility have severed many of the links between a family unit and the larger family organization. Beyond her husband and children, and perhaps some friends and civic groups, the homemaker is socially unconnected.

The return of extensive family linkages seems unlikely, and, though formalized collective living will satisfy the needs of some families, others will prefer not to commit themselves so fully to collective arrangements. For many, a more acceptable strategy for organization is the establishment of new networks among the homemakers now living in nuclear families.

Such networks can serve two purposes. First, they can help home-makers deal with the isolation that is so often a part of their jobs. Second, they can provide an important base for homemaker influence, a grass-roots foundation for increasing economic and political power.

What would an organization of homemakers look like? The basic unit would be the neighborhood network. This would consist of a small group (three to twelve members) of homemakers living relatively close to each other. Such groups would have several advantages. The closer the homemakers are to each other, the less dependent they are on trans-portation and the more likely they are to see each other frequently. They will have issues in common besides their problems as women and as homemakers—their children will be attending the same schools, their investments in the neighborhood will be similar, their political units will be the same. Also, their socioeconomic status will probably be comparable, a fact that should eliminate some of the psychological bar-riers to organizing.

At the community level one can imagine an organization represent-ing a coalition of the neighborhood networks. This organization would be more likely to involve various socioeconomic groups, and it could represent homemaker interests in various community activities, from city council to school board. And then, ascending the organizational pyramid still further, there are the possibilities of state and national groups, both in contact with the grass-roots neighborhood networks.

The issues tackled at each level of homemaker organization would have in common the homemaker orientation, but they would probably differ considerably otherwise. The neighborhood networks would necessarily cope with the immediate and personal issues of home-making. Psychological satisfaction with the job, the need for contact with other adults, and planning for homemakers' financial security would all be addressed at this level. Community, state, and national organizations would be more heavily invested in issues involving or-ganizations for political action, and they would be in a better position to keep track of the overall status of homemakers.

In the next several pages we will look at just what might be accom-plished by homemaker organizations. In some cases I have made artifi-cial distinctions in order to make a point. For instance, I will discuss separately groups organized for consciousness-raising and groups or-ganized for sharing work. Obviously, in the real world one group may serve both purposes. The main purpose of the discussion is to indicate some of the goals that homemaker groups may want to set for them-selves. But there are no rules.

Consciousness-Raising

Consciousness-raising groups, also known as rap groups and, by some, as bitch sessions, have been a keystone of the women's movement. Half a dozen years ago they were springing up everywhere. They were an important way of creating and spreading the ideas of women's libera-tion.

Women changed their lives in those groups. They got support for leaving bad marriages. They heard that other women were frustrated and angry too. They learned that women don't have to compete with each other, and they made lifelong friends. They realized that they wanted more out of life than being "just a housewife."

Often the rap session led to activism. Women joined feminist organi-zations, or they took jobs and fought for equal employment opportuni-ties. The movement spread because through consciousness-raising it had touched women's lives.

Where is consciousness-raising today? To some extent it has been institutionalized. Training groups for women have assumed some of the old functions of consciousness-raising. Assertiveness training, transactional analysis for women, even training programs for women managers often include basic elements of feminist consciousness-raising. Women's studies programs at all educational levels have also fulfilled many of the same functions. NOW chapters still make an effort to run groups as part of their formal programs. For women in current groups, the old power of consciousness-raising is probably still there. But, for the movement as a whole, the excitement of consciousness-raising seems to have faded. Much less is heard about it than before; less energy is put into it.

Maybe consciousness-raising should be revived, and revived specifically with the homemaker in mind. It seems that, among women today, homemakers are the ones most in need of sharing their frustrations and problems, of creating a new self-consciousness and a new thrust of feminism. A logical place to start would be to organize rap sessions among homemakers who are neighbors, thus promoting neighborhood networks.

Like other consciousness-raising sessions, homemakers' sessions would make a special point of letting each woman tell her story fully, at her own pace and free from interruptions. The most important purpose of the group is sharing, rather than criticizing or even offering helpful suggestions. Like traditional consciousness-raising sessions, the homemakers' session would include efforts to find common threads among the participants' life stories.

However, to be effective, homemakers' consciousness-raising should provide a more focused perspective than traditional rap groups have given: while the traditional groups have usually been organized around women's issues in general, these groups will be organized around homemakers' issues, and there is a difference.

Picture two scenarios. In the first rap group, women share their stories and eventually arrive at the synthesis "we are oppressed in such and such a way because we are women." In a second group, members share their stories and arrive at the synthesis "we are oppressed in such and such a way because we are women and because we are homemakers." In the first group, the members have become more aware of the disadvantages of being female, which is a useful state of consciousness in itself. But in the second group the members will have the additional consciousness of the disadvantages of their work role, and to the extent that they see themselves as an oppressed set of workers their group will have more focus.

No one can be sure what effects this will have on the consciousness-raising effort. I would guess that, when a woman wants some changes in her life, heterogeneous consciousness-raising groups would be likely to encourage her to quit her homemaker role rather than to improve it, while homemaker consciousness-raising groups might have some tendency to improve the homemaker role rather than to avoid it. Since changes in the homemaker role are drastically needed, this is all to the good and should be a goal of these groups. But homemaker consciousness-raising groups will have to be especially sensitive to the tension between their group goals and the needs of their individual members. In some cases changing the role will not be possible; leaving it will be the only answer. The stories of six women who are or have been homemakers are included in chapter 4. These women range from the contented homemaker to the displaced homemaker and the battered homemaker. My interviews with them are included here in the hope that they will be useful as a tool in consciousness-raising.

Study Groups

A slightly different approach to organizing is to establish a study group for homemakers on homemaking. Several years ago this goal would have been laughable, but today there is much to study. The women's movement itself now has a history, and it has recaptured older feminist history. It will be important to understand the homemaker movement in context. Also, legislation of importance to homemakers has already been passed, NOW and the International Women's Year have taken stands on homemaker issues, and research on homemakers' lives has been published.

The organization of this book itself can be used to suggest topics and readings of specific interest to homemakers. The Introduction raises the basic issue of feminism and homemakers. To what extent do group members identify with the feminist movement? Do they have feminist friends? Are the friends homemakers or employed women? Do the friends believe in the importance of the homemaking role?

Chapter 1 can be used to spur discussion of homemakers' problems. We all know homemakers who have been poor, displaced, or disadvantaged in the job market. Group members will have—or may worry about having—similar issues in their own lives. Chapters 2 and 3 may help them put these issues into perspective and can encourage the reexamination of both personal and cultural values about homemaking and sex roles, work, and money.

Homemakers will want to test the ideas of chapter 5 against their own intuitions and informal experiments. They will want to compare themselves with the women studied in the chapter on the psychology of homemaking. Do they feel the same way as others about housework?

What do they believe about family power? They may want to read the chapter on alternative life-styles and ask what elements of such experiments are valid for their own ways of living.

And so on, through the book. Of course there are many other ways to organize the study group. Sessions organized around "What would you do if..." questions are often useful: What would you do if your husband decided to divorce you? What would you do if you became disabled? Or several sessions could be organized around comparing housework with other kinds of work in basic areas like compensation, security, safety, and opportunity for personal fulfillment and growth.

Service Co-ops

Service cooperatives provide yet another rationale for organizing: the common desire to minimize drudgery and expense by sharing housework. In recent years this has been the form of homemaker organization most often seen, and in some places it is quite common. Probably the most frequently enountered forms are baby-sitting cooperatives and bulk food-purchasing co-ops. Co-ops organized to share other aspects of homemaking are rarer. Occasionally two or more families will share cooking responsibilities. It seems that homemakers share routine housecleaning even less often, though this is probably the aspect of homemaking that is the most boring and that could be most improved by companionship.

One thing that is happening, of course, is that (for those who can afford it) commercial services are replacing homemaker services. This is especially true with meals—families are spending more and more money on restaurant foods. In terms of cost, quality, and companionship, however, one would think that the benefits of cooperative arrangements would outweigh the convenience (and often the inconvenience) of eating out. Frankly, why more homemakers do not organize to fight fast foods is a mystery to me.

Cottage Industries

Earning money at home seems to be one of the homemaker's fondest dreams. Yet I have many reservations about whether cottage industries will do more to help or to harm homemakers. On the one hand, working for money at home sounds like a reasonable idea—there is the reward of money itself, and if more than one homemaker is involved there is the potential for fighting isolation. There may also be dignity and satisfaction in the work. On the other hand, establishing a successful cottage industry is extremely difficult given homemakers' lack of resources. The potential for exploitation of the homemaker by various interest groups (mail-order businesses, to name one) is large; the homemaker's lack of mobility works against her ability to know the realistic outlets for her product.

Nevertheless, many homemakers seem determined to earn money at home. The question then is which cottage industries will best serve their needs. One can imagine two kinds. In the first, individual women take work into their homes, often on an hourly or piecework basis. Sometimes they do the traditional things—typing, tutoring, baby-sitting. Industries are becoming more interested in this arrangement. For instance, one typesetting company has provided dozens of individual homemakers with machines for doing their work; the women work when they can and are paid by the page. In another case the Prudential Insurance Company has established an experimental cottage industry for homebound new mothers who are already company executives. The women do special writing assignments such as proposals for group-insurance contracts or real-estate purchases. Both the company and the women benefit from the arrangement, in income and in employee continuity.[3]

Obviously this kind of cottage industry can benefit individual homemakers. Women can be near their families and earn money at the same time. It is important to recognize, however, that the benefits derive not from the homemaking, but from the employment. The woman's status may improve once she has contacts outside the home, and money, and a measure of independence because of the contacts and money. Her personal situation may be improved overall, but the status of her homemaking has not changed. Furthermore, this kind of cottage industry will not alleviate all the homemaker's problems: she will still be relatively isolated. She will still probably be underemployed. She may be bored. And she will be relatively powerless.

I hold out more hope for a second kind of cottage industry: work groups run for groups of homemakers. Such industries would make a point of getting women together to work, and as a group women may have more choices about the kinds of work they will do. These industries can provide the kind of forum that will create homemaker networks. Just getting homemakers together to discuss the need for a collective cottage industry may encourage discussions similar to those encountered in consciousness-raising and study groups: homemakers will be more likely to go into the industry with their eyes open to the need for maintaining the dignity of homemaking itself. Of course, most employers will not be motivated to organize their employees in this way; this kind of cottage industry is much more likely to be an enterprise owned by the homemakers themselves. As such it can combine the advantages of income with the advantages of group consciousness, interaction, and energy.

Homemakers Hiring Homemakers

The notion that homemakers can hire each other and thus qualify for government benefits like Social Security retirement and disability insurance is what first made me think seriously about homemakers as workers. Unlike cottage industries, this approach deals directly with the issue of compensating people for homemaking. It is a rather simple plan, requiring only rudimentary knowledge about qualifying for the government plans and a minimum of organization—any two homemakers could initiate it immediately. The plan may be an excellent way for homemakers to protect themselves while waiting for Social Security reform.

Dr. Jessie Hartline, associate professor of economics at Rutgers University, first proposed the idea in 1976. Basically, her strategy is as follows: Two homemakers agree to clean each other's homes for pay at whatever the representative rate for such work is—say $30 a day. By law, some of that pay must be contributed toward Social Security benefits. As employers, the women will also be required to contribute toward their employees' Social Security. However, most of the $30 will simply be exchanged equally, at no real cost to either woman. And both women will qualify as workers for purposes of Social Security benefits, workers' compensation for disability, and the Individual Retirement Accounts for the self-employed.

Hartline points out, "The reason I don't believe this has been thought of before is because most economists are men. They go home and their house is clean and dinner is ready . . . . This isn't a gimmick at all. If I put an ad in the paper to hire a housecleaner, and it turns out that the lady across the street answers the ad, that's fine, right? I would pay her for the work and if I choose to clean her house she would pay me . . . . The barrier to the idea, if there is one, isn't legal at all. It's psychological and organizational . . . women just have not thought along these lines."[4]

The response Hartline has received has ranged from "crumpled-up, chewed-up dollars from old ladies to help me in my work" to "male chauvinist letters written by women who think I'm terrible for proposing that their husbands be forced to pay for their work."[5]

Let us look at exactly how the system would work. A primary goal would be to earn credits for the Social Security benefits of retirement income, disability insurance, and life insurance (called survivors' insurance in the Social Security Administration literature). Credits are called quarters, based on credit for one-quarter year of work. Before 1978 most employees got credit for one-quarter year of work if they were paid $50 or more during a three-month calendar quarter (starting with January, April, July, or October). However, since 1978 all employees get one quarter of coverage for each $250 of earnings received during the entire year. To earn four quarters of credit, the employee must earn $1,000 during the year. No more than four quarters may be earned in any one calendar year, though if an employee earns more than $1,000 he will eventually get higher benefits because of his higher lifetime average earnings.

This means that a homemaker-employee must earn at least $250 to gain one quarter's credit. Suppose she is paid a wage of $30 a day. She will have to work a little less than eight and a half days to earn one quarter's credit. Since she is going to swap roles and pay her employer $30 a day, she will break even on the bulk of the $250. But the Social Security tax must be reckoned in as a real cost. In 1979–80 the tax is 6.13 percent each for employer and employee, or $15.33 per quarter (in 1981 it will be 6.65 percent, and it will rise to 7.65 percent by 1990). A homemaker-employee will have to pay the tax once as an employer and again as an employee for a total of $30.66 for each quarter of coverage. If she earns only the $1,000 minimum for the year, and if she pays only the $1,000 minimum, her annual Social Security cost will be $122.64. The only other additional cost would be the income tax she would pay, according to her family tax bracket.

According to the Social Security Administration, household workers include "maids, cooks, cleaning women, gardeners, handymen, etc., who perform housework in or about a private home. Babysitters, whether adult or teenage, are also included if they come to a private home to care for children."[6] Thus the range of duties for which you may employ someone in your home is quite large.

The bookkeeping involved is not extensive, but it is important; it establishes a record of the employer/employee relationship, and it provides the means for sending the necessary money to the Social Security Administration. Two forms must be filed. The first is a quarterly report. Before the end of the month after the calendar quarter the employer must send the taxes and a wage report (IRS form 942, the "Employer's Quarterly Tax Return for Household Employment") to the Internal Revenue Service. The second is an annual report. After the end of the year the employer completes IRS form W-2 and sends copies of it to the employee and to the Social Security Administration.

And just what does this time, effort, and investment buy? Several things, the usefulness of which depends on the financial situations of individual homemakers.

Perhaps the simplest benefit to calculate comes from Social Security life insurance. If a worker dies who has earned credits for at least one and a half years of work within the three years before death, benefits will be paid to the surviving spouse and children. This benefit may be particularly important to homemakers, who currently are likely to be out of the paid work force for several years or more. Of course the potential Social Security benefits must be weighed against the cost of privately sponsored life insurance policies. The benefits would be in monthly payments, the amount of which will depend in most cases on the amount of the worker's average covered earnings.

Another benefit is disability insurance. A worker is considered disabled if she cannot work because of a severe physical or mental impairment that has lasted or is expected to last for at least twelve months. Disability insurance will give her a monthly check, again based on her average covered earnings. Eligibility requirements for disability insurance fall into two areas. First, the worker must be "fully insured" according to Social Security definitions. The requirement for this status varies with age. For instance, you are fully insured if you are thirty-two years old or older and have ten quarters of credit, or if you are twenty-eight years old or younger and have six quarters of credit. Today many homemakers have worked in traditional jobs for a year or two before taking on full-time housekeeping responsibilities, and so many will be fully insured. However, those who may need this protection the most—those who have not worked outside the home at all—will not have met this standard.

The second eligibility requirement for disability insurance is that of recently earned quarters. A worker thirty-one or older must have credit for five years of work within the ten-year period ending when she becomes disabled, or, if the worker becomes disabled between ages twenty-four and thirty-one, credit is needed for half the time between age twenty-one and the time of disability. Consider this typical case. A woman graduates from college and is employed for three years. At the age of twenty-four she begins a stint of full-time homemaking. Unless she accumulates additional credits, she will be eligible for disability coverage only until she is twenty-seven. After that she should try to earn credits for at least half of every year in order to maintain her eligibility until she is thirty-one (at which point the requirements change slightly). On the other hand, consider the situation of an older woman who has been out of the paid work force for ten years or more.

She will have to start from scratch and accumulate twenty quarters of coverage.

The eligibility requirements for retirement benefits are similarly based on a minimum required number of quarter credits. However, in this case, quarters earned at any time in a person's life may be counted. No one needs more than forty quarters of work to qualify for at least the minimum benefits. Whether the retirement benefits will be important to homemakers depends greatly on individual circumstances. Most homemakers will be married, and if married at least ten years will be eligible for a spouse's benefit when their husbands retire. These women can choose either the spouse's benefit or the benefit they would earn on their own employment record, whichever is greater. Earning the minimum amount in any given quarter may boost their average lifetime earnings somewhat, but not much. (As it is, years out of the paid work force are averaged in as "$0.") On the other hand, some homemakers may not stay married long enough to qualify for the spouse's benefit, and simply getting quarters of coverage at *any* rate may be important to them.

These, then, are the primary Social Security benefits for which homemaker-employees would be eligible. They would also be eligible for other government programs. As workers not employed in companies with pension plans, they would be eligible to establish Individual Retirement Accounts covering a percentage of their annual income. And they would be able to deduct their cleaning materials, transportation expenses, and other business expenses just as any other self-employed businessperson can.

A basic question underlying the whole proposal is whether it is legal. At this point it is certainly not illegal—there is no law or rule against it. Under some conditions even relatives can hire each other and thus qualify for Social Security benefits. Probably then there is ample justification for two unrelated persons hiring each other.

If the homemakers-hiring-homemakers arrangement is ever challenged, a number of court decisions have set some precedent in favor of it. In one case a United States District Court judge stated that, "Although individuals can arrange their affairs in a manner which allows them to qualify for Social Security benefits, the Secretary is not bound to accept allegations of services performed in the absence of proof thereof." Note first here the assumption that individuals can arrange their affairs in order to qualify. In this case it was further noted that the testimony of the plaintiff and the alleged employer is not sufficient proof of the arrangement. More acceptable proof would be such things as registration with appropriate state agencies and a requirement to work definite hours.[7]

Another court decision accentuates the need to keep records at the time of the employer/employee relationship. In denying eligibility, a court stated that, "The late filing of certain of the returns cast doubt as to whether they stood for a valid employer-employee relationship."[8]

A 1972 decision is reassuring about the legitimacy of homemakers' intentions to be eligible for Social Security: "The fact that the claimant's work was motivated by a desire to establish eligibility for benefits was irrelevant."[9]

Aside from the obvious financial and security benefits, the plan will have other important effects on homemakers' lives. Perhaps most important, it will encourage interaction and organization. Of course the simplest arrangement is one in which two homemakers hire each other. Even working in pairs can help homemakers overcome isolation—it will require a certain amount of interaction. It may also help them overcome any sensitivity about the habitual state of their households. The mere fact that one homemaker will be doing another's housework is a bit revolutionary. One may hope that the old cliché about cleaning before the maid comes will fall by the wayside.

More complex arrangements involving three or more homemakers are of course possible and provide even more opportunity for interaction. Possibilities may arise, too, for specialization of labor. Within a team, a homemaker may specialize in a task she prefers—and then hire herself out to homemakers who loathe that particular chore. The efficiency of the team effort may also create more free time for the homemakers involved.

A typical plan might look like this: Sara and Jane and Fran all have preschool children and work full time as homemakers. The three women are all in their late twenties or early thirties. Two of them live near each other; the third has access to a car twice a week. Together the women decide what they want from their homemaking co-op: Sara and Jane have been employed before and feel they need only enough quarter credits to keep their entitlement to disability and survivors' benefits—they want to earn enough money to qualify for two quarters a year. Fran, on the other hand, has not been employed and wants more than two credits: she hopes to become entitled to at least three or even four quarters of credit by continuing co-op work and outside work. The women have decided they do not have the energy or resources to start a cottage industry, but they do want to get together more often and to increase their free time.

The women note that summer (June through August) is a hectic time for their families, primarily because of outings and vacations, and that the holiday month of December is also busy. They decide to confine the co-op to the other eight months of the year. They determine that a reasonable rate for their services is $35 a day, and that to earn the qualifying minimum of $500 they must each work about fifteen days during the eight months. This works out to about one day every other week, but the women want a regular weekly schedule. They decide that they will work Mondays, Wednesdays, and Fridays, one day at each home, from 9 A.M. until 1 P.M., for fifteen weeks.

The basic kinds of work to be done are determined in advance. Sara, for instance, hates doing dishes, so she makes it clear that she plans to leave some from the night (and maybe even the week) before. Fran has decided to take a part-time job during the four hours when the team is at her home, and she has made it clear that one of her homemaker-employees' jobs will be baby-sitting. In all cases it is assumed that the employer need not be present as supervisor—for those four hours a week she is free to do as she likes.

I have already discussed the obvious advantages of such group systems. There are some other interesting points. With a group of three, a homemaker-employer is not dependent on the availability of one other homemaker. With two homemaker-employees working at a time, there is a built-in backup system in case any one of the dozen things that might happen in a family does. The co-op thus gives Fran a relatively reliable base for her part-time job. Also, each home worker will have a companion, which would not necessarily be true if only two homemakers had exchanged services. All this, and financial protection for themselves and their families as well—at a cost to each woman of about $5.36 per month plus tax. (Fifteen days × $35 is the total wage paid per homemaker-employee, amounting to $525 a year; 6.13 percent of that total is $32.18, to be paid twice by each partner, for a total of $64.36 in annual costs per homemaker-employer.)

Local Political Action

It will also be useful for homemakers to have more representatives in local government. The constituency for this representation can be the aware homemakers of the community—those who are dedicated, at least for the time being, to improving, rather than leaving, their jobs. A constituency of homemaker networks will not be essential, but it will probably be useful in supporting representatives who will face interest groups that are far more powerful in commanding resources and money. To represent the interests of the relatively resourceless, unpaid homemaker in the mire of local politics will indeed be challenging.

The kinds of part-time political positions that may be of particular interest to homemakers themselves will probably involve community planning—positions on zoning boards, city councils, township boards, community planning and management commissions, housing commissions, parks and recreation commissions, and public works of all kinds.

They will often be most interested in power issues central to the future of their communities: where to put a shopping center or a park, how much money should go to one neighborhood versus another, whether to support public transportation. In all these decisions women, and particularly homemakers, have a stake, yet they tend to be largely unrepresented (even by their husbands.)

If the idea of homemaker-politicians seems farfetched, consider the following. Reading what sociologists and urban planners tell us about the importance of our physical environment can raise our consciousness of how that environment shapes our lives. It can help homemakers see how affecting local policy can create a better life-style.

For instance, in his 1977 book comparing an American suburb with a Swedish suburb, sociologist David Popenoe shows us how women's lives are affected by their physical community.[10] Popenoe compares Levittown, New Jersey, and Vallingby, near Stockholm, both planned suburbs constructed in the fifties. Though different in major environmental characteristics, both were built to house similar populations.

I cannot do justice here to the richness of Popenoe's study, but I can point out a few salient ideas. In one section the author describes the types of people for whom a suburb like Levittown is detrimental. (He notes that, paradoxically, the individuals involved do not want to leave Levittown, and that in general Levittowners are well pleased.) One of these types is the trapped housewife. Popenoe found fewer of these women than he had expected, perhaps because his sample tapped very few women with young children. One that he does describe is the mother of a two-year-old boy. She has lived in Levittown for three years. Her husband is a construction worker. She has no car, and, though she occasionally goes out with her husband, her social life centers on her woman friends in the neighborhood. All her friends lead similar lives, and so even socializing with them does not provide the stimulation and variety that this homemaker needs. Levittown is a typical suburb consisting primarily of single-family dwellings; it does not offer much else.

A similar story is that of the dependent woman. She is a widow, or perhaps a divorcée. She has no job and, perhaps suddenly, she is without income. Living in Levittown exacerbates her dependency: "The lack of public transportation will keep her employment situation problematic, maintenance of the house will tax her ingenuity and her resources, her home-bound life will offer little variety, and she will find it difficult to make ends meet financially."[11] Without going into detail, Vallingby has the public transportation, the cheaper housing, and the richer local culture that this homemaker needs, and the people there seem to be better off because of city design.

These then are some of the issues that should concern home-makers—public transportation, available jobs, social variety, and afford-ability of a dwelling. Others are the presence or absence of local public space, of sidewalks and bike paths, of retail services. As Popenoe notes:

> The pattern of environmental influence not only operates in situa-tions which we would label incongruent; on a day-to-day basis, over long periods of time, people are quietly and subtly adjusting their own behaviors, values, and even needs to the characteristics of the environments in which they find themselves. Many and perhaps most of these adjustments may be of little importance both for the individuals involved and for the society around them; and the ad-justments will often be overwhelmed by the more powerful in-fluences of nonenvironmental factors such as family, income level, religious beliefs, or messages from the mass media. But some may also have lasting personal and social significance, more than is com-monly realized.[12]

Nonpolitical Local Organization

The scope of nonpolitical kinds of organization is as broad as the imagination. Let me list just a few ideas. Within existing organizations, homemakers can organize subcommittees and task forces for non-political purposes. From women's clubs to the National Organization for Women, many groups will be receptive to special programs for homemakers. These programs may at first set out to inform, perhaps later producing homemaker networks of the kinds I have described. Or homemakers may continue as an ongoing interest group within these organizations.

Furthermore, civic groups designed especially for homemakers could be started. Where now we have the League of Women Voters and Jay-cees' Auxiliary, we could also have a homemaker's organization dedi-cated to service projects of special relevance to them.

Another way homemakers might wish to organize would be related to their spouses' paid work: homemakers married to employees of a given company might organize to provide a united front in support of desirable company policies. Companies may be glad to be systemat-ically in touch with the opinions of employees' spouses, especially with regard to such issues as flextime, vacations, transfers, and other policies directly affecting whole families. For their part, the homemakers will want to suggest such options to employers who have not yet seriously considered them.

State Actions

The potential for action on the state level will develop out of a network of smaller homemaker groups, or it may be part of already existing larger programs such as those carried out by the National Organization for Women. To some extent the latter strategy has already been effective—homemakers have been an important part of NOW membership, and as such have had some influence on their own behalf as well as on behalf of all women. In some cases homemakers may choose not to affiliate with NOW—a group called, for instance, the Michigan Homemakers' Coalition, could have enormous media appeal. It would not run the risk of losing energy to other issues. It could emphasize to the public the importance of homemaking. And, depending on the state, it could tap the power of that large bloc of voters who are homemakers.

National Actions

On the national scene homemakers have the same choice: Should they organize a separate homemaker organization, or should they affiliate with other organizations? My own choice would be the latter, and I specifically suggest that homemakers affiliate with the National Organization for Women, partly because NOW is well organized and respected, and partly because it already has an operating homemaker task force. Through affiliation with NOW, homemakers can expect to tap legislative and other professional expertise that would be much more difficult to obtain on their own.

Separate organizations of homemakers on a national scale have been attempted with only small success. The Martha Movement is the best known of these. The Martha Movement gained national attention and began publishing its newsletter *Martha Matters* in 1976. It now seems that it has attracted some homemakers but has repelled many others. The newsletter, for instance, has been criticized for being a "how-to" piece resembling magazines like *Woman's Day*.[13] Lead articles have included "The Psychological Aspects of Housekeeping," "Self-Esteem, What It Is," and "Tips for Making Money at Home."

The organization ran into financial difficulties in late 1977. Its founder, Jinx Melia, had counted on attracting financial support as a nonprofit organization and had therefore not expected its low membership dues to fully support the organization. Publication of the newsletter was temporarily suspended until contributions ranging from $100 to $3,000 were arranged from the McDonald Corporation, General Mills Foundation, Life Cycle Ministries/Church of the Brethren, and individuals.

By winter 1978 only three Martha chapters had been chartered. The promise to announce more chapters in the next newsletter was not sustained. In later newsletters several dozen homemakers across the country have been reported as wanting to start chapters, though as of this time no new chapter charters have been announced. The Martha Movement may yet succeed, but the prognosis is not good.

Compared with what might be achieved through NOW, improvements in homemakers' status through the Martha Movement are likely to be slow in coming. In summer 1978 the movement was looking for a member to write a regular column on the homemaker and politics simply to inform its members; at about the same time, NOW was actually lobbying in Washington and the states for specific new legislation. Its finances and support are worrisome, too. With major funding from corporations like McDonald's and with board members from corporations like Avon, it seems likely that the organization might not be able to achieve the autonomy it needs to fully represent homemakers' interests.

Perhaps the Martha Movement can significantly increase communication among homemakers. It may reach and encourage homemakers who have been reluctant to identify with avowedly feminist organizations like NOW. But the Martha Movement and other potential national homemaker organizations need to reconsider basic issues like funding and goals if they are to gain a national constituency and the power to influence national policy.

Coalitions of Working Women

Many employed women have realized that, as women and as workers, they have many problems in common. Coalitions of employed women have been formed across industries, across women's organizations, and even across hierarchical levels within industries. Problems they have attacked range from equal opportunity to sexual assault on the job.

The need for coalitions between organizations in the women's movement and other workers' organizations has been widely recognized. In a speech before a convention of the International Union of Electrical Radio and Machine Workers at the Pittsburgh Hilton Hotel, Eleanor Smeal, president of NOW, said that labor's fight for justice on the job is women's fight, that women are the most underemployed and lowest-paid workers, and that to fight for women is to fight for all workers. Among the national organizations supporting the Equal Rights Amendment are the American Nurses Association, Federally Employed Women, the National Federation of Business and Professional Women's Clubs, and the AFL-CIO.

A number of writers have recognized that homemaker and employee issues—that is, worker issues—must be attacked simultaneously. Among them is Jean Tepperman, who describes actions to take when both the homemaker and the employee issues are embodied in the same women:

> When people in the Movement talk about women who work in factories, they ask whether these women are exploited basically as *workers* or as *women*. You can answer that only if you divide up what happens in an artificial way. A movement for the liberation of factory women would have to take a whole new form, one which dealt with the problems together, in a way that traditional male unionism or traditional middle-class feminism cannot. The movement would have to attack exploitation on the job and in the home simultaneously to win changes that would make a real difference. I have this personal vision of a factory women's movement that would fight against the plant, wage a campaign for state-supported day-care centers, abortions, etc., and all of whose members would take a pledge to do only 50 percent of the housework at home—all this backed up by support squads of women trained in karate.[14]

Moreover, when homemaker and employee issues are primarily embodied in separate women, the need for coalitions becomes especially important.

Housekeeping by Employees

About a third of all female employees work in clerical jobs.[15] Homemakers are likely to assume these jobs part time, or to move into them full time after a number of years in homemaking. For this reason alone homemakers and office workers have an interest in working together. As it is, homemakers make up a pool of cheap labor from which employers can draw, and thus they threaten the jobs of clerical workers. Unionization of office workers may make their jobs better paying and more secure.[16] Enlightened unionization—organizing so that flextime and part-time work become viable options—may be to the advantage of both homemakers and employees.

These days there is some sentiment among clerical workers that may be a barrier to their recognizing homemakers as a kindred group. I am referring, of course, to some secretaries' refusal to do personal and housekeeping business for their bosses. On National Secretaries' Day, one New York organization sponsored a contest to find the most ridiculous among such personal services. The winner was a secretary who was asked to take family-album photographs of her boss before and after he shaved off his moustache.

A more common complaint is the requirement to make the boss's coffee. I sympathize with the secretaries' position. They believe they are in the office to do a job, not to perform personal services. They want the power to define what their work will be. Many have sought employment precisely because they consider themselves independent women, not servants, and they see themselves as contributing real work to society—not doing housework for their bosses. Furthermore, they feel that, since their work has required training, it is more important than "other" work (like housework). The organization that ran the contest used the slogan "An office worker is trained, not maid."

I am concerned that there may be a lack of empathy here: the slogan shows a clear lack of respect for all "maid's work." The secretaries seem to be rebelling against the housework component of their jobs because they see it as demeaning. My argument in this book is, of course, that housework is not demeaning in and of itself, but only under certain social and economic conditions. It is not demeaning, but it is demeaned. A refusal to do housework because it is "dirty work" is, I believe, misplaced. (If it were inherently so demeaning, I would suggest that all homemakers quit immediately.) Instead, the housework component of a paid work role should be evaluated just as a homemaker should evaluate housework: according to the values she holds. What is the purpose of the task? Secretaries who are comfortable with making the coffee may well believe that in doing so they are saving their bosses' time, and that this is an important goal of their employment. On the other hand, if the boss stands by watching while the coffee is made, that is an entirely different situation.

It is unfortunate in the long run that housework done in the office has become the symbol of women's low status there. The result will be one more blow to the status of homemaking. The powerless, low-paid position of women, the fact that men usually are not secretaries (And would the boss ask a male secretary to make the coffee?)—these real problems will receive correspondingly less energy.

Coalitions of homemakers and clerical workers, of homemakers and any employees who do housework as part of their job, may be able to raise people's consciousness about these issues.

Domestic Workers and Homemakers

Forming coalitions of domestic workers and homemakers will also be important, but it will be difficult. This time the status differential will be in the opposite direction; while secretaries may see themselves as having a better position than homemakers, homemakers generally see themselves as better off than domestic workers. And yet homemakers and domestic workers have a great deal in common.

Often the role of the homemaker is presented as challenging and worthwhile, while that of the hired domestic worker, who is really the homemaker's closest counterpart in the paid labor force, is derided. Rarely is the hypocrisy of a double standard for paid domestic workers and unpaid homemakers squarely faced. Yet, if a domestic worker is deserving of only a low status, then so is the homemaker; if a domestic worker deserves only the lowest pay, then so does the homemaker. An analogous situation is the role of the day-care worker: these workers are paid very little because their work is seen as nearly valueless; after all, women have been doing it free for centuries. So, while the homemaker's status is low, it is not quite as low as that of these lowest-paid workers, and homemakers have resisted being associated with them.

Coalitions of homemakers and domestic workers may be especially difficult to form because of perceived class differences. At the very least women who are employers should not exploit their domestic workers. They should see to it that they have livable wages, Social Security coverage, vacations, sick days, accident insurance, paid holidays, decent working conditions, and reasonable performance standards. One might also expect homemaker organizations to fully support groups that are working to improve the status and the quality of working life for domestic workers.

Barriers

So far the tone of this chapter has been relatively optimistic. I have intended it to be, for I feel strongly that increasing homemakers' communication and group cohesiveness is important to improving their status over the long run.

But this organization will not come easily. To repeat: it is extremely difficult to organize people who work in separate buildings, on separate time schedules, and within different social settings (families). And as if these common characteristics of the homemaker's job weren't enough, there are also a number of other serious barriers.

Homemakers have limited resources at their disposal. They have time, but it is usually disjointed time, often dependent on young children or on schedules of other family members. One might hope that the homemaker would have at least one night out a week, but often she does not. Homemakers have some personal money, but usually not much. As we have noted, they may not even have consistent access to transportation.

Then there is the problem of awareness. How many homemakers know very much about their personal financial situation—their Social Security quarters, their disability insurance, and all the other things I have discussed in this book? How many know how to organize a co-op or run for local office? How many even know their own strength in numbers—that there are thirty-five million women in this country in just about the same position?

There are also several psychological barriers. Unfortunately, reform that has already been achieved through organizations like NOW, the Alliance for Displaced Homemakers, and the International Women's Year may actually hinder the formation of homemaker networks. Homemakers may feel that their work is being done for them; some of the urgency of their commitment may be lost. One trouble with this, of course, is that the organizations just mentioned deal primarily with state and federal issues and work mostly toward changing the law. The wide range of local government and community influence, and basic economic and psychological issues, are largely untapped by them. Much has been achieved without homemaker networks and coalitions, but with them much more could be done.

We cannot overlook the possibility that many women who are homemakers may be fundamentally different from women who do not choose that role. Maybe homemakers are particularly nonassertive; maybe they simply do not like joining organizations. Perhaps they for one reason or another are particularly susceptible to a "slave mentality"—that way of thinking in which a slave avers her eternal gratitude and satisfaction because she happens to have a benevolent master. If any of these propositions are true for a large percentage of homemakers—and at this point we have no idea whether they are— organizing homemakers will be accordingly difficult.

Another psychological issue is privacy. Under present ways of thinking there is something inviolable about a person's home, and perhaps even more so about a person's housework. Homemakers really do clean before the maid comes. Then too there is the desire for privacy in financial matters. These needs for privacy may be expected to interfere with housecleaning co-ops and with co-ops organized to improve the homemaker's financial status.

Finally, we have to deal with the American ethic of individualism. Homemakers are hardly exempt from our cultural belief in the merit of individual effort and the ability of the individual to overcome barriers to his or her goals. Thus, the most likely course for a frustrated homemaker is individual action—changing her own way of doing housework, or going back to school part time, or taking a part-time job. Individual strategies may be fine in some cases, but most often they involve getting away from homemakers' problems rather than solving them. Because individual strategies tend to avoid homemaking rather than to affirm it, they have limited usefulness in the long run and for homemakers as a class.

The idea of collective action is foreign, perhaps especially to women. Yet, if homemakers are to get the moral support and the resources they need to challenge social institutions, they must organize. They must resist the American ethic of individualism. If they do not, they will continue to be divided and, effectively, conquered.

The Displaced Homemaker

9

They were Total Women. Perfect. Careerists in homemaking. Mid-game, the rules change: Marriage is no longer a lifetime engagement. "We've grown apart," Sam Buckley announces to Helen one night just shy of their thirty-second anniversary. (These are not their real names.) Two days later Sam departs. Helen has been fired from marriage. She is a walking obsolescence, tossed on the scrap heap of laid-off wives.

Erica Abeel[1]

These women are faced with every crisis you can think of. They are usually unemployed, unskilled, ignorant of money and credit matters, isolated, ill-equipped to care for themselves and, often, have no money.

Tish Sommers[2]

In 1974 in Oakland, California, Tish Sommers was working with a rap group of older women. Then in her late fifties, and national coordinator of NOW's Task Force on Older Women, she was concerned that the women were having trouble getting jobs because of their age. So Tish Sommers coined the term "displaced homemaker," a phrase she chose specifically to emphasize that these women are part of a whole group who have been forcibly removed from their occupations. These are women who through a divorce or their spouse's death or other sudden loss of income are compelled to leave their long-term jobs as homemakers to find salaried work in what is more often than not an alien environment. In May 1975 the Alliance for Displaced Homemakers, a grass-roots organization of older women and "honorary older women" who are interested in helping the displaced homemaker, was organized to lobby for the needs of women. Tish Sommers and Laurie Shields have been that group's national coordinators; to a large extent it has been their effort and leadership that have made the displaced homemaker a national issue. Today this organization has been supplanted by the Displaced Homemakers' Network, a national group headquartered in Washington, D.C.

There are at least three million displaced homemakers in America today. There is a national potential for millions more among the women

186

whose minor children now qualify them for various kinds of support but who will be without benefits when their children reach majority. All these women have been doing unpaid labor in the home and either have actually had or would have problems in getting jobs. They have been dependent on another family member for their financial support, but now that support is not longer available.

"What binds all of us together," says Laurie Shields, "is the belief that a homemaker's days of usefulness are not over when our husbands die or when divorce breaks up our homes. We are just finding our collective voice and what we are saying is that we are not ready for the scrap heap, we are not content to opt for general assistance in order to survive and even while we recognize that ours is a male-dominated, youth oriented society, we older women in the adolescence of our aging are not willing to bury our particular talents."[3] Or, as one California judge put it as he decided the case of a forty-four-year-old woman divorced after twenty-five years of marriage:

> A woman is not a breeding cow to be nurtured during her years of fecundity, and then, conveniently and economically converted to cheap steaks when past her prime. If a woman is able to support herself, she certainly should do so. If, however, she has spent her productive years as a housewife and mother and has missed the opportunity to compete in the job market and improve her job skills, quite often she becomes, when divorced, simply a "displaced homemaker."[4]

Who Are the Displaced Homemakers?

Displaced homemakers are our mothers, our wives, our daughters—or perhaps ourselves. They are all around us, yet each of them tells a story uniquely her own. Displaced homemakers may be women like Merle Nelson, who in testimony before the House Subcommittee on Employment Opportunities said, "I went through the process of being a displaced homemaker, and when I went to the Department of Manpower Affairs to seek a job, I was told that at 43, and married for 21 years (I had been a teacher) . . . that there was no place for me in the job market."[5] Merle Nelson is now the Honorable Merle Nelson, representative to the Maine legislature.

They are women like Jean Dixon, one of the first women helped by the Center for Displaced Homemakers in Oakland, California, who upon being displaced dropped from an upper-middle-class income to poverty level. (Finally, with the help of the center, she bounced back to get a decent job.) And they are women like the one who wrote the following letter to Sommers and Shields when they had made an appearance on the "Phil Donahue Show":

Dear Ms. Shields and Ms. Sommers,

Your appearance on the Donahue show this morning has made me feel like a person again for the first time in over two years. In 1974 my husband died suddenly and in a matter of a few horrible hours I became a 55 year old widow . . . a classic example of all the things talked about on the show. I spent 33½ years of my marriage making a home for my husband and 3 children. I have developed no working skills and have been unsuccessful in finding any sort of a job. The opportunities are limited in a small town and are naturally filled by the young. Consequently, my funds grow smaller along with my shrinking ego. The 2½ years until I reach 60 stretch interminably. 71½% of my husband's Social Security will be no big deal at best. Preoccupation with grief, unexpected responsibility, rejection by potential employers, limited funds has made me feel alone and apart from life. After months of desperation I have lately begun to think of death as an attractive alternative. Which brings me to this morning's TV show! Suddenly I don't feel quite so hopeless and unworthy. As I watched and listened I began to see that I am not alone. Indeed, my situation is anything but unique. I think I might even have one or two faint assets.

This letter was only one of thousands that Sommers and Shields received.

Rose House, a displaced homemaker from Baltimore, told the following personal story in testimony before a House of Representatives subcommittee considering displaced homemaker legislation:

After nearly 42 years of happily married life, I was widowed in 1975. I had only worked outside my home for six years during my life, and I had stopped working several years earlier when my husband became ill. When I worked, I worked in a library referencing books, and this allowed me some money of my own to pay for extras. When my husband died, my only income became a little insurance he had carried. I wasn't yet eligible for Social Security, and at my age, I knew finding employment would be difficult.

I asked myself was I going to collapse or build a new life? I had raised five children of my own and two others, and I thought I was strong enough to begin anew.

But it was hard. For the first time in many years, I had to live on next to no income. I applied for a widow's pension, but I was not yet eligible. I started looking around for work, and nothing was available.

Even with the widow's pension I would need to find another source
of income. I was depressed and began to feel like nothing was going
to help me. I went back several times to agencies that said they could
find work for older women, but nothing happened for me. I wanted
very much to stay in my own home, but I knew I had to find work to
do.[6]

We don't know much about the millions of women who may be in
similar positions, because homemakers are excluded from conventional
data collection systems. Further, most helping agencies have not directed their services to these women, and thus they have no estimates of
their numbers. In fact, when the planners for the Maryland Displaced
Homemaker Center, one of the first of two such centers in the country,
set out to poll more than two hundred agencies in their state about the
potential need for the center, not one agency that replied had identified
the displaced homemaker as a potential client, and none had any way of
counting these women.

Today Maryland estimates that it has 286,000 displaced homemakers.
And the Alliance for Displaced Homemakers has estimated that nationwide there are potentially fifteen million. Of course, as the number of
older persons in the population grows, the number of displaced homemakers is also likely to rise.

According to Nancie Fadeley, the state representative who introduced a displaced homemakers bill in Oregon, "If there is one thing
we have learned in Oregon, it is that the general estimates of the target
population of displaced homemakers are far too low. Understandably
so, since hard figures are difficult to come by, given the fact that homemaking isn't counted as 'work' and therefore, out-of-work homemakers
aren't counted!"[7]

Help for the Displaced Homemaker

In response to a growing awareness of the problems of displaced
homemakers, many states have followed the lead of Maryland and
California and have established pilot centers to provide needed services
(see chap. 10). In general, all of the centers' services are available to
displaced homemakers of either sex, though the vast majority of their
clients are women. Their main emphasis is on training their clients to
be job-ready. One of the earliest and best-known centers is in Baltimore, Maryland.

The Maryland bill was introduced by Delegate Helen Koss in 1976. It
originally called for multipurpose centers in each county and in the city
of Baltimore, but it was severely amended by the state House Ways and

Means Committee so that at passage it authorized only one pilot displaced homemaker center. New Directions for Women received a contract from the Maryland State Department of Human Resources to set up the center, and the group worked closely with many private and government agencies to design their program.

Generally, programs initiated by legislative action have included five main components. First, peer counseling—usually older women counseling older women, displaced homemakers counseling displaced homemakers—is established. Second, there is an evaluation of the homemaker's native or acquired skills. Third is job training, and, fourth, job placement. Training without referral does not help, because the women still face subtle discrimination in the job market. So finally, and perhaps most important, the centers are to assist in identifying community needs and in creating new jobs in the public and private sectors that will use the skills the homemakers have developed.

The Maryland Center

Housed in a brick row house in a modest section near downtown Baltimore, the Maryland Displaced Homemaker Center is physically unimposing. A small sign for the program hangs in the front bay window, and you enter by a short flight of marble steps that are, I'm told, "typical old Baltimore." The office/reception room is decorated with cheerful graphics, and the open room beyond is a drop-in lounge, complete with pop machine and a perennial pot of coffee, and probably a few women chatting or working. Upstairs are two more floors of offices and meeting rooms.

It is a pleasant place, both physically and psychologically—impressive for an atmosphere both businesslike and welcoming. And it is reasonably well equipped, from the duplicating equipment down to the intraoffice memo device, a rope-and-basket affair that hangs down the stairwell from the third floor and runs strictly on woman-power.

It is obvious that the center has been well planned. After Helen Koss sponsored the law to fund it, and when the state of Maryland passed the legislation in the spring of 1976, the group selected to set it up was New Directions for Women, a private, nonprofit organization that has focused on the employment needs of women since 1973. New Directions for Women (NDW) has been funded by the Comprehensive Employment and Training Act of 1973 (CETA), the Maryland Commission for the Humanities and Public Policy, private foundations, contributions, and revenue from their Career Guidance program.

NDW is around the corner from the Displaced Homemaker Center and still maintains administrative ties with it. It is itself a model employment center, operating as a work cooperative and using tandem and part-time staffing patterns. It is no accident that NDW and the Displaced Homemaker Center are so close to each other: their proximity is part of a long-range community plan to consolidate some crucial social services in a relatively small and accessible area of Baltimore.

Using the experience of their staff, and in consultation with some outside agencies, NDW set the Displaced Homemaker Center in operation in November 1976. The center was originally funded at $190,000 a year for three years, the funds being administered by the state Department of Human Resources.

Originally the center had been projected to serve only thirty displaced homemakers. But the amount of time and money needed by each displaced homemaker had been overestimated; experience has shown that the range of needs is wide, and that many people can be helped in a less intensive program. Thus, in the first nine months of its operation, more than four hundred displaced homemakers received resource assistance, workshops, training, counseling, or employment assistance from the center, and more than one thousand persons received information and referral. Seventy persons have already become job-ready or have been placed in permanent employment. Director Cynthia Marano suggests that probably twice as many displaced homemakers could be trained if the funds for further traineeships were available.[8]

More than 90 percent of those who sought the services of the center have had incomes of less than six thousand dollars a year. Their educational range is broad, but only slightly more than half of the women who have used the center have finished high school. (In the overall American population, about two-thirds of the women have at least a high-school education.)

Betty June Bongiovanni is one of the homemakers who has been helped by the center. Her case is typical in that she has lost what she considered to be her job—homemaking—and has had difficulties in finding other work.

For twenty-one years she had built a life with her husband and three sons, living in a modest row house in northeast Baltimore, attending church, supporting the Boy Scouts. "Like Ethel Kennedy," she says, she married a man who seemed too good to be true. But her husband died at age forty-two, leaving her with few financial resources. Betty June did have a high-school diploma, but she had only two years' work experience, and that was from the 1950s. She could find only temporary office work.

After several years of inaction—she stayed home, didn't even visit relatives, and gained fifty pounds—Betty June found the center and found that she needed it. She doesn't like the term "displaced home-maker," because "It sounds embarrassing, like I couldn't do something, like I failed." But she has also come to a realization about her ability to help herself. "It's humbling to think that for months I kept saying, 'You can get a job, Betty June, you can get a job.' But I couldn't. So I needed the center."

Cynthia Marano points out, "People come to us in a crisis and often within a period of self-assessment, and find in that crisis an opportunity. They come to us with a lot of fears, often well-founded fears.... These people are unique in that they're not getting help from anywhere else."[9]

To be eligible for the center's training, homemakers must be over thirty-five and unemployed or underemployed. They must have been primarily homemakers—that is, they must have depended on the income of a family member and lost that income in part or wholly as the result of separation, divorce, or the death or disability of that family member. Or they may have depended on government assistance as the parent of dependent children—children under the age of eighteen who have lost a parent—and are no longer eligible for that assistance because the children have come of age.

Barbara Turner has worked as the Maryland Center's program coordinator. Like many of the staff members, she herself is a displaced homemaker. In a rap session for homemakers new to the program she told her own story:

> The women who come here are over 35.... They got married in a time when the world was so different. Twenty years ago or 25 years ago if you were married the only things you worried about were whether your husband had a good job, that you had a nice house, and that you had healthy children—and a lot of them. Twenty or 25 years later you're divorcing in a place where it doesn't matter where you live... [where you are asked] "why did you have all those children" and "what are you going to do with the rest of your life?" ... That was not the question 25 years ago. If I got married that was expected of me.
>
> And when I got a divorce there was nothing that I could hold onto from my past life that was of any value to me... nothing worked, it really didn't.... I really had to start from scratch. I had to make up new relationships with my kids that I was really comfortable with, because we had kind of gotten into playing games. We lived in the suburbs and we got into those traps.... Not that they're bad—if you can live in them and survive in them they're OK, but... we didn't.... So we just had to untangle ourselves from all that and that was really terrible.

I was like a stranger in a foreign land. I really didn't know the rules of this new place that I was. I've adapted . . . but I still find myself hesitant about a lot of things.

Fortunately I knew a woman who had done very pretty much the same thing and was a year and a half ahead of me in the process, so when I felt like I was going crazy I would call her and tell her basically what was going on . . . . That really was my salvation: . . . that somebody else had done it and had made it through.

The Training Experience

When a displaced homemaker like Barbara first comes to the center, she spends some time talking with an intake interviewer who is likely to be a displaced homemaker herself, and whose job as interviewer is probably part of her center training. The interviewer determines the woman's eligibility for the program and sets up an appointment with a counselor.

In the individual counseling session the women put their heads together to determine immediate and long-range goals. The counselor offers support, but not psychological services. Rosa Turner of the center staff has pointed out, "Many of the women who come through the doors have had psychological counseling and don't want that . . . . We deal more with trying to cope with what's happening *now*, rather than the orientation to why you're feeling this way." As one displaced homemaker put it, "When I walked in, I felt like somebody cared what happened while I was wondering where I was going, what I was going to do, and how I was going to do it. After the staff put a few ideas into my head . . . I did it." Today she's happy with her job.

In her congressional testimony in support of HR 28, the Displaced Homemakers Act, Marano has said, "It is not the training alone that makes the center work. At the Maryland Center, displaced homemakers are, in a sense, trained to be trained."[10] She summarized the needs of the displaced homemaker:

1. The chance to assess their skills related both to their homemaking experience and to their volunteer work.
2. The opportunity to see these skills as related to employment and occupational areas.
3. The opportunity to assess the emotional and substantive obstacles to the job search, and assistance in identifying manageable steps to conquer these obstacles.
4. Assistance with a career investigation matching personal skills with occupational titles.

5. Assistance in strengthening self-esteem, assertiveness, and job-seeking skills.
6. Peer support and the observation of others (models) who are making new lives for themselves.
7. Resource assistance, including: legal services; health and medical assistance; financial planning assistance; housing; etc.

Most of the center's counseling is done by peer counselors, who are being trained on the job by a head counselor. One of their main duties is to maintain contact with the displaced homemaker as she explores training and employment possibilities and adjusts to her new life-style—one that is probably a radical change from her accustomed way of living. When the counselor feels a woman is ready, she recommends her for the rest of the center's program—a job reentry workshop, a self-evaluation program, and, finally, job training.

The job reentry workshop is a cooperative effort by NDW, with its expertise in job placement, and the center staff. This is usually a one-time workshop with about twenty participants. Its goal is to inform clients about existing services and the realities of the job market before they make a commitment to the more intensive self-evaluation program. It includes information on job hunting, the employment outlook, the particular problems of displaced homemakers, and the center's services.

The self-evaluation program consists of fifteen hours of workshops held within a two-week period. About ten to fifteen displaced homemakers attend, and they do everything from role-playing to analyzing self-set goals. Basically, there are four goals in the self-evaluation program. The first is to confront present realities. The women are encouraged to accept the personal problems they are having, whether they are divorced, separated, widowed, or suddenly without support, and they discuss the dynamics of reaching out for help: Do they really want help? From whom will they accept help? What kind of help can they expect from the center? From themselves? Next the group works on building self-confidence through sharing ideas and feelings, examining personal needs and potentials, and strengthening self-image. Third, depending on the interests of the group, the women may then do such things as exploring the history of women or studying existing myths and stereotypes about being single versus being married. They are brought up to date on recent societal changes for women in terms of credit, legal rights, and employment opportunities. The final goal of the self-evaluation program is to develop personal goals and to carry them out.

A central part of the self-evaluation program is creating an experience of success for each participant. The women set goals for themselves and are given support to achieve them. The goals depend on the woman's job readiness and may be as elementary as reading the want ads and listing available jobs or as challenging as setting up a trial job interview. Whatever a woman's state of job readiness, the counselors are careful to create positive experiences for her; she is not encouraged to set goals they feel she will have a hard time achieving. The women are also urged to build their personal support networks by interviewing other women who are emerging from similar life situations. In general, they are expected to learn how to develop priorities, explore options, and manage time.

Self-evaluation programs begin monthly. The team leaders of the self-evaluation program meet daily to assess the progress of the group, and at the end of each program the individual participants are evaluated. Some women are referred directly to NDW for a job search; others are able to enter the Displaced Homemaker Center's training program. Some attend more workshop and counseling sessions, and some, whose family or other problems are blocking their progress, are referred to appropriate outside agencies. In every case the center maintains contact with them; at the very least, one month after the self-evaluation program ends the participants meet again to share their new experiences.

By the time the displaced homemaker reaches the job-training stage of the program, she is usually well motivated and knowledgeable. Her next step is to work with the director of training to explore training possibilities. To the extent that she is capable, the displaced homemaker is responsible for investigating possibilities for her own training. Joyce Shamer Keating, a training director of the center, has found that "usually, the woman has a good idea of what she wants to do.... That's the advantage of working with a mature woman." The training staff members suggest training sites and contact persons and accompany the displaced homemaker in initial visits if she feels she needs this support. Site exploration can take up to six weeks.

Basically, the center offers three kinds of training: on-the-job training, the voucher plan, and internships. On-the-job training is arranged for those women who already have marketable skills. For example, a woman who has had some office experience, whether paid or unpaid, may be placed in an on-the-job training position as clerk-typist or receptionist. The center pays her a minimum wage allowance for up to twenty-six weeks in such a position, and the woman not only updates her skills but also gains some recent experience to put on her resume. At the same time, the employer gains a free helping hand at the relatively small cost of supervision time and overhead. Sometimes the business even gains a useful permanent employee. As one satisfied employer wrote:

> When she first came to us, her typing and other clerical skills were so rusty that we could not possibly have afforded to bring her on our permanent staff. By the completion of her training period, however, her skills had improved markedly. Additionally, we found her to be a dedicated and congenial worker. Consequently, this week she began work here as a permanent, part-time member of our staff, and if additional funds should become available in the future, I'm sure we would want to increase her time with us. Of course, none of this would have been possible without the Displaced Homemakers Program.[11]

The voucher plan provides funds for the displaced homemaker either to continue her formal education or to start her own small business. The center pays for tuition, books, supplies, other training-related expenses, and institutional training fees, and it funds small businesses based on displaced homemakers' written proposals. It will fund only those plans through which the displaced homemaker has a reasonable chance for employment. Under the voucher plan, displaced homemakers are pursuing a variety of goals—getting their high-school equivalency diplomas, improving their typing, taking driver training, and earning bookkeeping certificates.

A number of the center's displaced homemakers take part in the internship program, which, like the on-the-job training and the voucher systems, pays them a maximum allotment of $1,625 for six months (in 1977 the pay was based on part-time work at $2.50 an hour). The internships are for displaced homemakers who want to work in an office but who have not worked for many years and would particularly benefit from a supportive, understanding environment. Most interns work regularly scheduled hours at the Displaced Homemaker Center or NDW in such areas as public information, job development, peer counseling, and bookkeeping. Some work in other relatively supportive environments, usually social service agencies.

A Chance to Grow

The center holds weekly lunches for the interns in training. I sat in on one of the sessions, which turned out to be a rather charming combination of business meeting and celebration. About fifteen women were present. During the one-hour session, checks for the intern allowances were distributed. Interns shared their experiences and problems. Two women were concerned that they were not learning enough on the job—they were being asked to do work like dishwashing, though they were supposed to be learning to keep books. The training director decided to arrange a conference with their supervisors. One woman stopped by to announce that she had gotten a "real" job—a permanent office position—and was greeted with applause and general delight.

Afterward I talked with one of the women about her training experience. Thirty-nine years old, the mother of four, she is in the process of getting a divorce. She lives with a daughter who goes to college. She says this of her internship:

> I got here through an advertisement in the women's newspaper and also through going to the women's fair at a local high school, where they advertised the Center for Displaced Homemakers. And I am a displaced homemaker. My husband has three of my children and I have one of the children. . . . We're in the process of getting a divorce at the present time.
>
> I had gone back to college and taken recreation leadership, but hadn't been able to get into it. Through the center they have placed me with Baltimore County, where I'm working with the Senior Citizens Centers in the west end of the county. I do bike from place to place because the bicycle is my transportation. My daughter has a car she lets me use rarely—very rarely because she also is in college and she works. I put in anywhere from ten to fifty miles a day going from center to center. We've tried to arrange my schedule so I can stay pretty much in one area.
>
> I had worked in offices as an accounting clerk off and on for many years, but that was just to help out, to get extra money because the family needed a few things. And I didn't like office work, so when I went back to college I sat down and evaluated what I wanted to do with the rest of my life and what I really enjoyed doing. Through the years I've been a Girl Scout leader, a volunteer in nursing homes, and I had done community work. To set your goals is something that I was never taught as a kid. I was taught you get married and you live happily ever after, but it didn't work out that way.
>
> When I decided that I wanted to go into recreation I went to college and I took the courses, but even so, after I graduated it was hard to get into the field at all. I went in as a [paid] activity director part time in a couple of nursing homes, but I didn't work with depressed people too well. But I do like working with the elderly, so I told that to my counselor here and she got me into the Senior Centers, which are places where the elderly are able to go—these are well, able people; they're not depressed, not completely unmotivated. The Senior Center can use my talents. . . . I'm also an arts and crafts and a music

person, not only an exercise person. Yes, [I do see possibilities for a job when the training is over] . . . . The Senior Citizens have 20 sites in Baltimore County now . . . . I'd prefer to go from site to site, but I can work into a site manager position. I would really need a car to cover the whole county as physical fitness coordinator.

[If the Displaced Homemaker Center hadn't been here], I'd probably be back in that darn office doing accounting—because that's where I had worked before—even though it wasn't what I wanted to do. This is a career that I really would like to do . . . . It's something I'm interested in and uses all my interests and my talents. And if I'm going to have work the rest of my life I'd better do something that I have skill in and that I enjoy. The Displaced Homemaker Center is a neat place to be. And the people here are fantastic . . . very supportive . . . they even put up with you changing your mind and not knowing what you want to do; they're really great. Even your peers here—everybody supports everybody. It's something that a woman who has gone through the traumatic experience of divorce and separation really needs, because you're way down . . . you lose support with married friends many times . . . it's nice to know what kinds of things there are in the outside world that as a housewife you can turn around and do.

The ultimate goal of counseling and of the self-evaluation and training programs is a permanent job. When the displaced homemaker has completed her center training, she works with a counselor at NDW, which receives job orders from many employers with a wide range of positions. Cynthia Marano believes that "the most saleable quality of the displaced homemaker is that she is looking for a job she's going to keep. Security is an issue that is extremely important to her." Though the center is young, already displaced homemakers have been placed in such jobs as project director of a small business training opportunities organization, site manager at a senior citizens' center, receptionist, clerk typist, and legal secretary. Trainees are also seeking such jobs as community home care aide, medical records worker, cosmetologist, floral designer, dental assistant, and offset press operator.

Having set up a successful program to meet the unique needs of the displaced homemaker, the Maryland Displaced Homemaker Center now has two additional goals—outreach and materials dissemination. It has very little money to reach out to help displaced homemakers in areas of Maryland beyond Baltimore—the original legislation setting up the center had included such a possibility but was amended. At this time, six counties in the state have requested a significant amount of help, and the center is searching for funding to meet this need. In addition, with twenty-nine state having already passed displaced homemaker legislation and many others considering it, the center has been deluged with requests for information and assistance of all kinds. As one of the few centers in operation, and as the more fully funded of the two original centers (the other is in Oakland, California), it has valuable expertise to share and is, again, searching for money with which to develop materials for program dissemination.

The Center Concept

With more than two dozen states having already passed displaced homemaker legislation, and many other states considering it, it is certain that a fairly large number of displaced homemaker centers will soon be in operation. But, even if every state funds a center (and at least one has merely passed legislation without appropriating funds), and even if the federal government appropriates money for fifty centers, only a small portion of the displaced homemakers' estimated need would be met. If, for instance, one hundred centers were to work with about the same number of people who have been seen in the Maryland Displaced Homemaker Center, in one year two hundred thousand out of the millions of displaced homemakers nationwide would have been helped, and of these only six to eight thousand would have received a stipend for training.

Clearly, the Maryland center's perception of the need for outreach programs is accurate. Perhaps centers must be funded to serve not only local but statewide clients. Certainly they should serve not only urban women but rural women as well.

One of the most important contributions to outreach the established centers can make is research on their own operations. For instance, we need complete data on their clients—their ages, incomes, work histories, job-search histories—and we need to know what happens to them as a result of center programs. We need to document the problems of displaced homemakers in various environments—city and country, suburb and inner city, small city and metropolis—to develop solutions appropriate to these environments.

And we need to know what particular problems displaced homemakers are having that may interfere with their job readiness. For example, the Maryland center has been confronted with a fairly high incidence of battery among the women it sees. The need for a crisis shelter is evident: women must have a place they can go, not only for a day or two but perhaps for several weeks, and not alone but with their children. Research is needed on the family background of the displaced homemaker to determine related problem areas. How much psychological and financial support does she get from her immediate family? Her relatives? Friends? What is her relationship with her children during the time she is displaced? How does she cope with being single again—finding new friends, facing rejection by some former friends? And so on. We are only beginning even to know which questions to ask.

In the area of training and jobs there is also much research to be done. The existing centers have neither time nor money for systematic, extensive efforts in this area, yet study of their training placements and of job development would be useful for future programs and for similar worker assistance programs. For instance, what are the characteristics of training placements that are most likely to further the paid careers of the displaced homemakers? What can we accurately say about transfer of homemaking skills to the job market? To what extent does the need to do housework interfere with the displaced homemaker's paid work? What are the experiences of the various centers in job development? How successful are they in placing clients? What regional differences are evident?

Ultimately, the knowledge accumulated through center research will aid in the design of outreach programs. In the short term, it will also provide centers with a systematic approach for analyzing and sharing information.

It is clear that the displaced homemaker centers are providing and will continue to provide important services. As they find out more about their clients, through experience and research, their goals may even be enlarged. But there are some problems with limiting aid programs to the center concept. For one thing, at this point funding for all the centers is short term—usually three years. Despite the tendency for bureaucracies to be self-perpetuating, extensions obviously will not be automatic. For another thing, the projects already funded have tight budgets, and because of this they can neither expand to more clients nor attract a broader range of clients. Some women simply cannot afford to participate in the traineeships, which, at part-time minimum wages, may not cover current expenses yet prevent a woman from working full time in another job. Even the staffs of the centers are working for minimal salaries; the maximum pay rate for staff members in Baltimore in 1976 was less than $13,500.

At the same time that women are fighting to get money for more and better centers, they need to be seriously considering additional

approaches—approaches like organizing both paid and volunteer action programs through local women's groups, marshaling extensive
publicity campaigns, and teaching professionals and government service employees about the special problems of displaced homemakers.

The Special Problems of the
Displaced Homemaker

An important question is what makes the displaced homemaker different from any other worker whose skills are outdated. Some would
agree that displaced homemakers are not different, and that there is no
reason to establish new programs for them. Differentiating the displaced homemaker from other workers who need training can be important in demonstrating to legislators that services requested for them
do not merely duplicate services already available.

One way displaced homemakers differ from other workers who lose
their jobs is that other workers routinely are financially compensated for
their job loss. Waged workers are eligible for unemployment compensation, usually for long enough to retrain themselves. Further, they may
belong to a union that protects them by specific contractual demands for
retraining. Homemakers have none of these protections.

The displaced homemaker is also unique in part because she needs
not merely training, but training for training. That is, she needs to
develop new contacts and interpersonal and technical skills, which may
be quite different from those appropriate to her homemaker role, before
she can know what kind of paid work she can do and will want to do,
and before she can reasonably be expected to enter a training program
for that work.

Other kinds of workers whose skills are no longer wanted may also
need to acquire new work skills, but most often they already have the
contacts and interpersonal skills appropriate to the workplace; many
such workers are men who have been trained all their lives to expect to
do paid work, to know how to seek it, and to know how to act on
the job.

As a displaced homemaker herself, Marie Parr of the Maryland center
says of displaced homemakers:

> Something has been happening in their lives which is different
> from what has happened to the men. It's not the loss of their job in
> life *only*, it's the fact that they've never been paid for what they did,
> and while our country says the most important thing a woman can do
> is run the home, be a wife and a mother, and we believe it, we don't

pay for it with money, and our society respects what gets paid for. And there's the unspoken thing where what you do at home is great but out there in the real world where people have to scramble to make it you wouldn't have a chance. This is what women have been buying for years and years while we've been doing a very difficult job that had its rewards that were not money. So when we go out to look for a job we don't see the connection between the skills we've used and what we have to offer. Besides that, if we've had a marriage that didn't work there's that thing that we're really failures. Now if you have the same man who has his marriage breaking up at the same time as he's having his job lost, he's dealing with many of the same things we are.

The displaced homemaker has usually been taught that her place is in the home, and therefore she has a whole set of skills appropriate mainly to the home. Some of her skills are transferable to the marketplace, but usually not without some additional training or experience. Most women who have managed a large household are probably also capable of managing a business project or an office staff, but they will not be successful at it until they learn the general customs and expectations of the paid work world and until they learn about the specific business and office routine.

In a well-meaning effort to bolster the homemaker's self-esteem and job-hunting assertion, many people today advise her that her home-making skills do indeed have market value. Unfortunately, this approach is likely to raise false hopes and to do real damage to a woman's self-esteem when she actually attempts to sell an employer on her skills. One article addressed to homemakers suggested that the following abilities are of "real value" to the business world: listening, taking direction, analyzing instructions, creating new ways to handle old problems, motivating others, arbitrating arguments, keeping cool under pressure, working alone, organizing materials, people, and time, and asserting oneself. Of course these skills are all necessary for getting a paid job—they are the absolute basics any employee should have—but they are hardly sufficient for being hired. Homemakers, and those who are trying to help them, need to appraise their skills realistically, in terms employers understand. Unfortunately, it is probably still true that a man with only these basic necessities is more likely to be hired than a woman with only these basic necessities. To be hired, the woman has to be better, and for displaced homemakers this means demonstrating skills that have already been accepted as valuable—skills that have titles like "typing" and "machine operation" and "accounting." This is not to

argue that these are the kinds of skills that ought to determine
hiring—though to argue against them hardly seems logical either—but
rather to point out that for better or worse they are the kinds of skills
that are used.

The Challenge of Job Creation

Displaced homemakers and their advocates are only beginning to realize the challenges and frustrations of job creation—making up new
combinations of skills that may be valuable to employers or that may be
marketable as new services.

The Maryland center stipulates that women must enter programs
through which they have a "reasonable" expectation of finding employment, but of course they know that the job market is highly volatile
and that the laudable notion of "reasonable" may sometimes resemble
nothing more than anybody's guess. Creating jobs, rather than training
for already existing titles, is one approach to this problem.

Further, if women are to escape their traditional housework-related,
low-paying jobs, they are going to have to find something else to do,
and one approach is to create that something else.

Internships and traineeships themselves tend to create new jobs.
Rather than simply applying for advertised positions, displaced homemakers who want traineeships may, with the assistance of their job
counselors, approach companies they are interested in and investigate
the possibility of creating temporary positions. As we have seen, in
some cases, the employer later finds that the newly created position is
useful and makes it into a permanent job.

Some entrepreneurial efforts also create new jobs. Women who set up
housecleaning services or other small businesses are creating positions
for themselves by finding a need in the marketplace and filling it directly. Such ventures by displaced homemakers—indeed by any
woman—are still relatively rare, and we need to know more about their
potential.

It is worth noting an irony in the Maryland situation. The Displaced
Homemaker Center in Baltimore was originally funded by the state of
Maryland for $190,000 a year for three years. It estimates that in its first
year of operation it cost about $2,500 to put a client through counseling
and training and into a job. At about the same time, the city of Baltimore received $5.7 million in job-creation funds, part of $2 billion in
local public works funds voted by Congress in the fall of 1976. According to *Wall Street Journal* figures, Congress expected the initial $2 billion

to create 300,000 jobs nationwide. Current estimates are that in Baltimore the creation of each job is costing $36,000,[12] a cost fourteen times as high as the job-creation program of the Displaced Homemaker Center.

The goals of the center and the Congress are the same; to enable people who want to work to find paying jobs. The problems they are facing are similar: many people need to be trained for available jobs; both homemakers and the low-skilled unemployed have trouble finding work, even getting the public works jobs; and in either case it seems there aren't enough jobs to go around. However, the cost difference between the two approaches is extreme. Further, the expensive federal program is aimed mainly at the traditionally male jobs of construction and related services.

What can we deduce from the wide divergence in total amount of money spent, and from the fact that the program to help primarily men is receiving a great deal more than the program to help primarily women? What do we learn when we compare the $2,500 per job spent by the Displaced Homemaker Center with the $36,000 spent by the Baltimore public works projects? Before drawing any firm conclusions, we would have to study each project in detail. But some areas of concern are immediately obvious.

Even if the federal government spends $10 million the first year and $15 million the second year to establish displaced homemaker centers nationwide, this will be nothing compared with the $2 billion voted in 1976, and the additional $4 billion voted in 1977, for reducing unemployment particularly among construction workers. Displaced homemakers are also unemployed. Why are our national priorities so heavily weighted against them? How can the balance be shifted?

During the time that we are considering our priorities, how can women take advantage of the present funding? For example, not all the jobs in the Baltimore public works projects require physical strength beyond that of most women. How can we encourage more women to seek such nontraditional jobs—and how can we encourage employers to hire them?

It seems possible that a project like a displaced homemaker center may be more efficient in creating jobs than is a more elaborate, better-funded program. Why is this? One hypothesis is that success is a function of project size. Small may indeed be beautiful. Joyce Shamer Keating, training director of the Maryland Displaced Homemaker Center, asserts that whenever projects—and usually it is large ones that work this way—attempt to fit the workers to the jobs, rather than the jobs to the workers, the result is inefficiency and waste of human resources. If this is true, to what extent can we expect the displaced homemaker centers to expand and still be effective? How can we reduce the bureaucracy and waste of projects like those in public works? On the other hand, perhaps displaced homemaker centers are more efficient partly because the women who run them are willing to work for less, or because they see what they are doing as immediately relevant and are thus highly committed. At present we are working with hypotheses; we need to follow the progress of both large and small projects closely before we can reach any conclusions.

We also need to be aware of the potential for sexism in the allocation of funding. The creation of jobs is one of the pressing problems of our time, and, based on present allocations, obviously male workers are ahead of female workers in the ability to command job-creation funds for themselves. If women are to move out of their status as low-paid, dispensable workers, they must learn to command funds for job creation without losing sight of the special qualities that make places like displaced homemaker centers effective.

"Displaced Homemaker":
The Term That Got Away?

As more people become aware of the problems of displaced homemakers, it is only natural that more people will want to do something to help them. But some problems are beginning to surface out of all the interest being generated. For one thing, though the term "displaced homemaker" originated out of the needs of older women, it is now being used to apply to a certain status regardless of age. There is some danger that the special needs of older women, for whom the burden of displacement is especially heavy, may be overlooked. As Laurie Shields has pointed out:

> One of the problems with the rapid acceptance of the term displaced homemaker, is that it is being co-opted to cover the problems of a status rather than being age-related. Women under 40 or 45 can be widowed and are being divorced. But by and large, their job options are better than the older woman's and so, too, are their chances for re-marriage. If they have children, they are far more likely to be eligible for governmental assistance than the older women. In Florida, for example, a private organization was recently granted $350,000 from CETA funds for a "displaced homemaker" program. A stipulation of the contract calls for 25% of the participants being under the age of 35. There is no such guarantee that the remainder or any part of it, will be women over 45.[13]

Another problem is that, as the term "displaced homemaker" gains currency and support among funding agencies, it may be misused. A center was funded in Gardner, Massachusetts, to train CETA personnel to handle displaced homemakers, to write a technical manual for CETA on dealing with displaced homemakers, and to train displaced homemakers for factory slot jobs. The directors of the center are men from the State Manpower Services Council and the local CETA office. NOW has opposed the Gardner center because it "won't properly benefit women" and because it feels the center benefits primarily CETA employees rather than displaced homemakers. It has also asserted that the establishment of the center was used as an excuse for postponing the passage of displaced homemaker legislation in Massachusetts.[14] Whether or not the center does provide some benefits for displaced homemakers, the fact is that relatively few displaced homemakers qualify for CETA programs. To train displaced homemakers only for factory slot jobs is, of course, an incredible proposition, and if this is indeed the center's intention it reflects an extreme lack of sensitivity to the problems and potentials of displaced homemakers and is an insult to all women. The need to remain vigilant over the future use of the term displaced homemaker is clear.

Today the displaced homemaker is becoming known, and her voice is being heard across the country. Those people who have pioneered in the effort to improve her status have begun a movement that is already having a broad conceptual and practical impact.

In her testimony before the House subcommittee, Oregon state representative Nancie Fadeley leaves us with the following reminder:

> In my own state, I am best known for my efforts to preserve our national resources. I have known, as you have known, the feeling of commitment to an issue. But never have I cared so much about a natural resource, as I care about the Displaced Homemaker—a neglected human resource. Why haven't we recognized her problem before, I ask myself, for haven't we had her with us always?[15]

Change in the House—
and in the Senate

10

At age 22, and rearing a two year old son, I'm just beginning my career as a professional parent. I want that idea to be respected and preserved for my sons and daughters . . . what attitudes I can instill in them at home, society can quickly undo . . . going through the legislature is the only way to get homemakers the social recognition and legal insurance for financial independence.

Correspondence received by the
NOW Task Force on Older Women[1]

Throughout the history of the United States, women's political role has been defined primarily by their domestic responsibilities. In colonial North America, voter qualifications based on property ownership effectively barred most women from political participation, and in the decades after national independence each of the states eventually inserted the term "male" into their descriptions of the qualified voter. A married woman was not recognized legally as a separate person: in most circumstances, and always in the case of the vote, she could act only through her influence on her husband.

It was not until 1838 that women gained some limited suffrage rights, and then Kentucky merely gave women the right to vote in school elections, a narrow political involvement presumably granted because of women's roles in motherhood and child-rearing.

The narrow scope of women's political involvement continued even after the Nineteenth Amendment to the Constitution gave women the right to vote in 1920. At first women themselves continued to avoid the political arena: initially they failed to use their potential political power and voted less frequently than men. Only after a generation of women grew up expecting to vote did women participate at the polls in numbers equal to those of men.

Still, as a group, their political power continued to be defined by their domestic roles. Their dominant voice was the League of Women Voters, a group originally especially concerned with issues of education and social reform. And because volunteerism was their primary method of community action—in organizations ranging from the Parent-Teacher Association to the Community Chest—they remained outside the mainstream of political power.

It was in the sixties that the women's movement finally demanded a new political role for women, one based not on woman's domestic responsibilities but on her equal rights as a citizen. Women began a campaign to gain broader powers, emphasizing the use of traditionally male political and legal means to improve their own status. Today women's political actions derive from a growing expertise in getting elected and in passing legislation.

However, the change has not been complete by any means. For example, it still seems that women, like many men, have some tendency to rely on the court system for action, as opposed to working for change through the legislatures. Seemingly, some have chosen to sit back and let the Supreme Court decide their fates, perhaps not realizing that, especially in the current court, this is not likely to effect much change. One of Chief Justice Burger's most cherished legal theses, for instance, is that Americans rely too much on the courts to solve problems that should be dealt with through legislation.[2] Burger court rulings in 1977 on disability benefits for pregnancy, Social Security payments for divorced mothers, and the issuing of a driver's license in a woman's married name all demonstrate the power of this conviction: the Court has refused to intervene for women's equal rights in these cases.

Women must use the legislative system to improve their status. If all this sounds a bit like a pep talk for political action, it is intended to. Women are only beginning to know about political power, and, among women, homemakers probably know less than anyone. The time has come for homemakers to start learning—and lobbying.

As always, solving homemakers' problems will not be simple. One barrier may be that a homemaker's political participation is intricately connected with her socioeconomic status. Indeed, it has been argued that a woman's socioeconomic self-image may be the most important determiner of her tendency to take part in professional political activity.[3] The kinds of changes I have discussed so far in this book—changes in the household division of labor, and in financial and psychological security—will help to create a new self-image among homemakers and therefore a new constituency for legislative action. Merely singling out homemakers as a group worthy of attention may help.

As a nation we need to ask ourselves whether homemaking is an occupation that deserves special social support. Is it in our best interest to allow the economic and social status of homemakers to remain in decline, while perhaps widening the welfare net to include those homemakers who happen to be poor, or do we want to single out homemaking as an occupation to be encouraged for its own sake?

One of the main problems with the plans for providing various homemaker benefits is the inadequate definition of a homemaker. For purposes of legislation, Bella Abzug has defined the homemaker as:

> An individual who, during a month (1) keeps house, not for pay, for a person who is employed full-time, and one person in the household is the individual's spouse, parent, child, brother, sister, aunt, uncle, niece, nephew, grandparent, or grandchild, (2) is between 18 and 65 years of age, and (3) is not employed full-time.[4]

Barbara Jordan has defined the homemaker as:

> A person who, during a month, (1) keeps house, not for pay,
> (2) is between 18 and 65 years of age, (3) is not entitled to a monthly social security benefit, and (4) is not employed for more than 135 hours.[5]

The problem with these definitions is that virtually anyone without a full-time job could be described as a homemaker and could therefore claim homemaker credits.

In general parlance, a homemaker is a person who cooks and cleans and shops, who cares for children, and who provides overall home and appliance maintenance. If we as a society are to support homemaking as an occupation, then homemakers must argue successfully that the country has a vested interest in one or more of their functions. It would be odd to argue that America particularly cares whether the Jones family has waxed floors and dusted window sills. It would be unusual, to say the least, if national policy were designed with the express purpose of maintaining a consumer in the home (though Galbraith has argued convincingly that this has been the effect, if not the goal, of our consumer economy).[6] But it would not be odd or unusual—indeed it would be timely and totally relevant to the state of our society—for homemakers to assert that America does have a vested interest in its children, and that therefore it has a vested interest in those people, generally called homemakers, who raise the nation's children.

The social cost of the economic status of homemaking will be measured in part by the children we raise. If homemaking continues to be a low-security, low-esteem position in our society—if it continues to be seen as a role to escape rather than to embrace—then most likely the children, and ultimately the society, will suffer. I would argue not that full-time homemaking provides a better child-rearing system than part-time homemaking, but rather that both full- and part-time homemaking seem to be adaptable options for child care, and that both should be supported to the fullest extent of our financial means.

The logical extension of the social role of homemaker goes beyond child care alone. Homemakers may also be the primary care-givers for the disabled and the elderly. Here too society has an interest. Beyond these kinds of caretaking services, however, lies a vast definitional problem in which our social values, at least at this point, show no clear direction. For the purpose of passing legislation, this problem is best simplified by concentrating on the homemaker contribution that is obvious and indisputable.

However, one issue remains. We have been talking about current values and expectations; indeed we may be talking only about the values and expectations of the younger generations. People who have called themselves homemakers in former times—women, for instance, who have not believed they should work outside the home yet have not had children or others dependent on them—should not be penalized for their values. Rather, society should bear the burden for change by establishing eligibility requirements for homemaker programs congruent with the expectations that homemakers of different generations can reasonably be expected to hold.

Once we have established our societal need for the services of the homemaker and have defined homemaker in a verifiable way, we can implement a program for change. Much, though obviously not all, of women's legislation proposed in the past twenty years has been aimed at women working outside the home. As a group, homemakers have received legislative attention only in the last few years, and there is still much work to do. In the rest of this chapter we will look at proposed legislation that will be important to homemakers, much of which was summarized in the Homemakers' Bill of Rights presented by Eleanor Smeal to the House Select Committee on Aging subcommittee in 1979 (see Appendix 1).

Homemakers and the
Equal Rights Amendment

The Equal Rights Amendment states that "Equality of rights under the law shall not be denied or abridged by the United States or by any State on account of sex." With the enactment of this constitutional amendment, homemakers will benefit along with all other people, men included, who have been the victims of sex discrimination.

As White House consultant on women's organizations, Jill Ruckels-
haus asserted in 1973:

> ERA is needed by homemakers as well as professional women. Today
> there are myriad laws in various states that discriminate against
> women in the areas of credit, loans, housing, education, jury service
> and job opportunities. The passage of the Equal Rights Amendment
> would make a final, legal and compelling commitment that all Ameri-
> cans are equal and individual before the law.[7]

Today the amendment remains absolutely essential. Martha Griffiths
points out, "Laws can be rewritten. Court interpretations can be overturned. For the assurance of women generally, equal rights should be
written into the Constitution."[8]

The amendment does not say what laws will be changed; it is merely
a statement of principle that courts and legislatures will have to take
into account and that will necessarily stir up a great many legal contests
over its application. The ERA has symbolic value as well; it will
establish a woman's place once and for all; women's independence and
equality—not women's dependence or women's second-class status—
will become the norm.

Specifically, it will provide a basis for a challenge of the Social Security Act's differential treatment of husbands and wives. Among other
things, this will mean that married women who work outside the home
(or who work for money inside the home) can no longer be discriminated against in the protection they are able to offer their families.

Spouses will become equal partners. For example, property and credit
laws preventing married women from running their own businesses
will be struck down. A woman at present is required to assume her
husband's domicile (his "permanent home") or else risk being charged
with desertion. A domicile is the determinant of certain rights and
privileges—the right to hold public office, to receive welfare, or to be
eligible for lower state university tuition. Under the ERA, women will
be able to choose their own domiciles and will have a legal right to enter
into the decision on where the whole family will live.

As an equal partner in the marriage, a wife will have more power to
protect her children: every legal right she gains for herself enables her to
make decisions to protect them. For instance, under present law, the
husband can decide the standard of living for the family, regardless of
his income. In one incredible case in Nebraska a husband owning more
than $100,000 in government bonds refused to put an indoor toilet in
his house, and the court refused to order him to do so.[9] The ERA would
provide a basis from which to challenge such inequities and to ac-

knowledge the contributions and rights of both wage-earning and homemaking spouses.

Also, the ERA will give parents of either sex a legal basis on which to challenge current sexual assault statutes, many of which now protect only female children.

Finally, the ERA will lead to the removal of sex discrimination in the Aid to Families with Dependent Children program (AFDC). Currently in this program the sex of the unemployed parent determines whether the family is given or denied benefits; in a two-parent family, only the father can qualify as the unemployed parent. Furthermore, under the Work Incentive Program (WIN), established in 1967 in part to train AFDC parents, all women are ranked below all men in the priority lists for enrollment in training or placement programs. As a result, in fiscal year 1975 about 90 percent of all adult AFDC recipients were women, but only 74 percent of WIN participants were women.[10] Clearly this is discrimination by sex, and clearly this represents a stereotypical view of homemakers: according to this way of thinking, only women are to be homemakers and child-rearers; only men are to get first choice at training and outside labor. The ERA would be a firm basis from which to challenge these guidelines.

Too often we tend to think that the ERA will benefit only women, forgetting that it will protect men as well. This may be especially pertinent for men who are full-time homemakers or who are considering becoming full-time homemakers. The ERA will be the basis for enforcing equal treatment for homemakers of both sexes. Legislated displaced homemaker protections will be available to both men and women. Both will be eligible for a credit or benefit system for purposes of Social Security. We can guess that men in general have more awareness than women do of the problems of being outside the paid work force. After all, they more often pay Social Security and other taxes directly, and therefore they have an immediate interest in knowing what security their money is buying for them. Thus we can expect men who are considering full-time homemaking to be particularly sensitive to the financial vulnerability inherent in the job of homemaker. That the ERA will not allow sex discrimination among homemakers should be an incentive to these men to consider homemaking seriously and to work for legislation that will benefit all homemakers.

Social Security

Each Congress sees its share of Social Security bills that are of interest to homemakers either directly or indirectly. Some of the bills aim to make small and simple changes in the Social Security Act; others attempt sweeping reforms. With each bill Congress must weigh costs and benefits. These days, with Social Security in dire financial straits, the costs of some reforms may seem prohibitive.

Aside from the overt sex discrimination in the act, in general the problem with Social Security from the individual homemaker's point of view is that she does not receive adequate recognition of her contributions to her family and to society. The problem is similar to that of the homemaker who wants her employed husband to help with the housework: he complains that he doesn't have time, that after all someone has to do it, and that it is a shame, but that person has to be her. His attitude is one of "I got there first, now you'll have to live with it." Under Social Security, waged workers, especially male waged workers, got there first. The challenge for homemakers is to gain recognition of their contributions in the face of this status quo and the Social Security program's limited financial resources.

From the government's point of view the problem is money. Certainly our legislators would like to give every citizen a decent retirement and aid in disability. But changes in Social Security laws, even simple changes, generally affect millions of people and tend to be expensive.

For example, former congresswoman Martha Griffiths sponsored a bill to gain death benefits for children whose mothers die after being out of the work force for more than a year and a half; the bill passed and cost $100 million in benefit payments in the first year. A Supreme Court ruling making 220,000 widowers eligible for survivors' benefits will cost $211 million in the first year. By government standards these amounts are not huge. But one recent challenge to the law would have made new benefit calculations for men retroactive for nine million retired men, raising their benefits immediately, and would have cost the government $13 billion by 1983. The Supreme Court recently disallowed this challenge.

In 1975 a trustees' report for Social Security's Old Age, Survivors, and Disability Insurance (OASDI) forecast that outgo would exceed income during 1975 and every year following unless tax income was increased. President Carter initiated steps to take some of the necessary money out of the General Fund, once considered a radical act. Solutions to inequities in the system will be found, and challenges to the assumptions of Social Security will go on, but the bottom line will also continue to be the dollar sign. Keeping this in the back of our minds, then, let us consider some of the proposed changes in the Social Security Act.

Of all the reform legislation proposed recently, perhaps the most ambitious is the Fraser-Keys bill entitled the Equity in Social Security for Individuals and Families Act. The bill was first developed by Arvonne Fraser, former president of the Women's Equity Action League, and Jane Chapmen of the Center for Women Policy Studies, and it was introduced in 1977 by Congressman Donald M. Fraser of Minnesota and Congresswoman Martha Keys of Kansas. A revised version of the bill was reintroduced in 1979 by Congresswoman Mary Rose Okar of Oklahoma. The philosophy behind the bill is that homemakers make important contributions to a marriage and that Social Security therefore should be given to them not as dependents but as persons useful in their own right.

One of the key provisions of the bill is Social Security portability: partners may marry, be widowed, divorce, or remarry without losing benefits. The credits they earn, whether as waged workers or as homemakers, are theirs alone and cannot be lost.

The bill offers two ways of crediting individual spouses. Under the first alternative each spouse receives 50 percent of the credit for their combined earnings. This would benefit the spouse who earns less: if each kept only his or her own earnings, because of their lower salaries, more than half the time women would be entitled only to minimum benefits upon retirement.

The second alternative is that each spouse gets credit for 75 percent of the highest salary earned. This alternative would apply only if there is one wage earner in covered employment or if one wage earner has a significantly higher salary in covered employment. The 75 percent split is similar to what happens now. The husband and wife get 150 percent of the benefits based on the husband's primary insurance amount (the amount of earnings used to calculate benefits) or 100 percent of each person's benefits based on the primary insurance amount, whichever is higher. Under either alternative, persons not in covered employment would maintain Social Security records through their spouse's covered employment.

There are two other major benefits of the bill. First, the homemaker would become eligible for disability insurance since she would have current quarters of coverage under Social Security. Also, the age of eligibility to receive Social Security benefits by widows or widowers would be reduced from sixty years of age to fifty, the approximate year in which most widowed women with children lose benefits because their children come of age.

In summary, the bill would attack the three major problems of the dependent wife under the present system: first, that she has no guaranteed share in her spouse's Social Security benefits; second, that the unpaid homemaker has no death or disability insurance; and, third, that a woman widowed after her children are eighteen but before she reaches sixty, unless totally disabled herself, receives no benefits.

The reader may find it interesting that the 1975 Department of Health, Education, and Welfare Report of the Advisory Council on Social Security declined to support proposals similar to these. The council recognized that housework has value but argued that payments to homemakers were contrary to the nature of Social Security, a scheme designed as an earnings-replacement program.[11]

Many other revisions of the Social Security Act have been suggested. For instance, it has been suggested that child-rearing years be excluded from the years used for income calculation, since they represent years of no earnings that, averaged in with other years, will pull down a person's retirement benefits. This is one of the changes that will not be covered by passage of the Equal Rights Amendment, since it is sex neutral, and that will require the legislature to make a commitment to the social value of those homemaking years.

To gain disability coverage for homemakers, it has been suggested that the quarters of coverage required for eligibility not be restricted to a particular time period: quarters earned over many years would be counted toward eligibility. Many women workers who left the work force to care for children in the home would thus become eligible for coverage.[12]

In 1977 former secretary of Health, Education, and Welfare Wilbur Cohen suggested that the original requirement that a couple be married for twenty years before the dependent is eligible for coverage be amended to read ten or five years or even one year.[13] A bill introduced by Bella Abzug would have reduced the period to five years. In 1978 the number of years was reduced from twenty to ten.

Other suggestions are to increase the minimum payment, thus helping our poorest workers; to abolish the reductions in benefits for those who retire early if they cannot work; and to provide some recourse for homemakers who have been declared ineligible when their marriages have been found to be invalid. In the last case, in 1976 the United States Supreme Court refused to aid a Wisconsin woman who found out after her husband died that she had not been legally married to him. Because a state court ruled that her Mexican divorce from her previous husband was invalid, she failed to qualify for federal tax and probably Social Security benefits.[14]

The Homemaker's Committee of the Commission on International Women's Year has emphasized that educating homemakers about their legal position is of primary importance. When one considers the intricacies of Social Security, one can see how right they are. (And not only homemakers, but all citizens need this kind of knowledge.) They have sponsored a state-by-state review of laws affecting homemakers (see Appendix 2).

Even the Fraser-Keys bill leaves many questions unanswered. For example, if a fifty-year-old widow becomes eligible for death benefits, will she also be given an incentive to go to work? What about the discrepancy between single-wage-earner and two-wage-earner families, through which the two-wage-earner family may pay more Social Security taxes than a single-wage-earner family with the same income and yet receive less retirement? And finally, what will the suggested reforms cost?

Individual Retirement Accounts

Beginning 1 January 1977, millions of homemakers became eligible for a benefit that their husbands had been receiving for three years—the option of opening a tax-free Individual Retirement Account (IRA) in their own names. Originally the law excluded spouses from the program: a husband could make his wife the beneficiary of his IRA, but it was hers only if he died, and joint accounts were illegal.

Under the new law, a person may open a regular IRA in his or her own name as well as a spouse IRA for a nonworking *(sic)* spouse of either sex. Further, while the regular IRA has a $1,500 maximum, the IRA that includes the spouse has a maximum amount of $1,750—a $250 incentive to open the spouse account.

The IRA is a good way for women who can afford it to accumulate some retirement money in their own name. Contributions have to be split evenly between the two separate accounts. Each person can still make the other a beneficiary, but the money cannot be removed by the other spouse. Whatever interest or dividends the account earns continues to grow tax-free until retirement. (Funds can be withdrawn without penalty at age fifty-nine and a half.) Important for many women, the program is available right now—it can be used right away, without waiting for any further legislation.

But there are some problems. The first is that tax law has exempted from estate taxes a survivor's annuity from an employer's retirement plan; in 1976 it extended this exemption to IRA but failed to extend it to the new spouse IRA. This is but one of many problems in the hastily assembled tax reform package of 1976, and plans to rectify it have been under way in Congress.

The other problem is that unless the employed spouse is employed by an organization that does not offer pension, profit-sharing, thrift, or stock bonus plans, she or he cannot start an IRA, and therefore neither can the nonemployed spouse be covered. In short, the homemaker in this case remains dependent on the wage earner's goodwill.

Homemakers need the right to start pensions in their own names regardless of their spouses' status as workers. Such a plan for pensions for homemakers was offered in Congress in 1977 by freshman representative Paul S. Trible, Jr., of Virginia, with support from conservatives who think such a plan will stimulate savings and from liberals who see its importance in terms of human rights. The Homemaker Retirement Bill, sponsored in the Senate by Senator Wendell Anderson, would allow homemakers to set up IRAs of their own in amounts up to $1,500 a year when they have no other retirement coverage. The IRAs would be tax sheltered, allowing homemakers to save about twice as much toward retirement as they would if the same money were put into a savings account.

Divorce Law

In general, divorce statutes are antiquated, complicated, and incredibly in need of reform. I can only touch on the needed changes here; each state differs. But this is a very important area of the law for a homemaker to know about and to work to change, and the time to learn about it is when a marriage is stable and relatively unpressured or, better yet, before marriage. Women are fast realizing that for them marriage may hold more pitfalls than promise.

Homemakers cannot count on the courts to assure them of a decent living, or even a reasonable period of economic adjustment, after divorce. In a report to the American Bar Association, a Florida lawyer recently pointed out that "if a woman has demonstrated a work history, she is unlikely to get permanent alimony, even after a marriage of long duration . . . . Rehabilitative alimony [is granted] for the shortest period deemed necessary to get the wife back into the job market."[15] Of course judges are not required to consider which job market the woman may be capable of entering after many years at home; a woman who worked to put her husband through college may not be granted the equivalent training for herself.

According to a 1975 survey, only one divorce in seven involves an alimony award.[16] This is roughly 14 percent. Given that 57 percent of all married women are unpaid homemakers, it seems likely that a good proportion of those divorcées who are getting no alimony are also homemakers. Only a fraction of states permit a judge to consider the homemaker's labor as a factor in deciding a financial settlement of a divorce. In California in 1979 a bill supported by Assemblyman Alister McAlister and later enacted requires divorce judges to consider, when ruling on alimony, "the extent to which the supported spouse's present and future earning capacity is impaired by periods of unemployment that were incurred during the marriage to permit the supported spouse to devote time to domestic duties." In New York State a bill including a similar provision has been defeated at least four times.

Another sobering statistic is that fewer than 50 percent of divorced women are granted financial support for their children. What happens to these children? Why are their fathers not required to support them? Why must women, who are likely to earn less money than men, and who are more likely than men to have a full-time job in housework already, be required to bear this financial burden?

The conclusion that must be drawn is that until divorce support statutes are reformed, a woman who opts for full-time homemaking and children—or for one or the other—is taking a considerable risk. She is likely to end up without alimony and without recent job skills to help her move into paid work. She is likely to end up supporting her children herself on whatever job she can get, or relying on the state to do so.

Among reforms that are needed are laws requiring the supporting spouse to make full financial disclosure at the time of divorce, better enforcement procedures, and better grievance procedures against judges and attorneys. An immediate need is public investigation and education, particularly by and for homemakers.

Displaced Homemaker Legislation

Of course, much of the proposed legislation that will help homemakers will have important effects on the displaced homemaker. Widows' benefits, inheritance-tax laws, and the ten-year marriage requirement for Social Security eligibility are all issues that affect her immediately. But, as you may well imagine, interest in displaced homemakers does not stop with such issues. Displaced homemakers are aiming to get both state and federally funded programs to provide retraining and job counseling.

The first state bill to fund a program for displaced homemakers was filed in California in April 1975. The bill, with a cost of $200,000, passed in 121 working days and established a center for displaced homemakers in Alameda, California. Within six months acts were also passed in Maryland and Florida. In Oregon a center funded by the state legislature started operating out of the University of Oregon's Center for Gerontology in July 1977. The 1977 Minnesota legislature funded two pilot projects—one in the Twin Cities urban area and one in a rural area. Texas has passed legislation and awarded contracts to private agencies in late 1977. Various counties in Florida have received CETA training grants to establish centers or to ascertain the needs of homemakers. And these are only a few of the states that have programs. In 1976, bills were filed in Minnesota, New York, Massachusetts, Ohio, and Pennsylvania. New bills were introduced in twenty-eight states in 1977, and in 1977 sixteen states had adopted legislation. By the end of 1979, twenty-nine states had adopted legislation.

Speaking at the NOW national convention in 1977, Laurie Shields reported on the astounding response to displaced homemaker legislation. "Telling you about bills that have passed is like telling you the story of a series of miracles," she said. "Women who had never been active in politics were suddenly turned on to this and realized they would have to act in their own behalf. The line is 'nobody sets you free, you set yourself free.'"[17] She went on to tell the story of the Nebraska "miracle." A young mother of four, appointed to the Nebraska Senate to fill a vacancy, introduced the displaced homemaker bill for the state of Nebraska on 24 January 1977. Senator Jo Ann Maxey was not collecting favors—she hadn't been in office long enough—but she spurred an intensive grass-roots effort, and the Nebraska legislature passed the bill in a clear response to the needs of their constituents. The bill passed on 16 March, was vetoed by Governor J. James Exon on 22 March, and became law when the legislature overrode the veto on 25 March.

Another miracle: there had been high hopes for a displaced homemaker bill in the South Dakota legislature, but three Democratic women who had supported it lost their seats in an election. However, Republican women picked up the legislative effort: this is not a partisan issue. As Shields says, "The only enemies displaced homemakers have are apathy, ignorance, and misunderstanding."[18]

Early in July 1976, candidate Jimmy Carter endorsed the passage of displaced homemaker legislation on a national level. Just after the Ninety-fifth Congress convened in January 1977, Congresswoman Yvonne Braithwaite Burke and Senator Birch Bayh introduced a bill to provide for the establishment of pilot training centers nationwide. (Senator Bayh *asked* to sponsor the bill.) This federal bill also called for feasibility studies to consider including homemakers under current federal programs such as unemployment compensation, the Comprehensive Employment and Training Act of 1973 (CETA), and related federal employment, education, and health assistance programs. The total cost of $10 million the first year and $15 million the second is a modest appropriation by federal standards. But, again, Laurie Shields has said in testimony to the House Finance Committee, "Sure this is a modestly funded piece of legislation. But we believe bigger isn't ALWAYS better, sometimes smaller can be smarter."[19] On 13 October 1978, Congress passed the CETA authorization bill, including the first national legislation to cite displaced homemakers as an economically disadvantaged group eligible for federal assistance programs. At this time, thirty-one new CETA Title III projects have been started, and half a dozen national demonstration projects, funded for a total of one million dollars, were scheduled to begin within the next six months. However, continued funding for the CETA projects was in doubt.

Flextime and Part-time Employment

Legislation aimed at encouraging part-time and flexibly scheduled jobs (known as flextime) can obviously benefit homemakers who need to or wish to work outside the home. It will also encourage greater male participation in homelife, allowing men to make a gradual shift into more home involvement without giving up the outside jobs with which they have come to identify so strongly. Two approaches to these new job designs have been suggested. First, it has been suggested that private industries be given a tax incentive to schedule part-time and flextime jobs. The Private Sector Part-time Employment Act, sponsored in the House by Congressman Barber B. Conable, Jr., of New York, provides employers with tax credits of up to 25 percent on wages paid to part-time workers. And, second, in the federal civil service, proposals have been introduced through Congress to encourage part-time and flextime jobs. A year-long experiment will be conducted in five federal agencies to test the feasibility of expanding the number of permanent part-time workers in the federal bureaucracy. In addition, several states are experimenting with flextime and part-time workers. In 1975 Massachusetts required that, within five years, 10 percent of all state jobs be part time and other jobs adopt flexible hours.

Pensions

Just as wives lose their husbands' Social Security credits upon divorce, so they lose any share in their husbands' personal company retirement plans, regardless of how the plans were paid for. Two schoolteachers in New York State agreed to live on the wife's salary and to save the husband's in a pension fund to give themselves a comfortable old age. The marriage ended after forty years, and by law the pension is all his, to share with his new wife if he wishes to.[20]

It has been suggested by Congresswoman Pat Schroeder of Colorado that former spouses of federal employees should be entitled to a share of retirement benefits if they were married twenty years (HR 3951). Since the twenty-year requirement for Social Security has itself been changed, the twenty-year suggestion for the federal pension programs, though a step in the right direction, should also be considered carefully. By law, pensions should belong equally to the employed and the nonemployed spouse and should be prorated for the term of the marriage. When the law for Individual Retirement Accounts was drafted, it included no-penalty provisions for splitting the account in case of divorce. Other laws are needed to do the same thing for Keogh and employer-funded retirement plans. Oregon, for example, has enacted legislation that empowers judges to allocate a portion of state retirement benefits to ex-spouses.

Marriage Contracts

Today many couples are entering marriage with a contract, either written or oral. The idea of spelling out the couple's expectations in advance is excellent: if nothing else, it may prevent some unpleasant surprises. However, most of these contracts are not legally binding, and if the couple later wishes to divorce, a judge is not required to consider the contract in his divorce settlement.

We need valid marriage contracts that contain real safeguards for both spouses. A bill to create a legal basis for such contracts has been presented by Laura S. Rasmussen in the Suffolk University Law Review[21] (see below). The bill can be used as a model for legislation in most states.

MODEL MARRIAGE
EQUALITY BILL

—AN ACT RELATIVE TO THE ESTABLISHMENT OF VALID CONTRACTS BE-TWEEN HUSBAND AND WIFE CONCERNING THE RIGHTS AND OBLIGATIONS OF THE SPOUSES.
Laura S. Rasmussen
SUFFOLK UNIVERSITY LAW REVIEW
Vol. IX: 185

Section 1   "A husband and wife may, during or in contemplation of marriage, enter into a written interspousal contract in consideration of the mutual promises contained therein, which apportions rights, duties, and obligations arising from the marriage and also regulating the control and ownership of property owned by either before marriage, or obtained by either or both during the marriage. The contract may provide for the division of property upon separation or divorce. Provision for subsequently acquired property or personal obligations may be included in the original contract or added to it through modification without additional consideration. The terms of such contract shall supersede the principles of the common law regarding rights and obligations between spouses. But no term on an interspousal contract shall be valid which attempts to abrogate the statutory or common law rights of the children of the marriage.

"An interspousal contract may, without limitation, provide:

1. for outside-the-home and inside-the-home obligations and duties necessary to the maintenance of the marital unit, both economic and physical, including division of the obligations of economic support and care of dependent elders or children;

2. for calculation of the economic value to the marriage of home and child custodial duties performed by either of the spouses;

3. for the establishment of community property with joint control;

4. that arbitrators are to be consulted in case of serious disagreement between the spouses, either during the marriage or after separation or divorce, and for selection of arbitrators;

5. for reasonable liquidated damages in case of breach.

"Property held in the name of one spouse shall not, except as provided by the Uniform Fraudulent Conveyance Act be reached by creditors of the other spouse, and property held by the spouses jointly shall be available to creditors of either spouse. An interspousal contract shall be recorded at the Registry of Deeds for the county of domicile if it is to be effective against third parties who do not have actual notice. If the contract is unrecorded, it shall be valid only between the parties thereto and their heirs and personal representatives.

Section 2 "Interspousal contracts may be enforced in the probate courts, as set forth in Section 3 of this Act, by actions at law for breach of contract or in equity for specific performance, upon a showing by the petitioner of a substantial and intentional breach by the respondent. Upon a finding that the contract was entered freely and with full understanding by the parties, and that its terms are essentially reasonable, the court shall adjudicate the rights of the parties under the contract; but an interspousal contract shall be presumed valid.

Section 3 "Except for a contract dealing solely with property or of a contract term which specifically concerns the exchange of rights in property, any dispute concerning a promise which is part of an interspousal contact shall be submitted to neutral arbitrator(s) selected by the spouses according to the terms of the contract."**"If the parties do not comply with the decision of the arbitrator(s), the arbitration award may be enforced in the probate court according to the provisions for the enforcement of arbitration awards.

"If one spouse seeks enforcement of an interspousal contract dealing solely with property, or a contract term which specifically concerns the exchange of rights in property, and if the contract does not provide for arbitration, the party seeking enforcement of such contract or term may petition the probate court."

Local Action

Other legislative actions that homemakers can initiate in their own behalf involve the myriad local laws that affect the way they live, where their children go to school, and how their community is organized. Zoning laws are one example. These local laws need to be reexamined and rewritten to create a better integration of home and outside work, a better integration of home and school activities, and decentralization of shopping and services. As I have already noted, this kind of change can combat women's isolation in the home, and it can promote the sense of community that so many people, men and women alike, are seeking today.

Media

Columnist Joan Beck has pointed out that "the media aren't going to start employing women in top-level, decision-making jobs or stop showing commercials about housewives too dumb to do laundry because the International Women's Year Commission recommends it."[22] However, television and radio in particular are vulnerable because stations must renew their licenses every few years. Homemakers can challenge the licenses of stations that continue to show objectionable commercials and programs; they can demand, for instance, that men as well as women be shown working in the home and that homemakers not be portrayed as stupid. Some stations and sponsors are beginning to get the message, and they should be commended. But more need to hear— and make some changes.

Enforcement

"Where there's a bill there's a way." Or is there? Women have found out that the Equal Employment Opportunity Commission can work very slowly, that the Equal Credit Opportunity Act doesn't always work, that alimony doesn't always get paid.

One of the most severe problems is husbands or ex-husbands who fail to maintain payments to their wives. HEW estimates that more than 650,000 families have court orders of support that husbands have evaded. The lost payments to families amount to $800 million per year, a bill that the taxpayer ultimately pays through increased welfare payments. Fewer than 50 percent of alimony payments arrive regularly, and payments come less and less frequently as the years pass.

Enforcement is obviously essential. The problem is compounded by laws that allow a spouse to avoid payment and prosecution simply by leaving the state. Wisconsin had refused to issue a marriage license to a divorced man until he proved that he was not delinquent in payments to his first family. However, in what the *Wall Street Journal* termed a "broad interpretation of the 'fundamental right' to wed" the Supreme Court banned states from refusing to give marriage licenses to men behind in child-support payments.[23] Even if a husband doesn't move out of state, however, enforcement is irregular. As one frustrated Long Island woman says, "I know where he is . . . . I've told welfare. I've told the court. The finance company camped on his lawn and got their money. Why can't I get mine?"[24] Indeed, why can't she? Is it because enforcement is really so difficult or expensive, or are apathy and disdain the reasons?

One amendment to the Social Security Act known as the 4-D program may help. If the state cannot find the nonsupporting spouse, under this amendment a federal Parent Locator Service will be empowered to obtain his current address from federal Social Security and Internal Revenue Service files. Though it will not address the problem of unmet alimony payments, this program may save the country millions of dollars in child support. The service will be available free for AFDC mothers and at a fee for nonwelfare women.

Tax Reform
"The Widows' Tax"

Among proposed tax reforms for homemakers, one of the better-known concerns the so-called widows' tax, the federal estate tax that treats a widow like any other inheritor unless she can prove that she has contributed money—not merely labor—to her husband's estate. A NOW publication asserts that the federal government says it has been unable to change this tax law because of difficulties in finding a formula that would equate the wife's work with a financial contribution (see a counterargument in chap. 2) and because of loss of income to the government.[25]

Establishing a dollar value for the homemaker's work is not a simple matter. Even within the same financial bracket, households vary in their complexity and in the skills needed to run them. Are homemakers to be given credit for training and skills, as other workers are, or merely for hours worked? The homemaker who manages a large and expensive dwelling is likely to see herself as more valuable than the homemaker who runs a modest household. Again, is the homemaker to earn credit for the type of household she manages—the Plaza as opposed to Joe's Motel, as it were—or for the effort she expends?

Most researchers who have attempted to place a dollar value on household work have simply estimated the number of hours a homemaker works per week and applied a dollar-per-hour valuation to this time to come up with some figure for an annual salary. Even using such an uncomplicated formula, however, different groups arrive at different figures, though it is important, too, to note that the figures are all in the same range. Chase Manhattan Bank estimates that it would cost $12,241 per year to replace a homemaker. *Changing Times* says her services are worth roughly $8,060 per year. As a home economist, the homemaker is worth between $8,500 and $12,000 a year.[26] And a report by the New York State College of Human Ecology at Cornell indicates that a nonemployed homemaker with two children contributes $10,000 worth of household work in a year.[27] The average of these four estimates (based on taking the mean where a range is given) is $10,138. This figure does not take into consideration either inflation in the years since the studies or, in all cases, quality of work done. The Cornell study, for instance, is most recent, yet it figures the hourly wage on the basis of what it would cost to hire someone to do the task in question, not what it would cost to replace the family member doing it.

Two points are worth making here. First, the homemaker's work does have value, and that value is high when seen in terms of dollars. As Secretary of Commerce Juanita Kreps points out, "The important consideration is not the failure to measure the value of home work, but the tendency to impute a low market value to those services which, being customarily performed in the home, have commanded no price at all.... Not only has the buyer been conditioned to view these services as cheap; the women who do the work are conditioned to think of them in the same way."[28]

Second, for computing work credit, a simple wage and hour formula to ascertain the value of homemaking, while not perfect, is workable.[29] No homemaker should be denied work credit merely because someone claims that an exact dollar value cannot be agreed upon for all home work. Too often the argument that one cannot place a dollar value on housework is mere camouflage for a more painful truth—that the homemaker's dollar value is so high that paying it may be exceedingly costly.

To add insult to injury, if a woman who has been a homemaker all her life dies, everything in the couple's estate automatically belongs to the husband, without tax.

In accepting the Report of the National Commission on the Observance of International Women's Year in 1976, President Ford cited the case of Mary Heath, fifty-five, a widow who had worked alongside her husband on their ranch for thirty-three years. When she became a widow in 1974, Mrs. Heath learned that she would have to pay an inheritance tax of $35,000 unless she could prove she had contributed money, not merely labor, to the purchase or improvement of the ranch. This was true even though the ranch was in both their names, and even though, had she died first, her husband would not have had to pay the same tax. It is as though a woman's lifetime of hard work—whether explicitly homemaking or farm labor or a combination of both—had been worth nothing at all.

The same problem exists on the state level. As of April 1977, only Wisconsin had enacted legislation recognizing a surviving wife as a fifty-fifty owner of joint property. The legislation was originally introduced by Wisconsin's only woman senator at the time, State Senator Kathryn Morrison.

Even when the property is held jointly—is listed in both names—in many other states the wife must prove her financial contribution to it or pay an inheritance tax. In Wisconsin in August of 1977, the state supreme court held that a wife could acquire interest in jointly held property through her services, industry, and skill in the joint operation of the couple's farm.

Other Taxes on a Woman's Work

Tax laws on a wife's work vary from state to state, and Minnesota is only one example of the various problems that can be encountered. In Minnesota a farmer can either put his wife on the payroll and claim her wages as a business expense when filing state tax, or he can form a partnership or corporation with his wife and get a better tax break. In the former case he does not have to pay Social Security or federal unemployment tax, but his wife does not qualify for the resulting benefits; in the latter case he must pay these taxes and she qualifies, but the cost of payments may offset the tax break. Because wives often earn more Social Security benefits as dependents than in their own right, the second alternative may seem more attractive, especially for the short term, except that women who are not paying into Social Security are not covered by disability insurance and are not gaining any credits toward retirement. As we have seen, neither can they count on inheriting their fair share of the farm. This particular combination of incentives may turn out to disadvantage the women in the long run.

Child-Care Centers

Another proposal for tax legislation concerns deductions for child-care centers in the home. The 1976 tax act imposed strict rules on deductions for business activity in the home. According to the *Wall Street Journal,* exemptions have been sought for day-care centers run in the home.

Tax Averaging

One new tax reform idea originated when homemaker Barbara Markana, of Ann Arbor, Michigan, learned from an accountant friend that women who divorce get inequitable treatment in regard to tax averaging. Ms. Markana called the Internal Revenue Service for information and, even before she could state her concern, heard the woman on the line say that women are getting a bad deal from the IRS. Ms. Markana investigated tax averaging and, supported by her local chapter of NOW and by national NOW, presented a proposal for one simple revision of the IRS code to her congressman, Carl D. Pursell. Pursell agreed to support her idea. The bill Ms. Markana has suggested is simple:

> Proposed: A bill to amend the federal income tax regulations on tax averaging in order to allow a person who filed a joint income tax return in the base year, and who is single or remarried to another spouse in the computation year, to compute their base income according to their pro rata share of joint taxable income in that filing year. [H.R. 8615, the Tax Averaging Equity Act]

As the tax law now stands, many dependents other than homemakers and full-time students do not have to consider their benefactors' incomes when tax-averaging. Homemakers, on the other hand, do have to consider their husbands' incomes. The purpose of the tax-averaging reform is to ease the burden of readjustment for displaced homemakers of any age by permitting them the benefits of tax-averaging based solely upon the income they personally earned during the base years, if that income would qualify them to tax average.

For example, consider two cases. In one case a homemaker has been supported for four years by her husband, who makes $20,000 a year. In the other case a dependent who is not a homemaker is supported for four years by a person making the same amount of money. In a fifth year the homemaker and the other dependent each earn $15,000. The non-homemaking dependent, for example, a child over the age of twenty-five, can forget about his benefactor's income: he or she is not assumed to have been entitled to half of it. The tax liability for purposes of averaging would be $15,000 over the five years for the former dependent who was not a homemaker. The homemaker's liability, by contrast, is approximately $55,000. She is assumed to have earned half of what her spouse made, though of course she probably never called that money her own. The bill would merely provide homemakers with the same benefits as any other taxpayer—like other dependents, homemakers would not be penalized for their former dependent status.

Conclusion

Staying informed is essential if homemakers want to see changes made in these areas that so directly affect them. One particularly useful source of information is the brochures on laws affecting homemakers, state by state, that have been published by the Homemaker Committee of the International Women's Year. Of course, local government agencies and elected officials also have information on current and pending legislation.

The laws are often so complex that working with a lawyer or other expert may be essential. And there are so many laws that could be improved that it may seem easier to stay home and bake a cake. Yet, after all their years of dependency, it seems to me that homemakers deserve to bake the cake and eat it too, and if the grass-roots support that publicized bills have begun to receive is any proof, they just may do it.

Women's Work
in the World

11

*We work like our husbands, often in the same shop, but in the home the
duties are unequally divided . . . and when you ask a husband to help, the
answer is always the same: "Do you want me to do a woman's work? Why,
the neighbors would laugh at me."*

Letter by a group of women to
a Moscow newspaper[1]

*Men are superior to women because of the qualities whereby God has made a
distinction between them, and because they expend their wealth to cover the
cost of housekeeping.*

The Koran[2]

*The women of the world are serving notice . . . . We are serving notice to you
that we intend to be paid for the work we do. We want wages for every dirty
toilet, every painful childbirth, ever indecent assault, every cup of coffee and
every smile. And if we don't get what we want, then we will simply refuse to
work any longer.*

A letter to all governments from the Wages for
Housework May Day Rally, Toronto, 1975.[3]

To some extent writing this chapter is an act of faith. The existing
statistics on women in the world, let alone on homemakers in the
world, are few and uncorroborated. One of the better single sources of
current statistical information on women is *The Handbook of International Data on Women*, which grew out of a project undertaken to
survey existing United Nations data on the position of women. Elise
Boulding's *Women in the Twentieth Century World* is also extensively
documented. But, as Boulding herself points out, many of the data are
unreliable. She cites, for example, important limitations on United Nations data on women in agriculture, including the fact that some countries do not report any data at all on their female agricultural workers,
and that some countries simply group female agricultural workers and
all unpaid family workers under the category "other."

229

The trouble is that many nations seem to find other issues more compelling. What they see as the questions of modernization—industrialization, urbanization, and education—occupy their attention, while the problems of women must wait their turn. Yet the women of the world are as deeply affected by cultural change as the men are, and all too often the concerns of modernization come to be synonymous with exclusively male interests and male values. In effect, then, to put the problems of modernization ahead of other social problems has been to put male interests ahead of female interests. Women of so-called modern cultures know only too well that taking a back seat to men is not exclusively characteristic of developing countries. Throughout the world, women are not counted—literally or figuratively—in the same ways that men are.

Yet, in spite of the difficulties, a body of research and policy on the international status of women is beginning to emerge. At the very least we can begin to see the tremendous diversity among women's roles, and at the same time to understand the remarkable commonalities in women's lives worldwide. We can begin to see how the status of homemakers in the United States, the central concern of this book, is related to the status of women around the world.

If we look at women's roles in various countries, we quickly see that words like homemaker, housewife, and housework seem primarily relevant to the United States and Canada, somewhat relevant to other industrialized nations, and only marginally relevant to the less developed countries. (Indeed, a cross-cultural study of the words used to describe the work women do could be fascinating.) If we examine the meanings of the terms closely, we can readily see why this is so. For example, perhaps the simplest definition of housework is the literal one: "work done in the house." This seems fairly straightforward until we realize that an activity like gardening is often included in our notion of housework though it does not fit our literal definition. And, if gardening is included by custom, where does one draw the line? Is partially supporting the family through keeping a large garden to be called housework? What about running the family farm? Analogously, does housework include making the family clothes? What about weaving them? Some may wish to declare that housework includes anything done for the sustenance and physical survival of the family, but this concept, though pertinent abroad, invalidates our American notion of housework in which many activities like specialized cooking and the purchase of elaborate ornamentation are clearly not geared to physical survival.

Furthermore, the American concept of housework commonly includes the notion that it is unpaid: whenever labor is waged, it is called something other than housework. (I have disputed the usefulness of this way of conceptualizing housework; see chap. 2.) By this way of thinking, the term housework seems particularly impotent when applied to other cultures. Yoruba women seldom cook at home; instead, they buy all their meals in the village from women who earn money for this service. Is this meal service then in some sense to be considered housework? If yes, then it is unusual by American standards because it is waged. And, if no, then what constitutes housework in Yoruba society? What happens if women exchange goods instead of money for such services? Does this make the services any more like housework? As we can see, our American term "housework" does not go far toward describing the work women do around the world.

The concept of homemaker is perhaps even more difficult to transfer to other cultures. What happens to the concept of home when a family is polygynous and the husband spends most of his time in the country with one wife while his other wives live in town? What is home for a nomadic woman? Furthermore, the American connotations surrounding the home are analogous to but far from identical with some Western European ideas. The French, for example, associate homemaking with refinement and culture; Americans generally do not. Obviously the strictly American notion of home—let alone homemaker, even with all of its connotations about emotional attachment and tradition—is not sufficient to encompass the variety of dwelling places and family arrangements that exist in the world.

Since these common American terms do not readily describe the practices of other cultures, what will be our basis for comparing women's housework and homemaking roles internationally? How are we to compare our American homemakers with, for instance, the market tradeswomen of Nigeria or the nomadic women of Somalia? It is probably not to anyone's advantage to try to fit the work women do in other countries into the mold of language for women's work in the West. A more fruitful approach will be to set aside our terminologies for the moment and examine the facts about the work women actually do.

I have chosen to include six examples of the work lives of women, each of which for one reason or another is unique. The diversity of women's work roles worldwide is in itself interesting, and examining some of the extremes of these roles opens our eyes to the many possibilities and problems that exist for women today. The countries included are not intended to represent all the different kinds of women's work in the world, but rather are meant to exemplify a possible range of differences and to encourage readers to learn more about how other women live. Later we will move on to consider some of the common denominators in the experience of these and other women. The eventual goal, of course, is to discover the commonalities in women's experience so that women can better organize their resources for change.

Next let us briefly consider the lives of women in Somalia, Nigeria, Ghana, France, Sweden, and China.

The Somali Nomads

In one sense the Somali woman is about as far removed from the concept of homemaker as she can be, for she is not bound to any physical home. Most of the Somalis are nomadic, following their herds throughout the arid lands of their own and neighboring countries. Furthermore, the Somali woman is anything but the stereotype of the dependent homemaker. By the time she is five years old, the Somali child is not afraid to go thirty miles alone, and she knows the genealogy of her clan over seventeen generations. She can milk, and thus she can feed herself: Somalis eat nothing but milk and camel meat.

And yet, for all her uniqueness, for all her independence, the Somali woman has much in common with other women in the world. For one thing, Somali women are controlled by their men. Female children are looked upon as possessions and have sometimes been sold as slaves. Somali men, who consider it beneath their dignity to tend anything but the camels, cattle, and ponies—the tribe's main assets—force the women to do most of the heavy and menial work under threat of physical violence.[4]

Today there are great pressures upon the Somalis to change their life-style, pressures that may in fact endanger their very existence and that, as elsewhere, weigh particularly heavily on the women. According to Boulding, Somali people are very interested in modern education. They envision using new technologies to promote communication about the condition of their lands and herds, and they can see the possibility of moving schools for their children. However, in recent decades the nomads have been encouraged by ruling authorities to settle down and take up agriculture, a policy the Somali women have fought vigorously. As one sociologist points out, "They know that the first consequence of the transplantation of a nomad group into an agricultural region (in Africa) is an enormous increase in the habitual unrequited work of the women. In Arabia it means, of course, veiling and seclusion."[5] They also know that settlement brings disease—respiratory complaints and tuberculosis at higher rates than for nomadic people—and that settlement may mean an almost total disruption of their culture. Naturally the Somali women have resisted. In 1947, for example, as a symbol of their rebellion toward town and sedentary life, they goaded their men into massacring a number of foreigners. Unfortunately, the Somalis are considered so backward that data on the proud Somali women are relatively rare, and, although the United Nations has made an attempt to enfranchise them, few people have paid attention to these women's pleas for preservation of their preferred way of life.[6]

Two Nigerian Tribes

The Yoruba and the Hausa women, members of the two main tribes of Nigeria, are primarily traders. They are accustomed to leading productive, dignified lives in spite of certain obstacles.

The Yoruba women, in fact, have been called the most independent in Africa.[7] The Yoruba culture has had urban centers since ancient times, and all but the youngest of the Yoruba wives trade and live in these centers. The women do very little farming, accounting for only 10 percent of the tribe's agricultural labor as opposed to as much as 75 percent done by women in other agricultural societies.[8] Their trading activities are organized through their long-existing trade guilds, powerful organizations that regulate standards and protect member interests, even to the point of extensive political involvement.

Among the Yoruba all household tasks are done by paid specialists. Women do practically everything, from sewing to hairdressing, as paid services to each other. Even meals are usually eaten out, though they may sometimes be prepared at home. In Nigeria, homemakers hiring homemakers is a way of life.

The Yoruba keep the incomes of husbands and wives separated; spouses buy from and sell to each other, and they contribute specified financial shares to their children's education and upbringing. Child care, by the way, is no problem. Children are spaced about two and a half to three years apart and are carried on their mothers' backs until they can walk. By the age of three they can be sent on errands around their compound, an area the size of a city block in which any adult will aid a child in need. By the age of eight the girls are helping their mothers in trading.

The Hausa women, in contrast, are secluded in their husbands' compounds, yet they also manage to live full trading lives. The only service to husbands that is required of the Hausa women is cooking; otherwise husbands must pay them for everything—including, for example, threshing. Even from seclusion women may perform many different kinds of tasks, including farming, midwifery, spinning, and market trading. A woman may buy a product from her husband, process it, and resell it for her own profit; children and women past menopause are not secluded and act as intermediaries in these transactions. Needless to say, the woman who can thus trade is relatively autonomous, and some women are wealthy even though married to poor men. They invest in goats and sheep and cloth and household trading stock and loans to husbands. Among the Hausa, 80 percent of all married or widowed women belong to the female-initiated and female-administered rotating credit associations.

We are not talking here about remote and inconsequential cultures. Together, the Yoruba and Hausa tribes represent approximately twenty million people. And yet, in spite of their prominence, Nigerian economic planning does not take into account the economic productivity of the Yoruba and Hausa women; it in fact tries to decrease that productivity in order to incorporate so-called modern methods of trade, all without consulting the women themselves. The result is that men are gaining more and more economic power, while women are becoming more dependent. As Boulding notes:

> Nigeria would appear to be a classic example of a country that has ignored the economic roles of women during the modernizing process, since the country . . . has developed a well-trained indigenous bureaucracy and an active indigenous middle class; yet there are not comparable showings for the participation of women in the modern sector.[9]

The Akan of Ghana

The Akan are a large ethnic group living in southern and central Ghana.[10] Among them, women have traditionally held a high status: descent has been reckoned through the female side of a family, historical chronicles have given a prominent place to women, and the Ohemaa, or queen mother, has had power separate from, but very nearly equal to, that of the chief. Traditionally, men and women have shared the economic responsibilities of children. Women have had some domestic responsibilities as well, but these duties have been considered part of a partnership with men, not an indication of lower or dependent status. Work roles have been seen as complementary: women plant, men harvest; women trade in the market, men trade over longer distances. Traditionally, husbands and wives have had separate savings and investments and have been entitled to any profits made from their own labor or trade; husbands and wives do not necessarily inform each other about their financial status.

Today Akan women are fighting what may be a losing battle to maintain this traditional independence. In general, colonialism and modernization have already greatly diminished their status and freedom. The traditional division of labor has been greatly altered because men were recruited into the colonial network as clerks and workers, while women were simply left in the villages. It was not until 1965 that the British colonial service was open to women. Within a system that gives status to white-collar and bureaucratic organizational work, the trading woman in the village has lost status. Of course, relative to her wage-earning husband, she has also lost income. In addition, men are given more educational opportunities, a policy that continues to widen the gap between males and females.

Today Akan women face pressures from both government and church to establish nuclear families in which wives are subordinate to their husbands and families have common funds. The present system allows two parallel modes of marriage, one on a Western Christian model and one on a customary model. Under the customary law men have responsibility for all children born to their wives, including "unofficial wives"—unmarried women who have borne a man's child. Women want this protection to continue in the urban sector as it has in the village, whereas those in power wish to adopt the practices of the "modern" cultures, which would mean that children born outside marriage as defined in the Western Christian model might remain unsupported.

Ghana has been widely recognized as one of the more progressive of developing nations, but modernization and even legal rights have not protected the country's women. As one author writes, "It is true . . . that women in Ghana enjoy most civic, social and political rights and that government policies prohibit discrimination on the basis of sex. The obstacles to women's full participation would appear, therefore, to be the result of practices which rest on cultural and institutionalized attitudes introduced into Ghana by male colonial agents, traders, and missionaries."[11]

France

Like her American counterpart, the French "femme au foyer" lives under a double standard: she is told that her contribution is priceless and, indeed, she earns very little for it.[12] French women have the additional burden of an even higher pedestal: being able to stay at home is a status symbol among the French, and women who do not have a domestic role are regarded as deprived. Further, the conceptualization of the French woman's home role goes far beyond the American notion of housewife or even homemaker:

> She is to charm, console, understand. Her role is that of a helpful, available assistant, but without initiative. She exists essentially in relation to others; her place in the scheme of things is not in the outside world of action, but in the privacy of the home, where she arranges and prepares the times of relaxation.[13]

The "femme au foyer" is to be a model of *politesse* and an agent of culture in the home.

The higher the social class, the less likely it is that men will help with the housework and the more likely it is that a woman's career will be seen as interfering with her household duties. Joelle Rutherford Juillard asserts that "in keeping with the compelling image of availability, women of all classes, except those with live-in servants, shine their husband's shoes."[14]

Many French women will declare that they do not want liberation in the home. "I don't understand this idea about making men wash dishes. That isn't a problem of life. American women's liberation has gone sour because American women don't like men. In France men and women like each other." The woman who said this is none other than Françoise Giroud, in 1977 secretary of state to the prime minister for the condition of women in France.

Giroud came to her new position with impeccable credentials and amid a great deal of publicity; and, indeed, since the creation of her job a number of important changes have occurred in the legal status of women in France. For example, female workers can now deduct childcare expenses from their income tax, widows can collect on their own pensions as well as on their husbands', and all levels and entrance examinations in the civil service are now open to women.

But in spite of some changes the French woman still gets an inordinately small amount of money for her labor, and she still does an inordinate amount of housework. In France more women work outside the home than in any other Western European country, but 56 percent earn less than $200 a month. Three-fourths of all French workers who earn less than $200 a month are women, and most women work in the garment industry, nursing, clerking, or canneries.

And housework in France is complicated. There are few supermarkets, so women shop in numerous small specialty stores; and, since there are few freezers, shopping is done frequently, often daily. Laundromats are rare, open at inconvenient hours, and extremely expensive. Schools and businesses usually close between noon and 2 P.M. for the main meal of the day, which it is considered the woman's duty to prepare.

In 1971 *Le Monde* reported that a French mother of two who works outside the home has an average workweek of eighty-four hours. When in 1971 representative French female workers were asked who did the housework, 54 percent said they did it alone.

In spite of these facts, a movement for change may not be on the horizon. About the situation in France in general, Juillard concludes:

> *Real* equality in the working and political worlds has not been achieved, nor has it been aspired to. Laws themselves, of course, have a limited scope of application unless they are enforced, and French women have been reluctant to challenge discriminatory practices. It does not seem probable that cultural attitudes and perspectives are changing rapidly or will change significantly in the near future.[15]

Sweden

In Sweden, when a child is born, either spouse is granted a six-month paid leave of absence from his or her paid employment. Joint taxation for couples, which had discriminated against the two-income family, was abolished in 1971. In 1977 close to 66 percent of married women worked outside the home (as opposed to 46.5 percent in 1969 and to 41 percent in the United States in 1977), and women earned 82 percent of the average male wage (compared with about 50 percent in the United States), the nearest approximation to sexual equality in wages in the world.

The Swedish government's ideological position is also unique: it asserts that women's two roles as homemaker and worker are both important, but also that it is essential that men participate in new roles. Women should not bear the brunt of change alone; men too have the responsibility to alter their accustomed life-styles—to become better fathers and to share home work equally. To these ends the Swedes are experimenting with parenthood training for both sexes, and both unions and management organizations are attempting to implement the new concepts. Trade unions and the organization of employers even have a joint collaborative body that works for equality between the sexes in accordance with this principle.

Still, the question of who will do the housework has not been resolved. It seems that in Sweden, as in many other nations, class status
and husbands' participation in housework are related. According to one
study of Swedes living in Finland, men in the Swedish middle and
lower classes are especially active in housework, while upper-class
Swedish men avoid household tasks more than do their Finnish
counterparts.[16]

Also, according to one source, the best-known feminist organization
in Sweden has asserted women's need to work outside the home, and
the need for child-care centers, but has failed to point out the importance of work at home. The same writer states, "Everybody knows
that the nurseries are there for the benefit of the employers—women
have to prove they are going out to work, otherwise the child loses its
place however much she/he might need the company of other children. . . . There is a great demand for women's cheap labour in under-
populated Sweden."[17] Other statistics bear out these charges. In
Sweden women still tend to be relatively undereducated and underemployed. Ninety percent of women in vocational schools take courses
that last a year or less, while 50 percent of the men take courses lasting
two years or more. Eighty percent of the women who work outside the
home are concentrated in twenty occupations. Even in Sweden there
seems to be much room for improvement.

China

One of the main goals of socialism in the People's Republic of China has
been the liberation of women. Mao said "Women hold up half of
heaven," and the Communist Chinese have worked to liberate women
from the confines of the home, from daily chores, and from economic
subjugation to men. In China today housework is reduced by widespread nurseries and collective eating places. Women are often reported
to earn equal pay for equal work (although this claim has been disputed).[18] Women are not economically dependent on their families.

Early revolutionary zeal was so strong that the Chinese public came to
frown upon women who stayed at home. "Family women," as they are
called, have been despised, and women have actually been afraid to quit
their paid work because they would face severe criticism. In the mid-
fifties the criticism was so strong that it prompted the editors of a major
women's magazine to publish an article entitled "A Correct Approach
to the Problem of Retirement of Women Cadres," in which they made
this statement:

Some women comrades erroneously think that returning home for household work would turn themselves into "parasites," fearing that they would be looked down upon when they are not economically independent.... It is essential that she be ideologically prepared, take a firm stand and has a strong conviction. She must not heed any sarcasm or ridicule but feel convinced herself that to take up housework is a glory, is beneficial to the nation and the people and carries with it a bright future.[19]

The controversy remains essentially unsettled. On the one hand housework and homelife are criticized on the ideological grounds that hedonism and individualism are detrimental to socialism and that love for the family is secondary to work for the people. On the other hand housewives are lauded for their revolutionary zeal. For example, the story of the housewives of Taching, the site of China's largest oil field, has become a symbol for women in other parts of China. In 1960 China was forced by a Soviet embargo to develop the oil field rapidly. As tradition dictated, workers' families followed them to the site, but many of the housewives found life too hard in Taching, and most were content to stay in their homes. However, one housewife conceived the idea of providing food for the new community. Without farm machinery of any kind, beginning with five housewives armed with spades, the women of the Taching village initiated a program that in the next ten years cultivated 434 acres of land and produced 374,000 pounds of grain, 1,200,000 pounds of vegetables, and 15,200 pounds of meat. The housewives eventually branched out into small local industries. They became the producers of food and the administrators of their community.

The question of equal treatment remains, and there is evidence that women have not achieved true equality in China. For instance, when employment drops, women are the first to be laid off. Also, according to at least one observer, the division of labor by sex has been untouched by socialism. The organization of the "iron girl brigades" is evidence of at least some resistance to these discrepancies in labor allocation—these groups of adolescent women challenge men's work teams to prove they deserve equal pay because they can perform equal labor, or to prove they are capable of doing work from which they have been excluded.[20]

Finding the Patterns in Diversity

These are only six of the thousands of variations on the theme of women's work in the world. Of course there are others even more unusual. Margaret Mead, for example, describes three extremely different New Guinea societies, existing within a hundred miles of each other: in one society growing food and raising children are the central preoccupations, in another fighting and competitive acquisition of women are central, and in the third the people live principally for art.[21]

What can we learn from this kind of diversity? At least two things. First, we can know that our own society is neither isolated nor immutable. Self-evident as this may seem, seeing the variety of individualistic and independent roles that women play around the globe can only be liberating. Studying the lives of other women may give us new ideas for ourselves; at the very least it will open up a new range of possibilities—possibilities like keeping spouses' funds separate as the Akan do, or paying each other for homemaking services as the Yoruba do. Women of the world need to study each other more, to communicate with each other more.

Second, we can begin to discover in diversity the ideas and ideals, problems and solutions, that women have in common. When we do this we find that we come up with a number of patterns that are visible around the world. To begin with, internationally women are bearing more than their equal share of the hardships of modernization. To many people the term modernization is automatically associated with progress, but the fact is that in many cases it means progress for only some people; others—including most women—are left behind in the old ways or, worse, exist in a culture in which old ways are derided and eventually disbanded but in which no alternatives are offered. The same things that happened in the United States when industrialization and the rise of capitalism removed production from the home arena are happening today elsewhere in the world. Women lose their directly productive work and subsequently become dependent on those people, usually their men, who have been assimilated into the industrial sector.

In some cases the schism between men and women is physical: men are recruited away from their homes to work in the city or in an industrial compound miles from their families. The women stay behind to care for farm and family. In American society this did not happen in quite the same way: in the agricultural sector families stayed together, though they diminished in numbers. It was when farm families moved to the cities that they were more likely to develop the schism created by the woman's being sequestered in the home while the man worked in a factory. It is notable that much larger physical distances between husband and wife have become commonplace in developing countries. The result is that transitions by women into the paid work force are even more difficult than for American women.

The differences between workers in the traditional sectors of a country and workers in the modern sector of that country are already large and are getting larger. Boulding points out that countries in the process of industrialization may enter a prolonged state of economic dualism in which there is coexistence of low-productivity subsistence agriculture and high-productivity agribusiness and industry. In the subsistence group, where one finds most of the women, people may actually be worse off than before modernization. The new high-productivity sectors usurp markets, labor, and raw materials, yet trade mainly with other sectors like themselves or with other countries because the subsistence group cannot afford their products. On the other hand, the high producers cannot absorb all the labor of the subsistence group and thus upgrade its status; neither is their technology very useful for increasing subsistence productivity. In short, the rich get richer and the poor get poorer. Of course, women tend to be excluded from the high-productivity agribusiness and industry, partly because the necessary technology is taught by individuals whose own cultures do not include women in these areas. The result, according to Boulding, is that:

> As societies have become more complex and more centralized, the women's sector has become progressively less visible, particularly as urbanization has created a class of male clerics and decision makers out of touch with the production system of their own economies. The imbalance between perceptions and reality has now gone very far, and it is dangerous to the future of the human community. All kinds of international hostilities pile on top of basic failures of perception regarding primary production processes. The problems of the new international economic order are not only problems for all states . . . of bringing domestic planning into line with a realistic assessment of world needs, in a way that will break down have/have-not dualism. They are also the problems of recognizing who the producers are in every society, and bringing the excluded partners into the planning process.[22]

There are other related problems. Even where men and women are not physically or economically separated, women often suffer more from the changes in their environment brought on by moving or, in the case of nomads, settling. We have seen how the nomads of Somalia have resisted efforts to make them settle down and farm. At the opposite extreme are those women whose lives are disrupted when they follow their husbands—for example, those women who follow America's corporate nomads. Whether in the United States or Africa, however, men who move are most often placed into some established role—probably a job—for which they have been chosen and in which they will, at least at the outset, be welcomed. Men join an organization, and that organization becomes the primary social system in which they will relate. Nomads may become farmers; corporate men may take on different jobs. Yet the women who follow must make their own way in a new environment without the institutional supports provided to the men. As men's lives change to meet the needs and values of a developing world—a world created by men and for men—women merely adapt as best they can.

The division of labor by sex, irrespective of individual differences, also continues worldwide. In developing countries, custom has clearly defined women's jobs, and they are the jobs that are underpaid and undervalued. (An interesting study would be a cross-cultural comparison of women's work in developed countries, to see if such things as women's interrupted careers, aptitudes, and housework duties, as opposed to factors like the cheapness and availability of the female labor pool and outright discrinination, can account for the concentration of women in certain jobs.) It is well known that, when women enter a job, men leave it, as in Russia where the formerly high-status job of doctor is now primarily women's work and has a low status. One country has attempted to combat this phenomenon: Sweden has established a quota system with the goal of having at least a 40 percent representation of the minority sex in every job.

In underdeveloped countries, women's work may also be clearly defined. For instance, Rajput women observe purdah, whose restrictions include confinement to the family courtyard and instructions to refrain from certain household tasks: their life has been described as one of "enforced leisure," which they use to cook, mend, and spin. Among the Nsaw of Cameroons women do virtually all of the labor necessary to maintain the family; men work no more than ten days a year and otherwise stay in the compound drinking and telling stories.

Custom is the usual explanation for such divisions of labor. Perhaps more useful than exploring the origins of these customs would be explaining the factors that currently maintain them. Anthropologist Judith K. Brown suggests that what seems like an unequal division of labor really represents a balance that maintains the conjugal family. For instance, "The apparent leisure of the Nsaw men [is] illusory. Socializing and wine drinking take up much of their time. However, their financial responsibilities to their family are heavy, and they are the agents through which the household enters the wider economic sphere of the market. The Rajput women fill their enforced idleness with domestic busywork, but their confinement is necessary for the caste status of the entire household."[23] We need to do more thinking along these lines. Why do extremes continue to exist? How do men and women in these societies feel when they learn that things are not the same in other parts of the world? More generally, why is it that labor is divided by sex, as opposed to ability or, for instance, seniority?

Another situation women have in common around the world is what has in the United States been called women's dual roles—as homemakers and as wage earners. Again the terminology does not transfer directly, for in many parts of the world women have more of the burden of work than men yet do not perform any waged work at all. What are seen as dual roles in the United States and parts of Europe and the Far East are what Boulding calls "the triple burdens of breeder-feeder-producer." Whatever the terminology, the fact remains that women do more work resembling housework than men do.

A UNESCO time budget study by Alexander Szalai including twelve countries clearly shows this triple role for the world's women.[24] As has been documented in the United States, Szalai's sample of cities shows that more employed women than men do child care and housework, including cooking, home chores, laundry, and marketing. Men in these cities never spend more than a half an hour a day on housework, while women never spend less than an hour and a half. In one city in the USSR women who work outside the home spend an average of 170 minutes a day on housework, while the men spend 28 minutes (child care is 30 minutes per person). This compares with 133 housework minutes a day for women and 31 minutes for men in one city in the United States and 156 minutes for women and 26 minutes for men in six cities in France. Women have substantially fewer minutes left for study and participation, use of mass media, or leisure than men do. In all these cases the women spend almost as much time as the men do in outside employment (generally within 10 to 15 minutes of the same time, the largest discrepancy being in Torun, Poland, where the men work outside the home an average of 73 minutes a day more than the women).

The pressure of these dual or triple roles—in short, this inequitable work burden—exerts pressure on many marriages. The phenomenon is by no means limited to the United States. Economist Lourdes Beneria of Rutgers University writes that, for instance, in Spain women who have moved into paid production have continued to be totally responsible for housework. Their problems have been aggravated by the lack of day care and collective services that might replace the homemaker's personal work. A particular difficulty is that in Spain role reversal by either sex is seen not merely as unusual but as positively deviant, and people who attempt it are ridiculed. Separation is on the increase, and women are realizing that traditional family life and economic independence may be incompatible.[25]

Similarly, in the countryside of Honduras, where *el hombre manda* ("the man rules"), some women are beginning to realize their exploited position. These women are constantly pregnant and do the worst of the housework—grinding corn, hauling wood and water, and cooking. The men plant crops, hunt, drink, and gamble. Perhaps most debilitating is the circumstance that, because the men resist marriage, women are often abandoned. One woman whose common-law husband left her raised her children alone for six years and trained to be a health worker with her local "housewives' club." When her husband returned shortly after her training, he was adamant against her club and her job; he beat her and threatened to shoot her if she continued. She refused to quit her club or her job. The village finally backed her, and eventually he left again. The woman is proud of her independence; she is one of the many women who are beginning to rebel at their multiple roles when they amount to mere servitude.[26]

Enclosure, another characteristic of women's lives around the globe, means that women are more restricted to activities within or near the home than men are. Enclosure ranges from purdah, the strict rules of veiling and seclusion for both Muslim and Hindu women, to the relatively free but nevertheless somewhat restricted life of the American woman in a nuclear household in the suburbs. It is difficult to determine whether enclosure exists because of a cultural ideology, as with the dicta of purdah, because of a need to protect women physically, or merely because of women's low status. It can even come about because of some seemingly tangential circumstance like zoning laws. The fact is that generally women are more restricted to the home than men are. (The exceptions are interesting to think about: the Tuaregs of the Sahara veil their men. Women own the property and manage it, and among the Tuaregs only the women learn to write.)[27]

Often, the higher the social class, the more likely it is that the women will be restricted in movement. Purdah is a luxury, aspired to by those who better their economic position. To a certain extent, the wealthier the man, the more restricted the woman, though this custom is changing as populations become more educated. The same mode of thinking—that men don't want their wives to work if they don't have to—remains strong in the West. Certainly men in the United States sometimes are proud because their women do not have to work. And of course the same notion is prevalent in France, where 84 percent of women who work do so solely out of economic necessity and where, as we have seen, being able to stay at home is a status symbol.[28]

As a result of enclosure, women may have less ability to trade and less knowledge and experience. They are likely to be seen as less valuable workers. As education becomes available—education that could lessen or even eliminate women's confinement—people wonder what use it is if women will only stay home anyway. "But what good does it do," asks an Indian village matron, "if housework is our goal? I've passed tests in water fetching, cooking, and childbearing without attending a single class."[29] A vicious circle exists: women are not trained for work that will expand their horizons, therefore women do not expand their horizons, therefore women's horizons are seen as limited.

Finally, almost all the women of the world have permanent relationships with individual men. Such relationships, one should remember, are not a necessity of life. All-female communities have existed quite successfully. An example is the Buddhist nuns of China, a highly prosperous group of communities that emerged in southern China from 1850 to 1930. The communities were a response to a unique economic opportunity for women: in those days a healthy silk industry hired only women and gave them the chance to be independent of husbands. These Chinese women based their communities on no special ideology. When interviewed, they told anthropologist Andrea Sankar such things as, "I wanted my freedom" and "I would be no man's slave," or "No one should tell us what to do with our lives." As we have seen, many women in the world support themselves economically, often not even living with their husbands. American women sometimes choose celibate lives, or lives with other women, or lives alone. It may be that there is indeed something valuable in the idea that women without men are better off—certainly, in some cases, they are better off economically. On the other hand, when their individuality does not receive a cultural sanction, they may suffer, even to the point where in some cultures they cannot survive.[30] The modern ability of an unmarried adult, whether male or female, to exist independently is a phenomenon whose impact we are only beginning to experience.

However, that most women have more or less stable relationships with men means that we are not dealing only with a woman's problem when we describe those things that are common among the world's women. We are also talking about a man-and-woman problem. For every woman that has been left in her village, there is a man who left her; status differentials for couples are not felt only by the woman—the man too must have thoughts about the distinction. The man who moves, taking his wife with him, must face her discontent. Such men see the poverty of women, and the anger of women, and the discrimination against women. How do these men deal with the discrepancies they see? What do they believe about these problems? Do they truly believe they are trivial, "women's" problems? Do they truly believe women are inferior? Are they truly absorbed by their desire to pursue their personal fortunes?

It is hard to believe that creating a gap between males and females is deliberate government policy in any country, though it is not so hard to believe that a developing country could adopt Western ideas about women's place, and it is easy to believe that a man would be reluctant to give up his wife's free labor. At any rate, the notion developing in this country that men too have more than one role and that men must change if women's status is to change is also true throughout the world.

The World Effort for Women

Let us now examine those policies and actions that are aimed at improving the status of women. I must begin with a caution: We will all do well to realize that countries do not necessarily conceive of their problems in the same ways; for instance, one country may not conceptualize a problem in terms of sex differences, not because the problem cannot be seen that way or because it is not useful to see it that way, but, in some cases, because other focuses are historically more acceptable or seem more immediately pressing.

Of course, some problems seem more pressing than others according to who is looking at them, and the problem-solvers with any power are almost invariably male. The unfortunate result may be that, for example, a country will concentrate on eradicating illiteracy, which on the face of it seems more important than some ideal of sexual equality, and indeed may make great progress in educating its population without ever educating its women. Or a nation may concentrate on eradicating poverty, in the process upgrading some of its male citizens and leaving women unaided or even worse off than before.

In the USSR, for instance, according to Stanford historian Dorothy B. Atkinson, women as a class do not seem to be aware that they have a problem, even though they are clearly burdened by their dual roles as employed workers and homemakers.[31] Many Soviet women believe that they alone should be primarily responsible for the care of their home and children, while at the same time 89 percent of all able-bodied women are working outside the home for a wage. Most of the women who work outside the home are full-time workers, since part-time jobs are very unusual in the USSR. It is difficult to know whether Soviet women do not know they have a problem or whether they simply do not dare organize to solve it. On the one hand, they probably lack exact information about their status. There has been no women's movement since the revolution, and publicity about, for example, sex differences in salary (even if those statistics exist) is nil. On the other hand, the revolution is supposed to have given women full equality once and for all. Lenin's Soviet regime announced very early that it was "the first and only government in the world to have completely abolished all the old despicable bourgeois laws that placed women in a position of inferiority to men."[32] Women were given the right to vote and were guaranteed full equality before the law. They were to have been spared the burdens of housework through communal dining rooms and child care. However, as Atkinson points out:

> Attitudinal changes have been slow to develop in the USSR partly because the liberation of women was never envisaged as entailing any modification of men's traditional roles. In the socialist blueprint, the state was supposed to solve all the problems of domestic management. But in the process of social reconstruction, other needs were judged more urgent by the men in political command, and these were given priority.[33]

Today in the USSR it is probably difficult to speak out against a system that the authorities have already hailed as successful. A recent Soviet sociological study discussing the lower income of women in general says the differences result from "the distinct sociobiological roles of men and women in the family which make men more responsible for material security and give women primary responsibility for domestic work."[34]

Of course many women elsewhere are already well aware of their status, and some are attempting to raise the consciousness of others. One of the best-known international groups lobbying for homemakers is the movement Wages for Housework, which reports on women's growing resistance to their exploitation, primarily in North American and Western European countries.

Wages for Housework is establishing a network among homemakers to discuss their common problems, and it is also demonstrating for their cause. In one consciousness-raising demonstration in London, twenty-five women marched from Marble Arch to Downing Street accompanied by a police escort, leafleting along the way and asking women such questions as how much they were paid for cleaning their houses.

The Wages for Housework group also publishes information on demonstrations held worldwide. They report, for instance, that in Bombay thousands of women marched through the streets banging pans and brandishing rolling pins in protest against rising prices. The rolling pin held in a clenched fist symbolizes the Women's Anti–Price Rise Front there.[35]

They also report that, in Portugal, a first meeting of concerned homemakers in December 1974 drew five hundred women. These women debated the slavery versus the nonslavery of housework, wages for housework, dependence upon husbands, unjust laws for women in Portugal, lack of education for women and lack of state nurseries. They decided to start a housework association, and fifty women came to the first organizational meeting: many were over forty years old and were attending without their husbands' permission. Part of the group later sponsored a demonstration to start International Women's Year, and twenty of them were stopped by two thousand men. According to a letter written to Wages for Housework by a woman from the MLM (the women's liberation movement) in Lisbon, the men who stopped them started out by hurling epithets—"Women only in bed"; "Go home and do your dishes"—and finished by abusing the women physically, including sexually. As a result, other nearby women were hurt—an old woman was beaten, and a sixteen-year-old girl was stripped naked. The police and the army did nothing but stand by and smile.[36]

Of course resistance by established powers is not always so crude. More sophisticated methods can just as effectively keep women in their place. All women can learn from the experience of the women of Ghana. In the fifties, two organizations represented the interests of most Ghanian women. One was primarily for educated, urban women and emphasized Western values; the other enlisted the support of Ghana's rural marketing women. The Convention People's Party, the revolutionary party that led Ghana to independence in 1957, wanted to consolidate these two organizations into a women's wing of the party. Other corporate groups in the country had already been organized as party auxiliaries, including the farmers in the United Ghana Farmer's Cooperative Council, the workers in the Trade Union Congress, and the youth in the Young Pioneers. Women had been sparsely represented in these other groups. To obtain the consolidation it wanted, the party called a conference of one hundred leading women and obtained a resolution from them calling for a national women's movement; it then created the National Council of Ghana women (NCGW) in September 1960.

The results of this consolidation have been to control the women's groups of the country and to give women a back seat in the party. As part of the incorporation, all women's groups in the country had to hand over their financial assets to the party. This policy included even the small trade and savings and loan associations of the market women. NCGW's established budget was small in comparison with those of other party auxiliaries, and so was its staff: its paid employees at national headquarters totaled 5, while the Young Pioneers, for example, had 129.

NCGW's main contribution for women has been its pressure on the government to change marriage laws. It has also attempted to get more secondary education for girls. However, it has never produced an official statement on the position of women in either traditional or modern Ghana. When the market women found their economic power waning as the party controlled import licenses and set prices on their products, the NCGW was useless to them. Instead of demonstrating in the streets over prices, as they had done when Britain instituted price controls, the market women instead talked to the party. And the party listened but did nothing.[37]

Consider also the case of Algerian women since Algerian independence in 1962. During the eight-year war for independence, women came out of purdah and left their traditional roles to take full roles as guerrillas, serving as everything from messengers to nurses to bombers. They shared the risks of the underground activity equally with men. When the new government was created, it called for full participation by women in public affairs and economic development and for active party support of women's equality in politics, in the party, and in the construction of socialism.[38] The new constitution guaranteed equal rights and responsibilities for women and men, and ten women were elected to the first legislature. Houari Boumedienne took over the government by military coup three years later and pledged to support the principles of the revolution, including women's equality. But in his 1966 address to International Women's Day he said that women already had their rights, that the progress of women must be within the framework of Islamic morality and not an imitation of the West, and that men could not be expected to suffer unemployment while the women worked. Only two women were elected to Algeria's second parliament, and none were elected to the third. And disciminatory laws continue—for example, punishment for adultery is twice as harsh for women as for men.

We can learn from the protesters in Portugal and India, the women's groups of Ghana, and the revolutionary women of Algeria, but only if we know about them. Exchange of information is essential. One thing women learn very quickly is that promises are not action: enforcement of policies of equality is difficult to achieve (perhaps because the idea of changing men's roles has not been incorporated into those policies), and women's issues get put on the back burner when the policymakers are all men. Women must establish their power to become educated and then to move those issues to the front of the stove where, as women's issues, they belong.

Fortunately for morale if nothing else, there are in existence some social programs that are worth examining and perhaps emulating. Of course, my selection of these programs represents my Western bias. I am writing here about programs that seem to me to be useful as models for the Western system; other women may perhaps be more critical of them and may find them less applicable to their own cultures.

In my opinion, then, the Scandinavian countries are ahead of other nations in their conceptualization of the problems—as I have already mentioned, Sweden in particular emphasizes that men must change as well as women, and that economic independence for all individuals is an important goal. Sweden had a long history of concern for women's rights. Among other early notions, in 1884 Strindberg's "Declaration of Women's Rights" included the suggestion of an allowance for housework.[39] A 1935 Swedish Commission report accused employers of "social misuses of their power" in hindering married women from obtaining work outside the home.[40] Today Sweden's educational system reflects this egalitarian heritage. Both boys and girls are required to take training in carpentry, metalcraft, domestic science, and child care. Textbooks reflect the newer ways of thinking, even to the point of attempting to change old ways. One text in family-life education includes the following statement: "One of the parents may want to stay at home and care for the children, at least as long as they are little. It need not always be the woman who has the greatest desire and aptitude for this."[41]

Denmark's national child-care system is also exemplary. Family helping agencies provide financial assistance whenever a family needs child care, youth club or special education fees, psychological help, the services of a homemaker, or short-term funds for food and necessities. This aid is based on the 1964 Child and Young Persons Act, which made services available to all families with children under the age of eighteen, but the social reform law of 1974 extended services to all citizens whether or not they have children. The Danes also have established, beginning privately in 1905 and sponsored since 1939 by the government, Mother's Help Centers for women with children under two years. Through these centers, "Overworked and exhausted housewives who are not eligible for the house-helper services, which is provided during sickness but not pregnancy, can get money for temporary domestic help."[42] This money can be used to pay for a homemaker to clean house for the first three months after childbirth.

Perhaps the most striking feature of the Danish system is the rest and recreation centers where "depleted" mothers may spend a week or a year. Each center houses about twenty mothers and thirty children. Each mother takes care of her room, feeds her child, and puts him or her to bed. But otherwise she has no housework to do. "She is spared all other responsibilities—the laundry, cooking, constant child care, housecleaning that have drained her energy. Perhaps for the first time in her life she gets a chance just to rest, read a book, chat. If she feels energetic, she might go to the craft room . . . . She can walk the spacious grounds, enjoy nature, or just sit. And there are consultation rooms where she might talk to a psychiatrist or a social worker about her problems or see a gynecologist if her physical condition worries her. She knows her children are playing happily with the child nurses."[43]

Norway's Family Council, a public agency, is doing some practical experimentation on role-sharing in the family under the direction of sociologists at the University of Oslo. Several couples are trying out the idea of sharing one job: they work either half-days or half-weeks or every other week and receive a full wage with all the attendant fringe benefits. A condition for participation is that home roles too must be shared equally. The study examines the effects of role-sharing on the marital relationship, the children, and job productivity. Results so far have been positive.[44]

Other innovations can be found in Canada, which, like some European countries, has a system of family allowances. (A similar system in Britain was originally conceived as pay for housework services but gradually was associated with having children.) In 1975 the Mother-Led Union, angry welfare mothers in Canada, protested the fact that the government increased the family allowance from $8 to $20 but informed welfare mothers that the increase would be deducted from their welfare checks. As one woman said, "But do we not work in the home? Yes, we do . . . . It works out to about 16 hours a day without pay. We would like to know how we are expected to do our jobs—the most important we believe—mothering . . . without the proper monies."[45]

Canada is also proposing changes in its pension system to allow the participation of housewives. The issues are similar to those now being debated in the United States: Should housewives be given credit for the work they do? And, if so, how, and who is to pay for it? The Royal Commission on the Status of Women recommends the exploration of a plan to credit the spouse at home with portions of the contributions of the employed spouse and of those contributions made by the employer for the employed spouse, and also on an optional basis, permitting the spouse at home to contribute as a self-employed worker.

International cooperation is probably the most promising way to bring women's collective expertise to those women who are ignorant of the global nature of their problems or who lack enough power in their own countries to do something about them. Even psychological support alone can be helpful. As a woman in Lisbon wrote, "It has been of great comfort to us, the way so many women's movements in the world are supporting us. The 'machismo' here is like a disease, a serious one. If it weren't for so many women around the world fighting for the same thing, we would feel quite lonely and hopeless."[46]

In any effort at international cooperation, avoiding cultural imperialism is essential. To take just one example, in some countries women may not even see the need or desirability of organizing special women's groups. Women's groups have been effective in creating change in the United States, but they are not necessarily able to effect change in countries where machismo reigns supreme. Developing countries are especially sensitive to the influence of Western culture on their life-styles. In many such cases Western women will do as well to listen and learn as to talk and teach.

At this point, simply gathering information may be a potent instrument for change. To gather information on women will represent a policy change for many governments, but it is a step that can be easily taken. Sharing such information internationally may allow women to see and to begin to work on their common problems. As the Power of Women collective has written, "Every worker, woman and man, knows that the more widespread your struggle, the more likely you are to win. But houseworkers understand best the weakness inherent in their isolated labour. We need, even more than other workers, to see that women in other situations, in this country and elsewhere, are demanding what we are demanding. Otherwise it is much more difficult to conceive of winning."[47]

Many organizations for international cooperation have already been established, though not explicitly with the problems of homemakers in mind. Aside from government and associated organizations, like the United Nations, other women's networks include WIN (Women's International Networks) and ISIS (Women's International Information and Communication Service). Nongovernment organizations that have the greatest contact with their female members are the World Association of Girl Guides and Girl Scouts, the Women's International Democratic Federation, the World Union of Catholic Women, the World YWCA, the International Council of Nurses, and the Associated Countrywomen of the World.[48]

With information assembled and efficient networks established, women internationally can begin to look at their goals for women who are homemakers—or whose status resembles that of homemakers as we know them. The goals may differ among nations. One can easily imagine that women will arrive at a point where women in one culture, even though their own preferences may differ, will effectively help women in another culture to set their own goals and to become autonomous within that culture.

Problems
and Potentials

12

The role in our society of the homemaker must be fully recognized. Her difficult but highly creative job will shape the future of the American family, which in turn dictates the quality of American life. She passes on crucial, basic values, sets an example for her community, and sends a new generation out into the world. Her importance in our society, in all of its multidimensional aspects cannot possibly be emphasized enough.

Rosalynn Carter[1]

Every woman householder is daily a practicing futurist. Because their responsibilities and experiences tend to be local, they do not think in terms of large-scale systems or world futures. Precisely because of their intimate knowledge of local social terrains, however, they will be increasingly important in the development of the self-help systems that must replace poorly functioning centralized systems.

Elise Boulding[2]

The homemaker movement today presents some unusual challenges and some far-reaching potentials. Foremost among the challenges is the fact that the movement is significantly different from efforts to obtain equality in employment. It may well be that efforts to get women employed in positions high in power, status, and financial reward, and in nontraditional jobs, will seem like child's play compared with improving the status of women who work in the home. This is because the two efforts have one crucial difference: the former is in line with important basic beliefs about work held in this country and much of the world, while the latter runs directly counter to some of these beliefs.

To reiterate what I have stressed in earlier chapters, people in our society tend to believe that certain kinds of work should earn money, power, and prestige while certain others should not. Work considered deserving is that done in the marketplace for money; work that does not earn as much status is that done in the home without pay. Further, as a society we believe that most individuals will be motivated to earn increasing amounts of traditional rewards and that money, power, and prestige are the legitimate and appropriate rewards for those who work the hardest.

Within this belief system, the feminist thrust to improve the status of women who work for a wage has been recognized as legitimate by many people, irrespective of their views on sexual equality. Even those observers who fail to acknowledge the wider humanist goals of the feminist movement can see why individual women might want to earn for themselves the same rewards in the same kinds of jobs that have commonly been available to men. Efforts to gain status for women's paid work, difficult as the process is—and insufficient as it remains—are nevertheless efforts that conform to our traditional beliefs about the desire to work.

Efforts to improve the status of housework, on the other hand, are outside and even antithetical to the traditional belief system. For one thing, homemaker advocates want to take a low-status job and give it respect. In essence, they are asking society to accept a new standard for the valuation of work, a standard that considers the importance of a worker's social contribution alongside of or even instead of such attributes as educational degrees or position in the organizational hierarchy. The idea of upgrading the work rather than the worker is still relatively novel, and the concept is not nearly so engaging to the American imagination as is the cherished ideal of Horatio Alger individualism.

At the same time, the new homemaker movement does not endorse the pursuit of traditional rewards. The movement breaks with tradition because competition has virtually no role in its ideology. Its emphasis is more cooperative than competitive. The concepts of hierarchy and power are alien to most new movement homemakers. Their primary goals are not to move up or to control, but rather to gain fair distribution of available rewards of all types. Homemakers want more of the tangible rewards like money, but they are also emphasizing satisfaction, personal growth, and, especially, social contributions. The new homemaker movement asserts that a reasonable share of available rewards and personal fulfillment is the right of any worker who makes a contribution to society, not merely of those few who are skillful or lucky enough to come out on top of the status pyramid. This threat to our traditional belief in the nature and purpose of work may partially account for the wide range of negative responses that homemaker advocates encounter.

Another challenge posed by the new homemaker movement is the impossibility of using strictly traditional methods for improving the homemaker's status. Several important issues are apparent. For one thing, new motivators must be developed. A typically important function of any organizational hierarchy is to provide a channel for the individual's upward mobility, and thus an incentive to work. Unlike most other work situations, housework has no hierarchy, thus eliminating an important avenue for the individual's increased status. Those who promote structures for collective rather than individualized rewards will see the absence of a hierarchy as an advantage, though they will also recognize the difficulties of establishing alternative structures. Yet it is not easy to invent new carrots, and many homemakers have been socialized to the traditional system.

Homemakers' "bosses"—their husbands, potential employers, and others who stand to lose from homemakers' change in status—will not willingly give up power to them. And the applicability of traditional models of power transition is often questionable when applied to the family unit. The individual homemaker can improve her status only to a point. After she has equalized her share of the housework and has gained respect for her housework among her family and her friends, she reaches a plateau. Individually she can go no further—there are no salary improvements or directorships built into her work system; she has no way of achieving a prestigious title tied to an elite job. She may not even be able to command reasonable working conditions. If the homemaker wishes to improve her status, it now seems that she must gain power and work for changes that will affect all homemakers as a group. Developing the knowledge and incentives to do this is problematic. This characteristic of the new homemaker movement is one of the most serious problems ever faced in the women's movement, and methods for dealing with it have yet to be developed.

The general challenge of the homemaker's isolation must continually be faced. The logistics of organizing individuals who work in millions of separate dwellings is enough to daunt the most fervent activist. As we have seen, a certain amount of change can be brought about through personal initiative aimed at revising specific laws and changing the behavior of one's own family. But at some point the work of isolated individuals is no longer enough. Homemakers will have to organize to bring pressure on powerful organizations or combat major interest groups. How likely is it that homemakers will band together to influence large corporations—for instance, insurance companies who refuse to grant them disability insurance? How likely is it that they will organize to demand their rights as workers? These are some of the difficult questions that homemakers and their advocates will need to answer if the new homemaker movement is to be successful.

In any system of homemaker organization, leadership may become an issue of contention, for two reasons. For one thing, system change usually proceeds from the top down. Leadership is traditionally seen as crucial to policy initiation and implementation. Change without traditional forms of leadership is possible, though generally more laborious. Then, too, if leadership is desirable in the homemaker movement, who will the leaders be? The women's movement still has a tendency toward schism—a tendency to alienate homemakers by more strongly legitimizing employed women. The language of the movement illustrates this. At this time, *MS.* magazine, for instance, continues to use the term "working woman" to refer to employed women rather than to both employed and homemaking women. Most women's magazines, whether avowedly feminist or not, do the same. If this schism widens—or even if it stays as is—one may expect homemakers to remain skeptical about forming coalitions with other women. Conceivably they may opt to choose leaders from among themselves only, which would be a pity, it seems, since employed women currently have a great deal more institutional and financial power and the two groups certainly have common interests. To a certain extent, the issues of cooperation among women are similar to those encountered in planning cross-cultural research or policy. All parties concerned should be fully apprised of goals and strategies. All should have input, decision power, and expected benefits from an enterprise, even from "pure" research. Only when such conditions are met can all sides be assured that they are neither exploiting nor being exploited. Homemakers and their employed advocates need to be sensitive to these concerns.

Efforts to improve homemakers' status by changing the language of homemaking are pernicious when they camouflage such organizational and leadership issues. Calling homemaking "home management" and home decision-making "management policy," as is done in some home economics research, is only using a Band-Aid if these true management issues are ignored. Closing the schism between homemakers and employed women, whether through enlightened traditional leadership forms or through collective structures, is one of the most serious challenges posed by the homemaker movement.

If the homemaker movement succeeds in organizing, its very size may give it far-reaching ideological and social power. It may be easy to explain efforts to improve the waged woman's status as a way for many individuals to better their personal status. It will be less easy to explain organized homemakers' campaigns by theories of individual self-gratification. On the contrary, the new homemaker movement will find advocates worldwide among both women and men who see in it possibilities for a renewed emphasis on family and community networks and for a reinvigoration of such values as nurturing rather than conquering and cooperation rather than competition.

Homemakers and the New Society

I think that meeting the special challenges posed by the new homemaker movement will be worth the effort. Improving homemakers' status has the potential to affect not only homemakers themselves, but also social systems around the world. For example, homemakers' support may help implement the decentralist world policy that has recently been advocated by such authors as E. F. Schumacher, whose *Small Is Beautiful* view of economics has captured the popular imagination, and Paul Ehrlich, whose books on the relation of ecology and social systems have been widely read. Specifically because of their position on the fringe of social power yet at the crux of many local social and ecological systems, homemakers can be important to the development of new social and ecological world systems. In *The End of Affluence*, Ehrlich delineates the kind of social change he feels we need:

> One area in which your personal efforts to change society are most likely to enhance the quality of your life in the future is your local community. If our predictions are correct, there will be an accelerating trend toward decentralization in the next few decades, and gradually your relationships with your neighbors and your local community will increase in importance while those with federal and (probably) state governments will tend to fade. Indeed, the strength and cohesiveness of your community may be *the* dominant factor in determining whether or not you can successfully ride out a time of troubles.[3]

What will be the homemaker's role in the development of these new social systems? Elise Boulding's analysis provides some basic concepts for understanding women's potential worldwide. Pointing out the marginality of women's status in the world, she asserts that the very fact that women are removed from the mainstream of political life may be advantageous for men and women alike in the long run:

> What is needed now? I would answer, a new set of images of possible futures that involve a decentralist yet still interconnected

and interdependent world, which will stimulate the development of a variety of new social techniques to enable that world to come about....

Who will create the new images? It will be those who are marginal to the present society, who are excluded from the centers of power, who stand at the world's peripheries and see society as with different eyes. All utopists, all visionaries have been marginal to the society they have lived in....

It happens that the category of human beings I have been writing about in this book fulfills the requirements of marginality, of exclusion from the centers of power, and of possession of practical everyday skills at the micro and intermediate levels of human activity—the family, the neighborhood, the town. Since they also represent approximately half the human race, their aggregate potential is incalculable. I am referring, of course to women.

The power of the marginals lies precisely in their lack of at-homeness in the world in which they live. Because they do not "belong" in the sense that they are never invited into society's back rooms where decisions that shape their lives are made, because they are usually treated as objects, never subjects, of the social process, they are driven to affirm belonging at another level.[4]

Of course the women who continue to be marginal to the present society will not be those who are most successful within the existing system—they will not be the highly paid, highly visible career women. They will be the homemakers.

Women are already in a position to make important personal contributions in the home. For example, they are the food policymakers for families all over the world. In this role they can to a certain extent manipulate the family's style of consumption, and in doing so they have great potential power to reflect various ecological and social concerns. On the other hand, because of the same role, women are also vulnerable to exploitation by some ever more popular ideas: the increased desire for pure homegrown and home-prepared foods and the ecological concerns about such convenience items as plastics and electric gadgets threaten to put an even heavier burden of work on the homemaker.

Ehrlich's advice to people who want to survive the predicted age of shortages is to know as much as you can about your immediate environment. Skills will become increasingly important; knowing how to grow your own food, fix your own heating system, and make your own clothes will constitute valuable survival expertise. Whether or not shortages and concurrent social crises occur, the homemaker can make use of Ehrlich's advice today, for most homemakers really know very little about their homes. The more the homemaker knows, the more autonomous and powerful she is in her own sphere. The homemaker is now at the mercy of her machinery, which most often she can neither repair nor replace without outside help. She usually has very little systematic knowledge about the basic chemistry of gardening or about the construction of furniture. She cannot fix her own plumbing or electricity, and so she waits for the repairman or her husband, while keeping herself ignorant and dependent. It has been suggested that future toy kitchens should include real plumbing under the sinks.

Giving such knowledge to a homemaker professionalizes her job at home in a way that can be extremely valuable to her family. And it is also valuable to society because it makes us more capable of national adjustment in emergency situations and more open and able to accept the concept of decentralization as a workable plan for a new society.

It is obvious that women cannot accomplish what Boulding hopes for them, and what Ehrlich hopes for the community at large, merely by virtue of their marginal existence. They must become aware of the nature of marginality, and they must be educated to the broad problems facing the world. They must make a conscious effort to develop alternative life-styles. In their revealing article "Women and Environments: An Overview of an Emerging Field," three members of the Faculty of Environmental Studies at York University in Toronto state the problem this way:

> Men are *dominant* (in a control sense) at the scale of the "world," city, and region by virtue of their political, economic and employment roles. Women on the other hand, tend to *occupy* spaces at the home and neighborhood levels, and exercise some degree of personal control over them. However, despite women's numerical concentration at the home and neighborhood scales, key decisions about these spheres tend to be made by institutions at the city-wide, regional, and national scales.[5]

Thus, while women are uniquely situated and while their value systems may be uniquely suited to the trend toward a "small is beautiful" view of society, they also tend to operate strictly within the microsystem rather than entering the wider authority system that largely controls their individual setting. The problem is clear. Boulding summarizes it:

> In part women need to uncover older preindustrial network skills; in part they need to unlearn socialization into male dominance systems; in part they need to be freshly inventive about new non-hierarchical patterns for working in large-scale entities. None of this can happen as long as women are attached to old status systems, and yet the old

status systems give them what recognition they do get from the "male world."[6]

It is not only recognition that they get from the "male world" through the old status systems; they get power as well. Experiments in women's centers and in other groups with nonhierarchical organizations run the risk of being overlooked as being well-meaning and interesting but not really applicable to larger organizations or societies. When groups do not seek power through conventional means, they are often seen as powerless. The quandary is an old one: whether to seek change from inside or outside the system. Women today are trying out both alternatives, though, as the discussion here suggests, perhaps they should be even more conscious about their choice of methods.

What Do Homemakers Really Want?

It would be delightful, wouldn't it, if we could arrive at some consensus about what all homemakers want. If we could establish concrete goals, it seems, we could more efficiently direct our efforts for change. Most people believe that goal-oriented behavior is more likely to succeed than is haphazard experimentation, and believers are doers. If homemakers had one clear goal, perhaps they could enlist more people for their cause, and perhaps they could get where they are going even faster.

Unfortunately, it is very difficult for the new homemaker movement to establish goals, because it concerns nothing less than the evolution of the family and of sex roles—two of the most enduring and yet unpredictable of all social institutions. It is far easier to say we will put a person on Mars by 1989 than it is to say we will change the structure of the family in the next three decades. We simply do not agree about what structure we want, and once we set the goal we still would not know what structure would actually work.

Thus we generally tend to take a problem-solving approach—the organization of this book is an example. We say that such and such is the homemaker's problem, then we set out to solve that problem—to make it go away. At this point we know only that women should not have to bear the burden of making their services available to society.[7] Our efforts to change this situation will undoubtedly create new social structures, but the forms they create will be born of problem-solving, not of planning. Foresight—ideas about what new social institutions could be created and about what new forms might be an improvement over present ones—is more difficult.

Most of this book has been devoted to presenting and analyzing the various change strategies that homemakers and their advocates have begun and are currently working on. I have emphasized the need for a systems approach to research and change, the need for model development, the need for increased communication among homemakers and between homemakers and their advocates. Of course this book has had to use piecemeal studies and information to create theoretical approaches for working with a broad category of individuals. I eagerly await data from much larger samples of homemakers, to use in refining and recasting strategies. I particularly look forward to discovering more data on homemakers in other nations and among minority groups in this country.[8] Occasionally I have mentioned the need for more research in a given area, or the need for more explicit statistics. In concluding, let me stress the need for an active approach to change. It is relatively easy, especially for a woman who is an academician, as I am, but also for women in general—since verbal abilities have been their stock in trade—to write about and analyze problems, to generate theories about housework and homemaking and how to change them. It is perhaps more difficult, and certainly is more unusual, for women to take action to change the status quo. And yet, without action, the theories are only so many words; without men and women working for change in their homes and communities and legislatures, a book like this is written in vain. As Boulding says, a "kind of wholistic, behaviorally oriented approach to problem solving...must replace a purely verbal facility with problem manipulation, if viable transition strategies to the gentle society are to be found."[9]

And I want to stress again that any homemaker, indeed any interested person, can make an important contribution. Individual actions are part of the grand network of interactions that make up the social system; homemakers' individual actions to change their own status are part of a network for change for all homemakers. Each homemaker who starts an Individual Retirement Account, or who teaches her daughter to mow the lawn and her son to sew, is contributing to the new homemaker movement. Whether her first step is to ask her spouse for help with the housework or to organize a homemaker co-op, or whether it is to propose some new legislation to her representative, her action is a revolutionary act in what may one day be remembered as one of the greatest of peaceful revolutions.

National Platforms for Homemakers' Rights

APPENDIX ONE

The National Organization for Women
National Conference Resolutions on
Homemakers, 1978

Homemakers' Bill of Rights

Whereas, the unpaid status of the homemaker has resulted in exploitation and injustice; and

Whereas, the National Organization for Women has pledged itself to achieving dignity and security for all women; and

Whereas, the Homemakers' Rights Committee has been charged with the duty of proposing a Bill of Rights for Homemakers;

Therefore be it resolved, that the National Organization for Women endorse the proposal of Economic Rights Within Marriage, as follows:

In recognition of marriage as a truly equal partnership, homemakers shall be granted equal access to, and control over, all money acquired during the marriages,

—through revision of Federal Income Tax forms and their interpretation, so that there is a clear indication that all income listed on a joint income tax return is co-owned;

—through abolition of gift taxes on interspousal transfers;

—through revision of state laws so that a homemaker has the right to obligate the family income through credit purchases, loans, and similar transactions;

—through evaluation and revision of state property laws so that the contributions of the wage-earner and the homemaker are given equal weight in determining ownership of marital property.

Homemakers in Transition

Whereas, the economic security of the homemaker rests entirely on the stability of the marriage; and

Whereas, a homemaker who is divorced, widowed, or abandoned is often left without adequate resources, and with bleak prospects for becoming self-sufficient because of ongoing economic discrimination against women, particularly older women; and

Whereas, the Homemakers' Rights Committee has been charged with the duty of proposing a Bill of Rights for Homemakers:

Therefore be it resolved, that the National Organization for Women endorses the proposal of Economic Rights for Homemakers in Transition, as follows:

In recognition of the fact that over one-third of all marriages now end in divorce; and that homemakers fare poorly in most states because division of property and recognition of entitlement is often inadequate and unjust; and that homemakers who are divorced have among the highest rates of unemployment and under-employment because of the lack of recent paid work experience, prejudice toward their marital status, age and sex discrimination, and the unwillingness to translate homemaking skills into marketable job skills; homemakers must be protected in divorce:

—through equitable division of property which recognizes the unpaid contributions of the homemaker in acquiring and maintaining the family's assets;

—through maintenance (alimony) awards to compensate for the loss of educational opportunities, seniority, advancement, benefits, and accrued protections the homemaker would have had if the homemaker had been in the paid workforce during the years of homemaking;

—through vigorous enforcement of court-awarded maintenance;

—through comprehensive legislation and funded programs to offer divorced and displaced homemakers job-entry education, training, counselling and placement, and supportive services;

—through recognizing the right of homemakers to unemployment compensation;

—through award of an equitable share of pensions, annuities, legislative protection, and other retirement securities;

—through mandatory disclosure of assets of both parties of a divorce, including those sold or distributed in anticipation of a divorce.

In recognition of the special problems a homemaker faces when s/he is widowed, the homemaker must be protected from the unfair burdens that add to her/his grief

—through continuation of pensions, family insurance coverage and other benefits;

—through abolition of interspousal inheritance taxes;

—through the right to continued access to the family savings accounts, checking accounts, securities and safety deposit boxes.

Economic Recognition

Whereas, society has not recognized the economic value of the goods and services provided by the homemaker to her/his family and the community; and

Whereas, the lack of value has resulted not only in the evaluation of homemakers as "non-working" women, but has also deprived the homemaker of job-related benefits that paid workers take for granted; and

Whereas, the lack of recognition of the economic value of homemaking has had an adverse impact on women in paid employment, especially in those occupations seen as extensions of a homemaker's duties, such as nursing, education, restaurant service, domestic service and office work; and

Whereas, the Homemakers' Rights Committee has been charged with the duty of proposing a Bill of Rights for Homemakers;

Therefore be it resolved, that the National Organization for Women endorse the proposal of Economic Recognition for Homemakers, as follows:

In recognition of the fact that it is not the homemaker who benefits most from her/his unpaid labor, but it is the community and family and through them all of society, homemakers should be granted the recognitions and rights of paid, skilled workers

—through independent Social Security coverage in her/his name, portable into and out of marriage and continuing as the homemaker leaves and re-enters the paid workforce, containing provision for disability and retirement benefits adequate to maintain a decent standard of living

—through inclusion of the value of goods and services produced and provided by homemakers in the Gross National Product;

—through revision of welfare laws so that a low-income homemaker can remain at home with her/his family, rather than be forced to take a second, paying, job;

—through development of flexible-time and part-time employment, and the development of adequate flexible-time and part-time child care facilities to make these jobs more available to parents of young children;

—through civil and criminal protection from spousal rape and domestic abuse;

—through providing the homemaker wth a safe workplace; adequate housing regardless of income;

—through comprehensive review of current domestic relations laws to challenge and change those laws, statutes, procedures and codes that deprive homemakers of dignity, security and recognition;

—through recognition of the right to retire or change jobs.

And be it further resolved, that the National Organization for Women adopts the proposals of Economic Rights Within Marriage, Economic Rights for Homemakers in Transition, and Economic Recognition for Homemakers as a comprehensive statement of a Bill of Rights for Homemakers.

Homemakers' Committee

Whereas, homemakers have contributed substantial efforts on behalf of the National Organization for Women; and

Whereas, resistance to the feminist movement has been identified as full-time homemakers; and

Whereas, ratification of the Equal Rights Amendment, as well as progress in other issue areas depends heavily on support of homemakers;

Therefore be it resolved, that adoption and implementation of a Homemakers' Bill of Rights should be a priority for the National Organization for Women; and

Further, be it resolved, that the implementation should include building a strong National Homemakers' Rights Committee.

The "Homemakers' Bill of Rights"
(Presented to the House Select Committee
on Aging Subcommittee at the Hearings
on "Problems of the Nation's Midlife
Women," 1979)

Homemakers' Bill of Rights

I. Educational Rights for Homemakers
   A. A tax policy which enables homemakers to deduct all educational expenses, including transportation costs and child care, over the entire period of their schooling;
   B. Revision of AFDC to cover all educational expenses and full costs of transportation and child care for homemakers who resume their schooling;
   C. Provision of loans at modest rates of interest to homemakers who wish to pursue vocational, professional, or graduate training;
   D. Incentives to businesses to train and hire homemakers, including a massive educational effort alerting corporations, organizations, and the government to the need to give special consideration to homemakers.
II. Economic Rights for Homemakers
   A. Rights for Women in the Home
      1. Revision of federal income tax forms to clearly indicate that all income listed on a joint income tax return is equally shared.
      2. Elimination of gift taxes on interspousal transfers.

3. Inclusion in the GNP of the value of goods and services produced and provided by homemakers.
4. Provision of independent Social Security coverage, including disability, in the homemaker's own name, portable in and out of marriage, and continuing as the homemaker leaves and re-enters the paid workforce.
5. Reform of the welfare system, including setting a Federal floor at the Bureau of Labor Statistics lower-living standard, and extension of coverage to all persons in need.
6. Increase and expansion of flexi-time and part-time employment and job sharing opportunities. Twenty-four hour child care facilities must be made available so that parents of young children can be free to work varied hours. All flexi- and part-time jobs must offer full fringe benefits.
7. Reform of civil and criminal laws to protect homemakers from spousal and domestic abuse.

B. Economic Rights for Homemakers in Transition
1. Equitable division of property and assets, including pensions and annuities, in recognition of the unpaid contributions of the homemaker in acquiring and maintaining the family's assets;
2. Vigorous enforcement of maintenance (alimony) orders to assure compensation for the loss of educational opportunities, seniority, advancement, benefits and accrued protection the homemaker would have had if s/he had been in the paid workforce during the years of homemaking;
3. Funding of programs to provide displaced homemakers with job-entry education, training, counselling and placement, and supportive service;
4. Eligibility of homemakers for unemployment compensation;
5. Revision of pension and Social Security laws so that divorced homemakers are entitled to retirement and disability benefits for their years of service, and so widowed homemakers are provided with special transition payments if they are not eligible for parent's or retirement benefits;
6. Assurance of widows' right to continued access to the family savings accounts, checking accounts, securities and safety deposit boxes, and continuation of pensions, family insurance coverage, and other employment-related benefits.

Sources of
Further Information

APPENDIX TWO

American Civil Liberties Union
600 Pennsylvania Avenue S.E.
Washington, D.C. 20003

Congressional Clearinghouse on Women's Rights
722 House Annex Building #1
Washington, D.C. 20515

Displaced Homemakers' Network
755 8th Street N.W.
Washington, D.C. 20001
(202) 347-0522

Guide to the Legal Status of Homemakers
   A pamphlet is available for each state at $1.25 per copy.
   Write: The Superintendent of Documents
          U.S. Government Printing Office
          Washington, D.C. 20402

KNOW, Inc.
P.O. Box 86031
Pittsburgh, Pennsylvania 15221
   The current publication list of this organization includes:
   Reflections of a Male Housewife, by Kingsley Widmer
   The Politics of Housework, by Pat Mainardi
   Should Wives Work? by Sylvia Hartman
   Why I Want a Wife, by Judy Syfers
   Married Women's Financial Subservience, by Hollie Hodge
   The Hand That Rocks the Cradle Should Be Paid, by Roberta
   The Bonnie Plan—for Economic Justice and Equality in Marriage, by
      V. Bonnie Cowan

The Issue: Minimum Wages for Babysitters? by the Feminist Theory
Collective of the University of Oregon

The Martha Movement
1011 Arlington Boulevard, Suite 305
Arlington, Virginia 22209

The National Organization for Women, Headquarters
425 13th Street N.W. #1048
Washington, D.C. 20004

Older Women's League, Educational Fund
3800 Harrison Street
Oakland, California 94611
(415) 658-8700
(OWLEF is a new group organized in part by the founders of the
Alliance for Displaced Homemakers)

Wellesley College Center for Research on Women
828 Washington Street
Wellesley, Massachusetts 02181
(617) 235-6360, 235-0320

Women and Environments International Newsletter
Faculty of Environmental Studies
York University
Toronto, Canada

Women's Equity Action League
733 15th Street N.W., Suite 200
Washington, D.C. 20005

Women's International Network NEWS
187 Grant Street
Lexington, Massachusetts 02173

Notes

Introduction

1. Betty Friedan, *The Feminine Mystique* (New York: Dell, 1963, p. 37).

2. See Appendix 2 for information on this and on other homemaker groups.

3. Betty Friedan, "Feminism Takes a New Turn," *New York Times Magazine*, 18 November 1979, pp. 40 ff.

Chapter 1: The Domestic Double Standard

1. Robert Lindsey, "Women Entering Job Market at an Extraordinary Pace," *New York Times*, 12 September 1976. See also "Women in Workforce to Hit Record," *National NOW Times*, August 1979.

2. United States Department of Labor, *Women Workers Today* (Washington, D.C.: Employment Standards Administration, Women's Bureau, 1976).

3. Harriet Martineau, *Household Education* (Cambridge, Mass.: 1880), Houghton, Osgood and Company, Riverside Press, p. 272.

4. Ibid., pp. 345–46.

5. Ann Oakley, *Women's Work: The Housewife, Past and Present* (New York: Pantheon Books, 1974), p. 240.

6. Pat Mainardi, *The Politics of Housework* (Pittsburgh: KNOW, Inc., 1968, 1970).

7. Survey of the National Assessment for Education Progress, reported in *Mother Jones*, February/March 1977, p. 8.

8. Kirsten Amundsen, *The Silenced Majority: Women and American Democracy* (Englewood Cliffs, N.J.: Prentice-Hall, 1971), p. 53.

9. Emma Goldman, "Marriage and Love," copyright 1917 by the author, reprinted in *Liberation Now*, ed. Deborah Babcox and Madeline Belkin (New York: Dell, 1971), p. 161.

10. Francine B. Rosen, "Someone Should Study the Studies," *Majority Report*, 2 October 1976.

11. Doris Deakin, "The Displaced Homemaker," *Dynamic Maturity*, January 1970, p. 30.

12. Rosen, "Someone Should Study the Studies."

13. Tish Sommers, "Social Security: A Woman's Viewpoint," *Industrial Gerontology* 2 (fall 1975): 270–71.

14. Ibid., p. 270.

15. Deakin, "Displaced Homemaker," pp. 30–31.

16. Sommers, "Social Security," p. 269.

17. Ibid., p. 272.

18. Virginia Reno, "Women Newly Entitled to Retired-Worker Benefits: Survey of New Beneficiaries," *Social Security Bulletin*, April 1973.

19. United States Department of Health, Education, and Welfare, *A Woman's Guide to Social Security* (Washington, D.C.: U.S. Government Printing Office, 1975).

20. Lucy B. Mullan, "Women Born in the Early 1900's: Employment, Earnings, and Benefit Levels," *Social Security Bulletin*, March 1974, pp. 1–25.

21. Reno, "Women Newly Entitled."

22. Ibid., p. 4.

23. "Women at Work," *Newsweek*, 6 December 1976.

24. S. L. Bem and D. J. Bem, "Case Study of a Non-conscious Ideology: Training Woman to Know Her Place," in *Beliefs, Attitudes and Human Affairs*, ed. D. J. Bem (Belmont, Calif.: Brooks/Cole, 1970).

25. Ibid.

26. Lorine Pruette, *Women and Leisure: A Study of Social Waste* (New York: E. P. Dutton, 1924), pp. xi–xii.

27. Elizabeth Barrett Browning, *Aurora Leigh* (originally published 1856), reprinted in *Women's Liberation and Literature*, ed. Elaine Showalter (New York: Harcourt Brace Jovanovich, 1971).

28. Television news report, 8 February 1977.

29. Hilda Kahne, "The Women in Professional Occupations: New Complexities for Chosen Roles," *Journal of the National Association for Women Deans, Administrators and Counselors* 39 (summer 1976): 183–84.

30. Sandra Newman, of the Survey Research Center's Urban Environmental Research Program, quoted in the newsletter of the Institute for Social Research, University of Michigan, 1976.

31. Erma Bombeck, *Detroit Free Press*, 8 April 1977.

32. Cornelia Butler Flora, "Changes in Women's Status in Women's Magazine Fiction: Differences by Social Class," *Social Problems* 26 (June 1979): 558–69.

33. Harry Braverman, *Labor and Monopoly Capitalism: The Degradation of Work in the Twentieth Century* (New York: Monthly Review Press, 1974).

34. Flora, "Changes in Women's Status."

35. Audrey D. Smith and Joyce O. Beckett, "Black Working Wives: Research Findings and Implications for Practice" (paper presented at the Sixth National Association for Social Work Professional Symposium, San Antonio, Texas, November, 1979).

36. R. Blood and D. Wolfe, *Husbands and Wives* (New York: Free Press, 1960).

37. O. Duncan, H. Schuman, and B. Duncan, *Social Change in a Metropolitan Community* (New York: Russell Sage, 1973).

38. Joseph Pleck, "Men's New Roles in the Family: Housework and Child Care" (paper prepared for the Ford Foundation/Merrill Palmer Institute, Detroit, November 1975), p. 54.

39. Ibid., p. 56.

40. J. Robinson, *How Americans Use Time: A Social-Psychological Analysis* (New York: Praeger, 1976).

Chapter 2: Perspectives on Housework

1. Ann Oakley, *Woman's Work: The Housewife, Past and Present* (New York: Vintage Books, 1974), p. 233.

2. Mariarosa Dalla Costa and Selma James, *The Power of Women and the Subversion of the Community* (Montpelier, Bristol, England: Falling Wall Press, 1972), p. 11.

3. Ibid., p. 38.

4. Ibid., p. 50.

5. Ibid., p. 48.

6. Jessie Bernard, *The Future of Motherhood* (New York: Penguin Books, 1974), p. 341.

7. Jessie Bernard, *Women, Wives, and Mothers: Values and Options* (Chicago: Aldine, 1975), p. 273.

8. Ibid., p. 26.

9. Bernard, *Future of Motherhood*, p. 350. An analysis of the 1972 American National Election Survey indicates that homemakers had higher political efficacy than women in nonindustrial blue-collar jobs. For higher-status occupations, working increased political efficacy. See Cornelia Butler Flora, "Working Class Women's Political Participation: Its Potential in Developed Countries," in *A Portrait of Marginality? The Political Behavior of the American Woman*, ed. M. Githens and J. Prestage, pp. 75–95 (New York: Longman, 1977).

10. Ibid., p. 361.

11. Bernard, *Women, Wives, and Mothers*, p. 27.

12. Ibid.

13. Juliet Mitchell, "Women: The Longest Revolution," *New Left Review* 17 (November–December 1966): 11–37.

14. Ibid.

15. Ibid.

16. Ibid.

17. Ibid.

18. Rosabeth Moss Kanter, "The Policy Issues: Presentation VI," in *Women and the Workplace: The Implications of Occupational Segregation*, ed. Martha Blaxall and Barbara Regan (Chicago: University of Chicago Press, 1976).

Chapter 3: Creating a New
Ideology for Housework

1. Silvia Federici, *Wages against Housework* (Montpelier, Bristol, England, and London: Power of Women Collective and Falling Wall Press, 1973).

2. Cited by Alice Lake in "The New Revolt of the Housewife," *Woman's Day*, 31 May 1977.

3. Daniel Yankelovich, *The New Morality: A Profile of American Youth in the '70s* (New York: McGraw-Hill, 1974).

4. Stanley E. Seashore, "Defining and Measuring the Quality of Working Life," in *The Quality of Working Life*, ed. Louis E. Davis and Albert B. Cherns (New York: Macmillan, 1975).

5. Sarah Fenstermaker Berk and Catherine White Berheide, "Going Back-

stage: Gaining Access to Observe Household Work," *Sociology of Work and Occupations* 4 (February 1977): 27–48.

6. Bill Hoest, "The Lockhorns," copyright by King Features Syndicate.

7. It is of course debatable whether one homemaker is an adequate substitute for another, especially in the area of child care.

8. For an insightful analysis of this issue, see Roslyn L. Feldberg and Evelyn Nakano Glenn, "Male and Female: Job versus Gender Models in the Sociology of Work," *Social Problems* 26 (June 1979): 524–38.

9. Richard E. Walton, "Criteria for Quality of Working Life," in *The Quality of Working Life*. Vol. 1. *Problems, Prospects, and the State of the Art*, ed. Louis E. Davis, Albert B. Cherns, and associates, pp. 91–104. New York: Free Press, 1975.

10. Charlotte Perkins Gilman, *Women and Economics*, ed. Carl Degler (New York: Harper Torchbooks, 1966), p. 144.

11. John Kenneth Galbraith, *Economics and the Public Purpose* (Boston: Houghton Mifflin, 1973).

12. Ibid., p. 193.

13. Karl Marx, *Capital*, vol. 1 (New York: International Publishers, 1970).

14. Mrs. Wibaut, "Working Woman and the Suffrage" (originally published in the 1890s); republished in *Women and Rebellion, 1900* (Leeds, England: Independent Labor Party, 1973).

15. Polda Fortunati, "The Housewife," in *All Work and No Pay: Women, Housework and the Wages Due*, ed. Wendy Edmond and Suzie Fleming (Montpelier, Bristol, England: Power of Women Collective and Falling Wall Press, 1975).

16. John Kenneth Galbraith, "The Economics of the American Housewife," *Atlantic Monthly*, August 1973, pp. 78–83.

17. Helena Znaniecki Lopata, *Occupation: Housewife* (New York: Oxford University Press, 1971).

18. Arlene Rossen Cardozo, *Woman at Home* (New York: Doubleday, 1977).

19. Kate Millett, *Sexual Politics* (New York: Avon Books, 1969), p. 216.

20. Ann Oakley, *Woman's Work: The Housewife Past and Present* (New York: Vintage Books, 1974).

21. Gilman, *Women and Economics*, p. 251.

22. Ibid., pp. 248–49.

23. "Rising Popularity of Eating out Puts a Pinch on Supermarkets," *New York Times*, 10 April 1977.

24. John Stuart Mill, *On the Subjection of Women* (1869). Quoted in Millett, *Sexual Politics*, p. 140.

Chapter 5: Equality Begins at Home

1. Ann Oakley, *The Sociology of Housework* (New York: Pantheon Books, 1974), p. 149.

2. R. Blood and D. Wolfe, *Husbands and Wives* (New York: Free Press, 1960).

3. L. Bailyn, "Career and Family Orientations of Husbands and Wives in Relation to Marital Happiness," *Human Relations* 23 (1970): 97–113.

4. Laura Lein, *Work and Family Life,* Final Report for National Institute of Education Project #3-3094 (Cambridge, Mass.: Center for the Study of Public Policy, 1974), pp. 62–63.

5. Jan Dizard, *Social Change in the Family* (Chicago: Community and Family Center, University of Chicago, 1958).

6. "Let George Do It," in *What Do Women Rally Want?* ed. Ellen Graham (Chicopee, Mass.: Dow Jones Books, 1970–74).

7. Graham, *What Do Women Really Want?*

8. Jane Hood, "Becoming a Two-Job Family" (Ph.D. diss., University of Michigan, 1980).

9. Ibid.

10. Jack Nichols, *Men's Liberation: A New Definition of Masculinity* (New York: Penguin Books, 1975).

11. Lein, *Final Report,* p. 64.

12. Ibid., p. 55.

13. Ibid.

14. Hood, "Becoming a Two-Job Family," p. 9.

15. Angela Barron McBride, *The Growth and Development of Mothers* (New York: Harper and Row, 1973), p. 118.

16. Hood, "Becoming a Two-Job Family."

17. Stephanie Roberts, "I Hereby Resign as Keeper of This House" *MS.,* May 1977.

18. See Barbara Pershing, "Family Policies: A Component of Management in the Home and Family Setting," *Journal of Marriage and the Family* 41 (August 1979): 573–82.

19. Pat Mainardi, *The Politics of Housework* (Pittsburgh: KNOW, Inc., 1970).

20. Blood and Wolfe, *Husbands and Wives.*

21. Stephanie Cleverdon, "On the Brink: Three Attempts to Liberate Women," *Working Papers for a New Society* 3 (spring 1975): 28–36.

22. Survey by the American Council on Life Insurance, reported in *Parade Magazine,* 12 December 1976.

Chapter 6: Psychology Looks at Homemaking

1. Some proposed research is presented in Joseph Veroff, "Women and Work at Home and away from Home." Unpublished paper, University of Michigan, ca. 1976.

2. Charles N. Weaver and Sandra L. Holmes, "A Comparative Study of the Work Satisfaction of Females with Full-Time Employment and Full-Time Housekeeping," *Journal of Applied Psychology* 60 (1975): 117–18. The satisfaction item was: "On the whole, how satisfied are you with the work you do—would you say that you are very satisfied, moderately satisfied, a little dissatisfied, or very dissatisfied?"

3. Carolyn B. Jarmon, master's thesis at Cornell University, 1972, reported in Louise Kapp Howe, *Pink Collar Workers* (New York: G. P. Putnam's Sons, 1977), p. 216.

4. Carol Tavris and Toby Epstein Jayaratne, "How Happy Is Your Marriage?" *Redbook*, June 1976.

5. Jean Lipman-Blumen, "How Ideology Shapes Women's Lives," *Scientific American* 226 (1972): 34–42.

6. Erma Bombeck, *The Grass Is Always Greener over the Septic Tank* (New York: McGraw-Hill, 1972).

7. American Psychological Association *Monitor*, September–October 1978.

8. Elizabeth Bates Harkins, "Effects of Empty Nest Transition on Self-Report of Psychological and Physical Well-being," *Journal of Marriage and the Family* 40 (August 1978): 549–56.

9. Robert L. Kahn and Robert P. Quinn, "Mental Health, Social Support, and Metropolitan Problems" (proposal to United States Department of Health, Education, and Welfare, 1976).

10. For an excellent though somewhat dated analysis of the psychological literature on marital satisfaction, see Judith Long Laws, "A Feminist Review of Marital Adjustment Literature: The Rape of the Locke," *Journal of Marriage and the Family* 33 (August 1971): 483–516.

11. L. J. Axelson, "The Marital Adjustment and Marital Role Definitions of Husbands of Working and Nonworking Wives," *Marriage and Family Living* 25 (1963): 189–95.

12. Lenore Radloff, "Sex Differences in Depression: The Effects of Occupation and Marital Status," *Sex Roles* 1 (1975): 249–65.

13. Ronald H. Gross and Richard D. Arvey, "Marital Satisfaction, Job Satisfaction, and Task Distribution in the Homemaker Job," *Journal of Vocational Behavior* 11 (1977): 1–13.

14. R. Weiss and N. Samuelson, "Social Roles of American Women: Their Contribution to a Sense of Usefulness and Importance," *Marriage and Family Living* 4 (1958): 358–66.

15. R. Blood and D. Wolfe, *Husbands and Wives: The Dynamics of Married Living* (New York: Free Press, 1960).

16. F. I. Nye, "Employment Status of Mothers and Marital Conflict, Permanence and Happiness," *Social Problems* 6 (winter 1958–59): 260–67.

17. F. I. Nye, "Personal Satisfactions," in *The Employed Mother in America*, ed. F. I. Nye and L. Hoffman (Chicago: Rand McNally, 1963), pp. 320–30.

18. Weaver and Holmes, "Comparative Study."

19. Myra Marx Ferree, "Working Class Jobs: Housework and Paid Work as Sources of Satisfaction," *Social Problems* 23 (April 1976): 431–41.

20. James D. Wright, "Are Working Women *Really* More Satisfied? Evidence from Several National Surveys," *Journal of Marriage and the Family* 40 (May 1978): 301–13.

21. Helen Weinreich, "What Future for the Female Subject? Some Implications of the Women's Movement for Psychological Research," *Human Relations* 30 (1977): 535–43.

22. Laws, "Feminist Review," p. 483.

23. Ann P. Parelius, "Emerging Sex-Role Attitudes, Expectations, and Strains among College Women," *Journal of Marriage and the Family* 37 (February 1975): 146–53.

24. Lipman-Blumen, "How Ideology Shapes Women's Lives."

25. Betty Yorburg and Ibtihaj Arafat, "Current Sex Role Conceptions and Conflict," *Sex Roles* 1 (1975): 135–46.

26. Sharon K. Araji, "Husbands' and Wives' Attitude-Behavior Congruence in Family Roles," *Journal of Marriage and the Family* 39 (May 1977): 309–20.

27. Walter L. Slocum and F. Ivan Nye, "Provider and Housekeeping Roles," in *Role Structure and Analysis of the Family,* ed. F. Ivan Nye (Beverly Hills: Sage Publications, 1976), pp. 81–99.

28. Carol Tavris, "Woman and Man," *Psychology Today,* March 1972. See also data from Joseph H. Pleck's 1975 paper "Men's New Roles in the Family: Housework and Child Care," as noted in chapter 1.

29. Margaret M. Poloma and T. Neal Garland, "The Myth of the Egalitarian Family: Familial Roles and the Professionally Employed Wife" (paper presented at the 65th annual meeting of the American Sociological Association, September 1970).

30. Laws, "Feminist Review," p. 491.

31. William A. Barry, "Marriage Research and Conflict: An Integrative Review," *Psychological Bulletin* 73 (1970): 41–54.

32. Sharon Price-Bonham, "Marital Decision Making: Congruence of Spouses' Responses," *Sociological Inquiry* 47 (1977): 119–25.

33. Linda Burzotta Nilson, "The Social Standing of a Housewife," *Journal of Marriage and the Family* 40 (August 1978): 541–48.

34. William J. Eaton, "Working Wife Likelier to Split," *Detroit Free Press,* 30 January 1978 (data from a study by the United States Department of Labor).

35. "Working Wives Prone to Marital Dissatisfaction," Institute for Social Research *Newsletter,* vol. 6, no. 1 (1978): 6.

36. Neil S. Jacobson, "Specific and Nonspecific Factors in the Effectiveness of a Behavioral Approach to the Treatment of Marital Discord," *Journal of Consulting and Clinical Psychology* 43 (1978): 442–52.

37. Sarah Fenstermaker Berk and Catherine White Berheide, "Going Backstage: Gaining Access to Observe Household Work," *Sociology of Work and Occupations* 4 (February 1977): 27–48.

38. Weinreich, "What Future for the Female Subject?" p. 538.

39. Joseph H. Pleck, "The Work-Family Role System," *Social Problems* 24 (1977): 417–27.

Chapter 7: Alternative Life-Styles
for Couples and Communities

1. James A. Levine, *Who Will Raise the Children: New Options for Fathers (and Mothers)* (New York: Bantam, 1977), p. 124.

2. Gunilla Hallberg and Goran Hallberg, "A Swedish 'Big Family,'" in *Communes: Creating and Managing the Collective Life,* ed. Rosabeth Moss Kanter (New York: Harper and Row, 1973), p. 423.

3. Nona Glazer-Malbin, "The Division of Labor in the Husband-Wife Relationship: Some Rethinking" (paper presented at the Conference on Family and Gender Roles, Merrill-Palmer Institute/Ford Foundation, Detroit, November 1975), pp. 13–14.

4. Jessie Bernard, *The Future of Marriage* (New York: World, 1972).

5. Ibid., p. 243.

6. Thomas H. Shey, "Why Communes Fail: A Comparative Analysis of the Viability of Danish and American Communes," *Journal of Marriage and the Family* 39 (August 1977): 605–14.

7. Richard Feallock and L. Keith Miller, "The Design and Evaluation of a Worksharing System for Experimental Living," *Journal of Applied Behavior Analysis* 9 (fall 1976): 277–88.

8. *Detroit News Magazine*, 29 October 1978.

9. Levine, *Who Will Raise the Children*, p. 141. Figures from the Bureau of Labor Statistics in *Employment and Earnings*.

10. Ann Quindlen, "Self-Fulfillment: Independence versus Intimacy," *New York Times*, 28 November 1977.

11. Levine, *Who Will Raise the Children*, p. 125.

12. Ibid.

13. Ibid., pp. 128–29.

14. Ibid., p. 130.

15. Kenneth Pitchford, "The Manly Art of Child Care," *MS.*, October 1978.

16. Shulamith Firestone, in Bernard, *The Future of Marriage*, p. 242.

17. Ibid.

18. Matthew L. Israel, "Two Communal Houses and Why (I Think) They Failed," *Journal of Behavior Technology* 1 (summer 1971): 13–15. Reprinted in Rosabeth Moss Kanter, ed., *Communes: Creating and Managing the Collective Life* (New York: Harper and Row, 1973), pp. 397–99.

19. For detailed information on the Center for Intentional Living, I am indebted to L. Keith Miller. Articles on the project include: Richard Feallock and L. Keith Miller, "The Design and Evaluation of a Worksharing System for Experimental Group Living," *Journal of Applied Behavior Analysis* 9 (fall 1976): 277–88. L. Keith Miller and Richard Feallock, "A Behavioral System for Group Living," in *Behavior Analysis: Areas of Research and Application*, ed. Eugene Ramp and George Semb (Englewood Cliffs, N.J.: Prentice-Hall, 1975). L. Keith Miller and Alice Ann Lies, "Everyday Behavior Analysis: A New Direction for Applied Behavior Analysis," *Behavioral Voice*, 1974. L. Keith Miller, Alice Lies, Dan L. Petersen, and Richard Feallock, "The Positive Community: A Strategy for Applying Behavioral Engineering to the Redesign of Family and Community," in *Behavior Modification and Families*, ed. Eric J. Mash, Leo A. Hamerlynck, and Lee C. Handy (New York: Brunner/Mazel, 1976).

20. Miller and Lies, "Everyday Behavior Analysis."

21. Rae Lesser Blumberg, "Kibbutz Women: From the Fields of Revolution to the Laundries of Discontent," in *Women in the World*, ed. Lynne B. Iglitzin and Ruth Ross, pp. 319–44 (Santa Barbara: Clio Books, 1976). I am indebted to Blumberg for many of the ideas in this section.

22. Martin Buber, *Paths in Utopia* (Boston: Beacon Press, 1958).

23. Benjamin Beit-Hallahmi and Albert I. Rabin, "The Kibbutz as a Social Experiment and as a Child-Rearing Laboratory," *American Psychologist* 32 (July 1977): 532–41.

24. Ibid., p. 540.

25. Blumberg, "Kibbutz Women," pp. 319 ff.

26. Ibid., p. 327.

27. Ibid., p. 321.

28. Ibid., p. 331.

29. Ibid., p. 322.

30. Kathleen Kinkade, *A Walden Two Experiment: The First Five Years of Twin Oaks Community* (New York: William Morrow, 1973).

31. Ibid., p. 43.

32. Ibid., p. 264.

33. Ibid., p. 171.

34. Susan, "Sexism at Twin Oaks," *Leaves of Twin Oaks*, no. 41 (August 1976), p. 7.

35. Henry David Thoreau, *Walden* (Boston: Houghton Mifflin, 1957), p. 78 (first published in 1854).

Chapter 8: Homemakers and Organization

1. Nickie McWhirter, "The Trapped Housewife Needs a Support System," *Detroit Free Press*, 30 October 1978.

2. Philip E. Slater, *The Pursuit of Loneliness* (Boston: Beacon Press, 1970), p. 68.

3. Jane Kronholz, "Women at Work: Management Practices Change to Reflect Role of Women Employees," *Wall Street Journal*, 13 September 1978.

4. Dick Pothier, "Economist Proposes Housewife Co-op for Pay," *Detroit Free Press*, 5 July 1976.

5. "Employment Plan for Housewives Is Urged by a Rutgers Economist," *New York Times*, 12 December 1976.

6. U. S. Department of Health, Education, and Welfare, "Social Security and Your Household Employee" (HEW Publication no. [SSA] 78-10021).

7. *Leoncia Gonzalez* v. *Secretary of HEW*, U.S. District Court, District of Puerto Rico, civ. no. 296-73, 2 December 1974.

8. *Acevedo* v. *Secretary of HEW*, U.S. District Court, District of Puerto Rico, civ. no. 788-71, 5 June 1973.

9. *Fancher* v. *Secretary of HEW*, U.S. District Court, District of Mississippi, civ. no. 4625, 29 June 1972.

10. David Popenoe, *The Suburban Environment: Sweden and the United States* (Chicago: University of Chicago Press, 1977).

11. Ibid., p. 153.

12. Ibid., p. 175.

13. *Martha Matters,* vol. 3, no. 3 (summer 1978).

14. Jean Tepperman, "Two Jobs: Women Who Work in Factories," in *Sisterhood Is Powerful*, ed. Robin Morgan (New York: Vantage Books, 1970).

15. KNOW, vol. 9, no. 4 (October 1978).

16. Joann S. Lublin, "Female Office Workers Form Groups to Fight Sex Bias, Petty Chores," *Wall Street Journal*, 24 February 1978.

Chapter 9: The Displaced Homemaker

1. Erica Abeel, "School for Ex-Wives," *New York Magazine,* 16 October 1978.

2. "Millions of Divorcees and Widows Become 'Displaced Homemakers,'" *New Times,* 1 January 1978.

3. Laurie Shields, testimony before the United States House of Representatives, Subcommittee on Employment Opportunities of the House Committee on Education and Labor, 14 July 1977.

4. Ibid.

5. Merle Nelson, testimony before the United States House of Representatives, Subcommittee on Employment Opportunities of the House Committee on Education and Labor, 14 July 1977.

6. Rose House, testimony before the United States House of Representatives, Subcommittee on Employment Opportunities of the House Committee on Education and Labor, 14 July 1977.

7. Nancie Fadeley, testimony before the United States House of Representatives, Subcommittee on Employment Opportunities of the House Committee on Education and Labor, 14 July 1977.

8. Cynthia Marano, personal interview, July 1977. Unless otherwise noted, all persons quoted in this section were interviewed at the Maryland Displaced Homemaker Center in July 1977.

9. Cynthia Marano, in "State Program Helps Displaced Homemakers," Baltimore *Evening Sun,* 16 June 1977.

10. Cynthia Marano, testimony before the United States House of Representatives, Subcommittee on Employment Opportunities of the House Committee on Education and Labor, 14 July 1977.

11. Ibid.

12. "Public-Works Grants Help Baltimore a Bit, the Jobless Very Little," *Wall Street Journal,* 21 July 1977.

13. Laurie Shields, testimony as cited above, note 3.

14. Stephanye Schuyler, "Setting an Example," *Equal Times,* vol. 1, no. 17 (10 July 1977).

15. Nancie Fadeley, testimony as cited above, note 7.

*Chapter 10: Change in the House—
and in the Senate*

1. Quarterly newsletter of the National Organization for Women Task Force on Older Women, vol. 4, no. 1 (March 1977).

2. "Pregnant Decisions," *Newsweek,* 20 December 1977.

3. John L. Stucker, "Women's Political Role." *Current History* 70 (May 1976): 213.

4. Report of the HEW Task Force on the Treatment of Women under Social Security, February 1978, p. 51.

5. Ibid., p. 52.

6. John Kenneth Galbraith, *Economics and the Public Purpose* (Boston: Houghton Mifflin, 1973).

7. Quoted in Claire Safran, "What You Should Know about the Equal Rights Amendment," *Redbook*, June 1973.

8. Martha Griffiths, "Requisites for Equality," in *Women and the American Economy: A Look to the 1980's*, ed. Juanita M. Kreps (Englewood Cliffs, N.J.: Prentice-Hall, 1976).

9. "Homemakers and the Equal Rights Amendment" (pamphlet published by the National Organization for Women).

10. Margaret J. Gates, "The Social Security Act and the Equal Rights Amendment," *Women's Rights Law Reporter*, September 1975.

11. Ibid., p. 19.

12. Ibid., p. 17.

13. Wilbur Cohen, interviewed in "Future in a Changing Society," in the video series *Worlds of Women*, University of Michigan Television Center, 1977.

14. *Wall Street Journal*, 14 December 1976.

15. *Do It Now*, June 1977.

16. Ibid.

17. Laurie Shields, "The Displaced Homemaker," workshop at the national convention of the National Organization for Women, April 1977.

18. Ibid.

19. Laurie Shields, testimony before the Finance Committee, United States House of Representatives, Columbus, Ohio, 30 March 1977. Bayh and Burke later filed companion bills calling for amendment of CETA to include the Displaced Homemaker Act as a special program under Title III.

20. *Do It Now*, June 1977.

21. Laura S. Rasmussen, "Model Marriage Equality Bill," reprinted in *Do It Now*, June 1977, from *Suffolk University Law Review*, vol. 9, no. 185 (1975).

22. Joan Beck, "Next Let's Have a Year of the Lady *and* the Tiger," *Chicago Tribune*, 12 July 1976.

23. *Wall Street Journal*, 19 January 1978.

24. *Do It Now*, June 1977.

25. "The Widows' Tax," *Do It Now*, April 1977.

26. James C. Hyatt, "What Value Housework?" in *What Do Women Really Want?* ed. Ellen Graham (New York: Dow Jones Books, 1970–74).

27. Kathryn E. Walker and William H. Gauger, *The Dollar Value of Household Work*, Information Bulletin 60, Consumer Economics and Public Policy no. 5 (Ithaca: New York State College of Human Ecology, Cornell University, 1980).

28. Juanita Kreps, "The Future for Working Women," *MS.*, March 1977.

29. For a consideration of methods for valuing homemaker services in trial practice and negotiation, see Nancy R. Hauserman and Carol Fethke, "Valuation of a Homemaker's Services," *Trial Lawyer's Guide* 22 (fall 1978): 249–66.

Chapter 11: Women's Work in the World

1. From the newspaper *Sovetskaia Rossiia*, quoted in Kent Geiger, *The Family in Soviet Russia* (Cambridge: Harvard University Press, 1968), p. 184.

2. Koran (London: Lazac and Company, 1956), p. 189.

3. "A Letter to All Governments," in *Wages for Housework: Women Speak Out,* Proceedings of the May Day Rally, Toronto, 1975 (Toronto: Amazon Press, a Feminist Collective, n.d.).

4. Peggy R. Sanday, "Female Status in the Public Domain," in *Woman, Culture, and Society,* ed. Michelle Zimbalist Rosaldo and Louise Lamphere (Stanford: Stanford University Press, 1974), p. 202.

5. Leo Silberman, "Somali Nomads," *International Social Science Journal* 11 (1959): 558.

6. Elise Boulding, *Women in the Twentieth Century World* (New York: Sage, Halsted, 1977), pp. 46–47. I am indebted to Dr. Boulding for many of the details in this and the succeeding sections.

7. Sanday, "Female Status," p. 203 (quoting a 1970 source).

8. Judith Van Allen, "African Women, 'Modernization,' and National Liberation," in *Women in the World: A Comparative Study,* ed. Lynne B. Iglitzin and Ruth Ross (Santa Barbara: Clio Books, 1976), p. 35.

9. Boulding, *Women in the Twentieth Century World,* p. 101.

10. Most of the information in this section is from Barbara J. Callaway, "Women in Ghana," *Women in the World: A Comparative Study,* ed. Lynne B. Iglitzin and Ruth Ross (Santa Barbara: Clio Books, 1976), pp. 189–99.

11. Ibid., p. 199.

12. Information for this section on French women has been taken from Joelle Rutherford Juillard, "Women in France," in *Women in the World: A Comparative Study,* ed. Lynne B. Iglitzin and Ruth Ross (Santa Barbara: Clio Books, 1976), pp. 115–26.

13. Ibid., p. 124.

14. Ibid., p. 125.

15. Ibid., p. 126.

16. Elina Haavio-Mannila, "Sex Differentiation in Role Expectations and Performance," in *Readings on the Psychology of Women,* ed. Judith M. Bardwick (New York: Harper and Row, 1972), p. 217.

17. Monica Sjoo, "Sweden, Now We Are 'Equal,'" in *Power of Women* 1 (summer 1975): 16.

18. Batya Weinbaum, "Women in Transition to Socialism: Perspectives on the Chinese Case," *Review of Radical Political Economics* 8 (spring 1976): 52.

19. Lucy Jen Huang, "A Re-evaluation of the Primary Role of the Communist Chinese Women: The Homemaker or the Worker," in *Readings on the Psychology of Women,* ed. Judith M. Bardwick (New York: Harper and Row, 1972), p. 231.

20. Weinbaum, "Women in Transition," p. 52.

21. Margaret Mead, *Sex and Temperament in Three Primitive Societies* (New York: Dell, 1935, 1963).

22. Boulding, *Women in the Twentieth Century World,* p. 109.

23. Judith K. Brown, "Leisure, Busywork and Housekeeping: A Note on the Unequal Division of Labor by Sex," *Anthropos* 68 (1973): 886.

24. Alexander Szalai, *The Situation of Women in the United Nations* (New York: United Nations, UNITAR, 1973).

25. Lourdes Beneria, "Women's Participation in Paid Production under Capitalism: The Spanish Experience," *Review of Radical Political Economics* 8 (spring 1976): 18–33.

26. Maricela Peraza and Harry Maurer, "Honduras: Did the Church Start Something It Can't Stop?" *MS.*, August 1977.

27. Judith Stiehm, "Algerian Women: Honor, Survival and Islamic Socialism," in *Women in the World: A Comparative Study*, ed. Lynne B. Iglitzin and Ruth Ross (Santa Barbara: Clio Books, 1976), p. 230.

28. Juillard, "Women in France," p. 125.

29. Doranne Wilson Jacobson, "Purdah in India: Life Behind the Veil," *National Geographic* 152 (August 1977): 289.

30. Brown, "Leisure, Busywork and Housekeeping."

31. Dorothy Atkinson, "American and Soviet Women: The Quest for Liberation," *Stanford Magazine*, spring–summer 1977.

32. Ibid.

33. Ibid.

34. Ibid.

35. "India Anti-Price Rise Front," *Power of Women*, vol. 1, no. 4 (summer 1975): 1–16.

36. "Letters from Portugal," *Power of Women*, vol. 1, no. 4 (summer 1975): 1–16.

37. Callaway, "Women in Ghana."

38. Stiehm, "Algerian Women," p. 235.

39. Stephanie Cleverdon, "On the Brink: Three Attempts to Liberate Women," *Working Papers for a New Society* 3 (spring 1975): 33.

40. Alva Myrdal and Viola Klein, *Women's Two Roles: Home and Work* (London: Routledge and Kegan Paul, 1956), p. 195.

41. Birgitta Linner, *Sex and Society in Sweden* (New York: Pantheon, 1967), p. 4.

42. Marsden Wagner and Mary Wagner, *The Danish National Child-Care System* (Boulder, Col.: Westview Press, 1976), p. 147.

43. Ibid., p. 156.

44. Ingunn Norderval Means, "Scandinavian Women," in *Women in the World: A Comparative Study*, ed. Lynne B. Iglitzin and Ruth Ross (Santa Barbara: Clio Books, 1976), p. 380.

45. *Power of Women*, vol. 1, no. 4 (summer 1975): 1–16.

46. Ibid.

47. Wendy Edmond and Suzie Fleming, eds., *All Work and No Pay* (London: Power of Women Collective and Falling Wall Press, 1975), p. 86.

48. Boulding, *Women in the Twentieth Century World*, pp. 205–6.

Chapter 12: Problems and Potentials

1. Rosalynn Carter, Women of Vermont Conference of the International Women's Year, 25 February 1977.

2. Elise Boulding, *Women in the Twentieth Century World* (New York: Sage, Halsted, 1977), p. 234.

3. Paul Ehrlich, *The End of Affluence* (New York: Ballantine Books, 1974), p. 181.

4. Boulding, *Women in the Twentieth Century World*, p. 227.

5. Rebecca Peterson, Gerda R. Wekerle, and David Morley, "Women and Environments: An Overview of an Emerging Field," *Journal of Environment and Behavior*, in press.

6. Boulding, *Women in the Twentieth Century World*, p. 217.

7. Bruno Bettelheim, "The Commitment Required of a Woman Entering a Scientific Profession in Present-Day American Society," in *Women and the Scientific Professions*, ed. Jacqueline A. Mattfeld and Carol G. Van Aken (Cambridge: MIT Press, 1965).

8. As Jualynne Dodson, project director of the Atlanta University School of Social Work, notes, "Because of stressful conditions of racism in this country we Black people created alternative family forms that helped us survive humanistically" (see newsletter for the Center for Continuing Education of Women, the University of Michigan, autumn 1979). The limited research evidence to date supports Dodson's claim. While it is clear that blacks are subject to a domestic double standard, they may also be among the first to escape from it.

9. Boulding, *Women in the Twentieth Century World*, p. 242.

Bibliography

Abeel, Erica. "School for Ex-Wives." *New York Magazine,* 16 October 1978.

Amundsen, Kirsten. *The Silenced Majority: Women and American Democracy.* Englewood Cliffs, N.J.: Prentice-Hall, 1971.

Araji, Sharon K. "Husbands' and Wives' Attitude-Behavior Congruence in Family Roles." *Journal of Marriage and the Family* 39 (May 1977): 309–20.

Atkinson, Dorothy. "American and Soviet Women: The Quest for Liberation." *Stanford Magazine,* spring–summer 1977.

Axelson, L. J. "The Marital Adjustment and Marital Role Definitions of Husbands of Working and Nonworking Wives." *Marriage and Family Living* 25 (1963): 189–95.

Bailyn, L. "Career and Family Orientations of Husbands and Wives in Relation to Marital Happiness." *Human Relations* 23 (1970): 97–113.

Barry, William A. "Marriage Research and Conflict: An Integrative Review." *Psychological Bulletin* 73 (1970): 41–54.

Beit-Hallahmi, Benjamin, and Rabin, Albert I. "The Kibbutz as a Social Experiment and as a Child-Rearing Laboratory." *American Psychologist* 32 (July 1977): 532–41.

Bem, S. L., and Bem, D. J. "Case Study of a Non-conscious Ideology: Training Woman to Know Her Place." In *Beliefs, Attitudes and Human Affairs,* ed. D. J. Bem. Belmont, Calif.: Brooks/Cole, 1970.

Beneria, Lourdes. "Women's Participation in Paid Production under Capitalism: The Spanish Experience." *Review of Radical Political Economics* 8 (spring 1976): 18–33.

Berk, Sarah Fenstermaker, ed. *Women and Household Labor.* Beverly Hills, Calif.: Sage Publications, 1980.

Berk, Sarah Fenstermaker, and Berheide, Catherine White. "Going Backstage: Gaining Access to Observe Household Work." *Sociology of Work and Occupations* 4 (February 1977): 27–48.

Bernard, Jessie. *The Future of Marriage.* New York: World, 1972.

———. *The Future of Motherhood.* New York: Penguin Books, 1974.

———. *Women, Wives, and Mothers: Values and Options.* Chicago: Aldine, 1975.

Bettelheim, Bruno. "The Commitment Required of a Woman Entering a Scientific Profession in Present-Day American Society." In *Women and the Scientific Professions,* ed. Jacqueline A. Mattfeld and Carol G. Van Aken. Cambridge: MIT Press, 1965.

285

Blood, R., and Wolfe, D. *Husbands and Wives: The Dynamics of Married Living.* New York: Free Press, 1960.

Blumberg, Rae Lesser. "Kibbutz Women: From the Fields of Revolution to the Laundries of Discontent." In *Women in the World,* ed. Lynne B. Iglitzin and Ruth Ross. Santa Barbara: Clio Books, 1976.

Bombeck, Erma. *The Grass Is Always Greener over the Septic Tank.* New York: McGraw-Hill, 1972.

Boulding, Elise. *Women in the Twentieth Century World.* New York: Sage, Halsted, 1977.

Braverman, Harry. *Labor and Monopoly Capitalism: The Degradation of Work in the Twentieth Century.* New York: Monthly Review Press, 1974.

Brown, Judith K. "Leisure, Busywork and Housekeeping: A Note on the Unequal Division of Labor by Sex." *Anthropos* 68 (1973): 881–88.

Browning, Elizabeth Barrett. *Aurora Leigh.* Reprinted in *Women's Liberation and Liberature,* ed. Elaine Showalter. New York: Harcourt Brace Jovanovich, 1971. Originally published 1856.

Buber, Martin. *Paths in Utopia.* Boston: Beacon Press, 1958.

Callaway, Barbara J. "Women in Ghana." In *Women in the World,* ed. Lynne B. Iglitzin and Ruth Ross. Santa Barbara: Clio Books, 1976.

Cardozo, Arlene Rossen. *Woman at Home.* New York: Doubleday, 1977.

Cleverdon, Stephanie. "On the Brink: Three Attempts to Liberate Women." *Working Papers for a New Society* 3 (spring 1975): 28–36.

Cowan, Ruth Schwartz. "The 'Industrial Revolution' in the Home: Household Technology and Social Change in the Twentieth Century." *Technology and Culture* 17 (January 1976): 1–23.

Dalla Costa, Mariarosa, and James, Selma. *The Power of Women and the Subversion of the Community.* Montpelier, Bristol, England: Falling Wall Press, 1972.

Deakin, Doris. "The Displaced Homemaker." *Dynamic Maturity* 12 (January 1977): 28–31.

Dizard, Jan. *Social Change in the Family.* Chicago: Community and Family Center, University of Chicago, 1958.

Duncan, O.; Shuman, H.; and Duncan, B. *Social Change in a Metropolitan Community.* New York: Russell Sage, 1973.

Edmond, Wendy, and Fleming, Suzie, eds. *All Work and No Pay: Women, Housework and the Wages Due.* London: Power of Women Collective and Falling Wall Press, 1975.

Ehrlich, Paul. *The End of Affluence.* New York: Ballantine Books, 1974.

Feallock, Richard, and Miller, L. Keith. "The Design and Evaluation of a Worksharing System for Experimental Living." *Journal of Applied Behavior Analysis* 9 (fall 1976): 277–88.

Federici, Silvia. *Wages against Housework.* Montpelier, Bristol, England, and London: Power of Women Collective and Falling Wall Press, 1973.

Fee, Terry. "Domestic Labor: An Analysis of Housework and Its Relation to the Production Process." *Review of Radical Political Economics* 8 (spring 1976): 1–8.

Feldberg, Roslyn L., and Glenn, Evelyn Nakano. "Male and Female: Job versus

Gender Models in the Sociology of Work." *Social Problems* 26 (June 1979): 524–38.

Ferree, Myra Marx. "Working Class Jobs: Housework and Paid Work as Sources of Satisfaction." *Social Problems* 23 (April 1976): 431–41.

Flora, Cornelia Butler. "Changes in Women's Status in Women's Magazine Fiction: Differences by Social Class." *Social Problems* 26 (June 1979): 558–69.

Fortunati, Polda. "The Housewife." In *All Work and No Pay: Women, Housework and the Wages Due,* ed. Wendy Edmond and Suzie Fleming. Montpelier, Bristol, England: Power of Women Collective and Falling Wall Press, 1975.

Friedan, Betty. *The Feminine Mystique.* New York: Dell, 1963.

———. "Feminism Takes a New Turn." *New York Times Magazine,* 18 November 1979, pp. 40 ff.

Galbraith, John Kenneth. *Economics and the Public Purpose.* Boston: Houghton Mifflin, 1973.

———. "The Economics of the American Housewife." *Atlantic Monthly,* August 1973, pp. 78–83.

Gates, Margaret J. "The Social Security Act and the Equal Rights Amendment." *Women's Rights Law Reporter,* September 1975.

Geiger, Kent. *The Family in Soviet Russia.* Cambridge: Harvard University Press, 1968.

Gilman, Charlotte Perkins. *Women and Economics,* ed. Carl Degler. New York: Harper Torchbooks, 1966.

Glazer-Malbin, Nona. "Housework." *Signs: Journal of Women in Culture and Society* 1 (1976): 905–20.

———. "The Division of Labor in the Husband-Wife Relationship: Some Rethinking." Paper presented at the Conference on Family and Gender Roles, Merrill-Palmer Institute/Ford Foundation, Detroit, November 1975.

Goldman, Emma. "Marriage and Love." Reprinted in *Liberation Now,* ed. Deborah Babcox and Madeline Belkin. New York: Dell, 1971. Originally published 1917.

Griffiths, Martha. "Requisites for Equality." In *Women and the American Economy: A Look to the 1980's,* ed. Juanita M. Kreps. Englewood Cliffs, N.J.: Prentice-Hall, 1976.

Gross, Ronald H., and Arvey, Richard D. "Marital Satisfaction, Job Satisfaction, and Task Distribution in the Homemaker Job." *Journal of Vocational Behavior* 11 (1977): 1–13.

Haavio-Mannila, Elina. "Sex Differentiation in Role Expectations and Performance." In *Readings on the Psychology of Women,* ed. Judith M. Bardwick. New York: Harper and Row, 1972.

Hallberg, Gunilla, and Hallberg, Goran. "A Swedish 'Big Family.'" In *Communes: Creating and Managing the Collective Life,* ed. Rosabeth Moss Kanter. New York: Harper and Row, 1973.

Harkins, Elizabeth Bates. "Effects of Empty Nest Transition on Self-Report of Psychological and Physical Well-being." *Journal of Marriage and the Family* 40 (August 1978): 549–56.

Hauserman, Nancy R., and Fethke, Carol. "Valuation of a Homemaker's Services." *Trial Lawyer's Guide*, vol. 22 (fall 1978).

Hood, Jane. "Becoming a Two-Job Family." Ph.D. diss., University of Michigan, 1980.

Huang, Lucy Jen. "A Re-evaluation of the Primary Role of the Communist Chinese Women: The Homemaker or the Worker." In *Readings on the Psychology of Women*, ed. Judith A. Bardwick. New York: Harper and Row, 1972.

Hyatt, James C. "What Value Housework?" In *What Do Women Really Want?* ed. Ellen Graham. New York: Dow Jones Books, 1970–74.

Iglitzin, Lynne B., and Ross, Ruth, eds. *Women in the World: A Comparative Study*. Santa Barbara: Clio Books, 1976.

Israel, Matthew L. "Two Communal Houses and Why (I Think) They Failed." *Journal of Behavior Technology* 1 (summer 1971): 13–15.

Jacobson, Doranne Wilson. "Purdah in India: Life behind the Veil." *National Geographic* 152 (August 1977): 270–86.

Jacobson, Neil S. "Specific and Nonspecific Factors in the Effectiveness of a Behavioral Approach to the Treatment of Marital Discord." *Journal of Consulting and Clinical Psychology* 43 (1978): 442–52.

Jarmon, Carolyn B. "Relationship between Homemakers' Attitudes toward Specific Household Tasks and Family Composition, Other Situational Variables and Time Allocation." M.S. thesis, Cornell University, 1972.

Kahn, Robert L., and Quinn, Robert P. "Mental Health, Social Support, and Metropolitan Problems." Proposal to the U.S. Department of Health, Education, and Welfare, 1976.

Kahne, Hilde. "The Women in Professional Occupations: New Complexities for Chosen Roles." *Journal of the National Association for Women Deans, Administrators and Counselors*, vol. 39 (summer 1976).

Kanter, Rosabeth Moss. "The Policy Issues: Presentation VI." In *Women and the Workplace: The Implications of Occupational Segregation*, ed. Martha Blaxall and Barbara Reagan. Chicago: University of Chicago Press, 1976.

Kinkade, Kathleen. *A Walden Two Experiment: The First Five Years of Twin Oaks Community*. New York: William Morrow, 1973.

Kreps, Juanita. "The Future for Working Women." *MS.*, March 1977.

Kronholz, Jane. "Women at Work: Management Practices Change to Reflect Role of Women Employees." *Wall Street Journal*, 13 September 1978.

Lake, Alice. "The New Revolt of the Housewife." *Woman's Day*, 31 May 1977.

Laws, Judith Long. "A Feminist Review of Marital Adjustment Literature: The Rape of the Locke." *Journal of Marriage and the Family* 33 (August 1971): 483–516.

Lein, Laura. *Work and Family Life*. Final Report for National Institute of Education, Project #3-3094. Cambridge, Mass.: Center for the Study of Public Policy, 1974.

Levine, James A. *Who Will Raise the Children*. New York: Bantam, 1977.

Lindsey, Robert. "Women Entering Job Market at an Extraordinary Pace." *New York Times*, 12 September 1976.

Linner, Birgitta. *Sex and Society in Sweden*. New York: Pantheon, 1967.

Lipman-Blumen, Jean. "How Ideology Shapes Women's Lives." *Scientific American* 226 (1972): 34–42.

Lopata, Helena Znaniecki. *Occupation: Housewife*. New York: Oxford University Press, 1971.

Lublin, Joann S. "Female Office Workers Form Groups to Fight Sex Bias, Petty Chores." *Wall Street Journal*, 24 February 1978.

McBride, Angela Barron. *The Growth and Development of Mothers*. New York: Harper and Row, 1973.

McWhirter, Nickie. "The Trapped Housewife Needs a Support System." *Detroit Free Press*, 30 October 1978.

Mainardi, Pat. *The Politics of Housework*. Pittsburgh: KNOW, Inc., 1970.

Martineau, Harriet. *Household Education*. Cambridge, Mass.: Houghton, Osgood and Company, Riverside Press, 1880.

Marx, Karl. *Capital*. Vol. 1. New York: International Publishers, 1970.

Mead, Margaret. *Sex and Temperament in Three Primitive Societies*. New York: Dell, 1935, 1963.

Means, Ingunn Norderval. "Scandinavian Women." In *Women in the World: A Comparative Study*, ed. Lynne B. Iglitzin and Ruth Ross. Santa Barbara: Clio Books, 1976.

Mill, John Stuart. *On the Subjection of Women* (1869). Quoted in Kate Millett, *Sexual Politics*. New York: Avon Books, 1969.

Miller, L. Keith, and Feallock, Richard. "A Behavioral System for Group Living." In *Behavior Analysis: Areas of Research and Application*, ed. Eugene Ramp and George Semb. Englewood Cliffs, N.J.: Prentice-Hall, 1975.

Miller, L. Keith, and Lies, Alice Ann. "Everyday Behavior Analysis: A New Direction for Applied Behavior Analysis." *Behavioral Voice*, 1974.

Miller, L. Keith; Lies, Alice; Petersen, Dan L.; and Feallock, Richard. "The Positive Community: A Strategy for Applying Behavioral Engineering to the Redesign of Family and Community." In *Behavior Modification and Families*, ed. Eric J. Mash, Leo A. Hamerlynck, and Lee C. Handy. New York: Brunner/Mazel, 1976.

Millett, Kate. *Sexual Politics*. New York: Avon Books, 1969.

Mitchell, Juliet. "Women: The Longest Revolution." *New Left Review* 17 (November–December 1966): 11–37.

Mullan, Lucy B. "Women Born in the Early 1900's: Employment, Earnings, and Benefit Levels." *Social Security Bulletin*, March 1974, pp. 1–25.

Myrdal, Alva, and Klein, Viola. *Women's Two Roles: Home and Work*. London: Routledge and Kegan Paul, 1956.

National Organization for Women. "Homemakers and the Equal Rights Amendment." Pamphlet.

Nichols, Jack. *Men's Liberation: A New Definition of Masculinity*. New York: Penguin Books, 1975.

Nieves, Isabel. "Household Arrangements and Multiple Jobs in San Salvador." *Signs: Journal of Women in Culture and Society* 5 (1979): 134–42.

Nilson, Linda Burzotta. "The Social Standing of a Housewife." *Journal of Marriage and the Family* 40 (August 1978): 541–48.

Nye, F. I. "Employment Status of Mothers and Marital Conflict, Permanence and Happiness." *Social Problems* 6 (winter 1958–59): 260–67.

———. "Personal Satisfactions." In *The Employed Mother in America*, ed. F. I. Nye and L. Hoffman. Chicago: Rand McNally, 1963.

Oakley, Ann. *The Sociology of Housework*. New York: Pantheon Books, 1974.

———. *Woman's Work: The Housewife Past and Present*. New York: Vintage Books, 1974.

Parelius, Ann P. "Emerging Sex-Role Attitudes, Expectations, and Strains among College Women." *Journal of Marriage and the Family* 37 (February 1975): 146–53.

Peraza, Maricela, and Maurer, Harry. "Honduras: Did the Church Start Something It Can't Stop?" *MS.*, August 1977.

Pershing, Barbara. "Family Policies: A Component of Management in the Home and Family Setting." *Journal of Marriage and the Family* 41 (August 1979): 573–82.

Peterson, Rebecca; Wekerle, Gerda R.; and Morley, David. "Women and Environments: An Overview of an Emerging Field." *Journal of Environment and Behavior*. In press.

Pitchford, Kenneth. "The Manly Art of Child Care." *MS.*, October 1978.

Pleck, Joseph H. "Men's New Roles in the Family: Housework and Child Care." Paper presented for the Ford Foundation/Merrill Palmer Institute, Detroit, November 1975.

———. "The Work-Family Role System." *Social Problems* 24 (1977): 417–27.

Poloma, Margaret M., and Garland, T. Neal. "The Myth of the Egalitarian Family: Familial Roles and the Professionally Employed Wife." Paper presented at the 65th annual meeting of the American Sociological Association, September 1970.

Popenoe, David. *The Suburban Environment: Sweden and the United States*. Chicago: University of Chicago Press, 1977.

Price-Bonham, Sharon. "Marital Decision Making: Congruence of Spouses' Responses." *Sociological Inquiry* 47 (1977): 119–25.

Pruette, Lorine. *Women and Leisure: A Study of Social Waste*. New York: E. P. Dutton, 1924.

Quindlen, Ann. "Self-Fulfillment: Independence versus Intimacy." *New York Times*, 28 November 1977.

Radloff, Lenore. "Sex Differences in Depression: The Effects of Occupation and Marital Status." *Sex Roles* 1 (1975): 249–65.

Rasmussen, Laura S. "Model Marriage Equality Bill." *Suffolk University Law Review*, vol. 9, no. 185 (1975). Reprinted in *Do It Now* (National Organization for Women), June 1977.

Reno, Virginia. "Women Newly Entitled to Retired-Worker Benefits: Survey of New Beneficiaries." *Social Security Bulletin*, April 1973, pp. 3–26.

Roberts, Stephanie. "I Hereby Resign as Keeper of This House." *MS.*, May 1977.

Robinson, J. *How Americans Use Time: A Social-Psychological Analysis*. New York: Praeger, 1976.

Rosen, Francine B. "Someone Should Study the Studies." *Majority Report*, 2 October 1976.

Safran, Claire. "What You Should Know about the Equal Rights Amendment." *Redbook*, June 1973.

Sanday, Peggy R. "Female Status in the Public Domain." In *Woman, Culture and Society*, ed. Michelle Zimbalist Rosaldo and Louise Lamphere. Stanford: Stanford University Press, 1974.

Seashore, Stanley E. "Defining and Measuring the Quality of Working Life." In *The Quality of Working Life*, ed. Louis E. Davis and Albert B. Cherns. New York: Macmillan, 1975.

Shey, Thomas H. "Why Communes Fail: A Comparative Analysis of the Viability of Danish and American Communes." *Journal of Marriage and the Family* 39 (August 1977): 605–14.

Silberman, Leo. "Somali Nomads." *International Social Science Journal* 11 (1959): 599–71.

Sjoo, Monica. "Sweden, Now We Are 'Equal.'" *Power of Women* 1 (summer 1975): 1–12.

Slater, Philip E. *The Pursuit of Loneliness*. Boston: Beacon Press, 1970.

Slocum, Walter L., and Nye, F. Ivan. "Provider and Housekeeping Roles." In *Role Structure and Analysis of the Family*, ed. F. Ivan Nye, pp. 81–99. Beverly Hills: Sage Publications, 1976.

Smith, Audrey D., and Beckett, Joyce O. "Black Working Wives: Research Findings and Implications for Practice." Paper presented at the Sixth National Association for Social Work Professional Symposium, San Antonio, Texas, November, 1979.

Sommers, Tish. "Social Security: A Woman's Viewpoint." *Industrial Gerontology* 2 (fall 1975): 266–79.

Stiehm, Judith. "Algerian Women: Honor, Survival and Islamic Socialism." In *Women in the World: A Comparative Study*, ed. Lynne B. Iglitzin and Ruth Ross. Santa Barbara: Clio Books, 1976.

Stucker, John L. "Women's Political Role." *Current History* 70 (May 1976): 213.

Susan. "Sexism at Twin Oaks." *Leaves of Twin Oaks*, no. 41 (August 1976), p. 7.

Szalai, Alexander. *The Situation of Women in the United Nations*. New York: United Nations, UNITAR, 1973.

Tavris, Carol. "Woman and Man." *Psychology Today*, March 1972, p. 57.

Tavris, Carol, and Jayaratne, Toby Epstein. "How Happy Is Your Marriage?" *Redbook*, June 1976.

Tepperman, Jean. "Two Jobs: Women Who Work in Factories." In *Sisterhood Is Powerful*, ed. Robin Morgan. New York: Vantage Books, 1970.

Thoreau, Henry David. *Walden*. Boston: Houghton Mifflin, 1957; first published 1854.

United States Department of Health, Education, and Welfare. *A Woman's Guide to Social Security*. Washington, D.C.: HEW, 1975.

———. "Report of the HEW Task Force on the Treatment of Women under

Social Security." February 1978.

———. "Social Security and Your Household Employee." HEW Publication no. (SSA) 78-10021. N.d.

United States Department of Labor. *Women Workers Today.* Washington, D.C.: Employment Standards Administration, Women's Bureau, 1976.

Van Allen, Judith. "African Women, 'Modernization,' and National Liberation." In *Women in the World: A Comparative Study,* ed. Lynne B. Iglitzin and Ruth Ross. Santa Barbara: Clio Books, 1976.

Wagner, Marsden, and Wagner, Mary. *The Danish National Child-Care System.* Boulder, Colo.: Westview Press, 1976.

Walker, Kathryn E., and Gauger, William H. *The Dollar Value of Household Work.* Ithaca: New York State College of Human Ecology, Cornell University, 1980.

———. "Time and Its Dollar Value in Household Work." *Family Economics Review* 62 (fall 1973): 8–13.

Walton, Richard E. "Criteria for Quality of Working Life." In *The Quality of Working Life.* Vol. 1. *Problems, Prospects, and the State of the Art,* ed. Louis E. Davis, Albert B. Cherns, and associates, pp. 91–104. New York: Free Press, 1975.

Weaver, Charles N., and Holmes, Sandra L. "A Comparative Study of the Work Satisfaction of Females with Full-Time Employment and Full-Time Housekeeping." *Journal of Applied Psychology* 60 (1975): 117–18.

Weinbaum, Batya. "Women in Transition to Socialism: Perspectives on the Chinese Case." *Review of Radical Political Economics* 8 (spring 1976): 34–58.

Weinreich, Helen. "What Future for the Female Subject? Some Implications of the Women's Movement for Psychological Research." *Human Relations* 30 (1977): 535–43.

Weiss, R., and Samuelson, N. "Social Roles of American Women: Their Contribution to a Sense of Usefulness and Importance." *Marriage and Family Living* 4 (1958): 358–66.

Weitzman, Lenore J. "Legal Regulation of Marriage: Tradition and Change." *California Law Review* 62 (1974): 1170–97.

Wibaut, Mrs. "Working Women and the Suffrage." Reprinted in *Women and Rebellion, 1900.* Leeds, England: Independent Labor Party, 1973. Originally published ca. 1890.

Wright, James D. "Are Working Women *Really* More Satisfied? Evidence from Several National Surveys." *Journal of Marriage and the Family* 40 (May 1978): 301–13.

Yankelovich, Daniel. *The New Morality: A Profile of American Youth in the '70's.* New York: McGraw-Hill, 1974.

Yorburg, Betty, and Ibtihaj, Arafat. "Current Sex Role Conceptions and Conflict." *Sex Roles* 1 (1975): 135–46.

Index